THE ARMY'S HANDYMAN

THE PIONEERS: A BRIEF HISTORY

ROMAN 66 AD (PRAECURIS)

BRITISH, PRUSSIAN, AUSTRIAN, FRENCH

1066 THROUGH 1799

AND A FEW
MODERN CONTEMPORARIES

William E. Eisenhauer
Pioneer (Ret.), 64th Regiment
of Foot in America, Ltd.

HERITAGE BOOKS
2012

HERITAGE BOOKS
AN IMPRINT OF HERITAGE BOOKS, INC.

Books, CDs, and more—Worldwide

For our listing of thousands of titles see our website at
www.HeritageBooks.com

Published 2012 by
HERITAGE BOOKS, INC.
Publishing Division
100 Railroad Ave. #104
Westminster, Maryland 21157

Copyright © 2012 William E. Eisenhauer

All rights reserved. No part of this book may be reproduced or transmitted in any form or by any means, electronic or mechanical, including photocopying, recording or by any information storage and retrieval system without written permission from the author, except for the inclusion of brief quotations in a review.

International Standard Book Numbers
Paperbound: 978-0-7884-5375-5
Clothbound: 978-0-7884-3425-9

THE ARMY'S HANDYMEN

MILITARY PIONEERS

COVER PHOTO: Brigaded Pioneers, assembled at
The 200th Anniversary of the British surrender at
Yorktown, Virginia October 1981
The Author is the 2nd from the left, front rank

V
TABLE OF CONTENTS'

DEDICATION - VI　　**ILLUSTRATIONS - VIII**
FOREWORD - X

ACKNOWLEDGMENTS - XII
INTRODUCTIONS - 15

CHAPTER ONE　　　　　　　　**PG. - 18**
　　THE BEGINNING - ROMAN ARMY OF 66AD

CHAPTER TWO　　　　　　　　**PG. - 33**
　　THE ENGLISH ARMY'S HANDYMEN
　　THE EARLY YEARS - 1066 to 1768

CHAPTER THREE　　　　　　　**PG. - 102**
　　ROYAL MILITARY ACADEMY

CHAPTER FOUR　　　　　　　　**PG. - 104**
　　1st SERIES OF LETTERS
　　1795 to 1779

CHAPTER FIVE　　　　　　　　**PG. - 114**
　　THOSE ARMY HANDYMEN

CHAPTER SIX　　　　　　　　　**PG. - 136**
　　CAPS, HATS AND HELMETS

CHAPTER SEVEN　　　　　　　**PG. - 170**
　　THE 64th REGIMENT OF FOOT - UNIFORMS
　AND ACCOUTREMENTS OF A BATTALION SOLDIER - 1768

CHAPTER EIGHT　　　　　　　**PG. - 188**
　THE CAMPS - PIONEER - ARTICIFER - TOOLS AND ACCOUTREMENTS

CHAPTER NINE　　　　　　　　**PG. - 222**
　FORTIFICATIONS - FASCINES - GABIONS, PARAPET CONSTRUCTION AND FIELD WORKS

CHAPTER TEN　　　　　　　　**PG. - 238**
　　PIONEERS - 1856 THROUGH THE GULF WAR

CHAPTER ELEVEN　　　　　　**PG. 284**
　　SO THEY LIKE MUSIC

THE AUTHOR - PGS. - 300 & 301
SOURCE LIST PG. - 305　　**INDEX PG. 311**

IN DEDICATION

TO THOSE WHO HELPED GET US STARTED AS RE-ENACTORS AND DEVELOP OUR SKILLS AS HISTORICAL INTERPRETERS.....

...... AND TO THOSE WHOSE FRIENDSHIP WE HAVE ENJOYED SHARING WAR STORIES AROUND MANY CAMP FIRES.........

WHO HAVE PASSED ON TO THAT FINAL CALLING...

YOUR COMRADESHIP IS SORELY MISSED

VII

1998

IN MEMORY OF

MAJOR LARRY BRADBURY

VIII

LIST OF ILLUSTRATION

Pg. 27 to 32 - Legionaries Tools, Hero's Staff, Legionaries Marching Camp
Pg. 46 - Colours and Gorget of the Articifer Corps.
Pg. 47 - Salaries of the Officers - c1701 - 1714 - Army of Queen Ann
Pg. 55 - British Army Rolling Stock - Wagons
Pg. 56 - Field Forges - British Army - c1700 - 1900
Pg. 58 - Diagram "A" - British Line of march - c1702 - 1761
Pg .60 - Diagram "B" - Battalion Formations - c1759
Pg. 63 - Diagram "C" - Battalion Formations - c1764
Pg. 66 - Diagram "D" - Pioneer Organization
Pg. 73 - Austrian Army - c1749 Pioneer manual of Arms with axe
Pg. 74 - Austrian Army Organization - Seven Years War
Pg. 94 - de Loutherbourg sketch; Lt. Infantry 69th Foot - 1778
Pg. 95 - Company of Guides and Pioneers - c1776
Pg. 95 - Company of Black Pioneers - c1777
Pg. 115 - Pioneer - King James Army - c1688
Pg. 117 & 118 - Pioneer - Guards Battalion - c1742 - 1759
Pg. 119 - Pioneer - 28th Regt. of Foot - c1759
Pg. 120 - Pioneer - 12th Regt. of Foot - c1761
Pg. 121 - Pioneer - 29th Regt. of Foot - c1768
Pg. 122 - Pioneer - 42nd Regt. of Foot - c1771
Pg. 123 - Pioneer - 23rd Regt. of Foot - c1775
Pg. 125 & 126 - Soldier Articifer Company - c1772 - 1789
Pg. 127 - Pioneer - 27th Regt. of Foot - c1785
Pg. 130 - Pioneer - 7th Regt. of Foot - c1789

IX

Pg. 132 - Pioneer - 66th Regt. of Foot - c1815
Pg. 138 - Pioneer - Hemet - Royal Warrants - c1768 and 1802
Pg. 139 to Pg. 145 - Pioneer - Helmet Designs
Pg. 147 & Pg. 148 - P.J. de Loutherbourg prints on the 3rd Buffs
Pg. 149 - Face Plate - Pioneer Helmet 59th and 64th Foot
Pg. 183 - Canteens and Knapsacks
Pg. 186 - Cartridge Boxes and Canteens
Pg. 189 - British Army Formal Encampment
Pg. 191 - Apron Design
Pg. 197 - 198 Axes, Saws, Hatches and Knives
Pg. 198 & Pg 199 - Axe Heads
Pg. 201 - 202 Entrenching Tools
Pg. 207 to Pg. 215 - The shops at Fort Sisseton, S.D.
Pg. 222 - Fortifications
Pg. 234 - Chevaux-de-Frise
Pg. 238 - Pioneers of the Regiments - British c1856 - Canadian c1792 to 1867 - French c1866 to 1875 and some modern Contemporizes
Pg. 253 - Equipment of Infantry and Pioneers - c1856 - Accoutrements, tools and appointments
Pg. 259 - French Army Sapeurs - c1766 to 1875 & Equipment
Pg. 264 - Some Notes
Pg. 269 - French Sapeurs after the Imperial Period c1857, 1860, 1861- Sapeur de Infantrue
Pg. 272 - British Forces in the 1st Gulf War - The Staffordshire Regiment
Pg. 281 - Battle of Eutaw Springs
Pg. 284 - So The Like Music - Regimental Marches

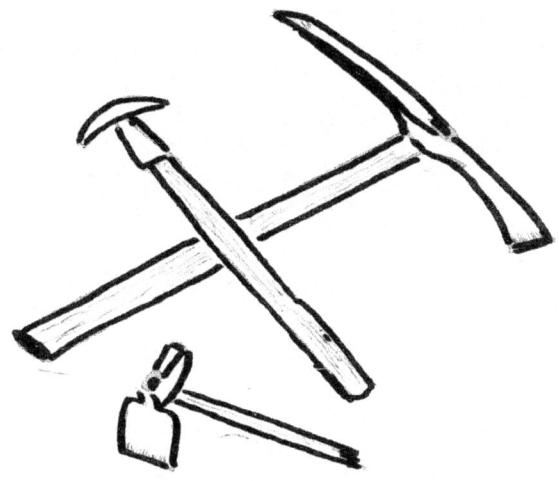

FOREWORD

Since 1978, when I first joined a reenactment organization such as the 64th Regiment of Foot, I had loved history, now is my chance to help recreate it.

But I did find one thing that was a bit disturbing, upon joining up, you put on that "Red Coat" and after some training, off you went to your first "Battle"; it appeared that few if any took the time to find out who a British Soldier was, not having documentation or records to fall back on to research didn't help.

As best as I can recall, an 18th Soldier was merely a "warm body, filling a space", he could follow orders, shoot a musket and march. I believe that it wasn't until the 1800's that soldiers were given a number along side their name. Thus at roll call, their number and name would be called.

Once I had "suited up" as a British Soldier/Pioneer, I wanted to know as much as I could as to what a "Pioneer" was and what they did, and I think after working on this project for the last 40 years I've come up with many great answers.

The one issue I wanted to settle was Beards or Facial Hair - Refer to the time period 1693 - Reign of King William III - "Pioneers were allowed to wear a full beard". But; moving into the periods 1789 (7th Regiment); 1815 (66th Regiment); General Order - November 1856 -"Pioneers are to wear their beards and mustachios unshaven"; Pioneer 59th Foot 1862; Pioneer, Fort Henry Guard 1867. Other than those mentioned, there are no beards or mustachios between 1768 and 1789.

I can only hope that the information collected herein will be a helpful tool to any new or older reinactors who want to portray a Pioneer.

I can only wish them good luck.

Regards

William "Ike" Eisenhauer

XI

ACKNOWLEDGEMENTS

Without the help of so many, this effort to bring to light the role of the "Pioneer" within an 18th Century British Regiment would still be just a dream. I can say what looked like an easy project has stretched out over 30 plus years and I was able to uncover the role of the Pioneers in other Centuries and in other Armies. We do have a varied and very interesting past.

First and foremost, **Col. John Elting**, U.S. Army (Ret), my mentor, who took the time to read what I thought was a well organized manuscript, which believe me as I was to learn, far be the case - it wasn't. Not even close, but his kind patience and attention to detail were immeasurable. His side notes and comments helped me later on to really pull it all together. But it remained a work in progress.

Allen Aimone - who works in the Rare Book Section at the West Point Military Library. Allen, like myself is a Revolutionary War rein-actor, who recreates an American Soldier; and is a member of the Brigade of the American Revolution. I don't know how many times I e-mailed him, seeking up dated information on various publishers I needed to contact so I could obtain their permission to use certain materials from various reference books. He also pointed me towards the many volumes of the Journal for the Society of Army Historical Research.

To those friends who in the early days of the Bi-Centennial helped form a small group of history lovers into the "Dutchess County Militia", sponsored by The Fishkill Historical Society. We participated in many mock battles, ceremonies and parades.

Fred Wahl - From the mid-60's to 1981, was the founder and Commander of One of the largest British Infantry Regiments, representing the rank and file Of the 64th Regiment of Foot c1775. Fred suggested I do the role of Pioneer and he continuely encouraged me to continue with my research. He helped get my kit together in time for the 200th Anniversary of the Battle of Brandywine, Pa.; where I had a chance to meet the current commander of the Staffordshire Regiment - Brigadier General Hargraves. Fred was one of several who was instrumental in establishing active relations with the Staffords, our parent organization in England.

Larry Bradbury - Picked up the rains as the Bi-Centennial started to wind down. His energy and constant drive kept us all going. His knowledge and enthusiasm never faltered regardless of the type of event, the weather, heat, rain, he was ready to guide us by example. His passing in 1998 was a loss which has been hard on all within the 64th Foot.

Mike Grienier - Our current commander, who has equaled Larry in energy and enthusiasm, has always been a great friend and ready to help if I needed it. His dedication to the 64th over the years was only equaled to that of Larry Bradbury and wife Jackie Bradbury; our ensign.

Dennis Krowe - Then the Commander of the newly formed, recreated 38th Regiment of Foot. His knowledge and access to many rare books helped to define the evolution of the Pioneer Helmet.

Mr. Loren Daniel Lillis - who put me into the various War Office Records in London, where I was able to locate reference to a Corps of Pioneers and my further contacts, such as Mr. Nicholas Coney, Research and Editorial Services, Dept. at the Public Record Office "The National Archives"

Mr. Rene Chartrand of Quebec who replied to one of my requests about an article he wrote on the Royal Highland Immigrants.

Mr. Dennis Farmer, then Curator at the Old Fort Niagara Historic Site Museum, Youngstown, New York.

Mr. Eric I. Manders, who provided information from the Kemble Papers.

Ms Janet Bloom - at the William L. Clements Library at the University of Michigan, materials she provided on the role that Free Blacks played in the American Revolutation.

Mr. Peter F. Copeland, member of the Company of Military Historians, for permission to use his color print of the 29th Foot in Boston.

Ms. Eleanor Gillers of the New York Historical Society

Ms Wendy Hefford and **Mr. Martin Durrant** of the Victoria and Albert Museum, London, England

Ms. Kate S. Woods - Dept. of Archives - **Mr. Peter B. Boyden and Ms. S.K. Hopkins** - of the National Army Museum in London, England.

Ms. Lindsay Stainton - Assistant Keeper - The British Museum - Dept. of Prints and Drawings.

Major (Ret.) P. C. Mulingani - Secretary, Regimental Assoc. and a **Ms.A.S. Elsom** of the Staffordshire Regimental Museum, Whittington Barrack, Litchfield, Staffordshire, England.

Mr. Ben Larosa - of San Antonio, Texas. Ben pointed out several items Which needed changing. Take the foot notes and put them in the back of the Book; justify all pages; explain further certain Officers names, especially those in the Austrian and Prussian Army, give more details as to who they were, their titles and responsibilities.

The Staff in the reference Departments in the Harte Branch of the Corpus Christi, Texas Library System and in the Bedford, Mass. Public Library System.

Mr. Erik Blakely - currently the Museum Curator at the Staffordshire Regimental Museum, Whittington Barrack, Litchfield, England.

Mr. Jeffery Elson - Staffordshire Regimental Museum, Historical Researcher. Litchfield, England.

Ms. Diane Brunner (*Ph.D in Medieval History*) of Fantastical Writing and Editing - Her very patient and professional approach to editing my manuscript was an immense help in getting this work printed - 411 Nordale Avenue, Dayton, OH. 45420 - Phone 937-830-2118.

I am sure there are others who have assisted in one way or the other, and names have been forgotten, since starting this project in 1978. But rest assured, I deeply appreciate the efforts of anyone who has helped me in the past and in the future to assemble this material from so many different sources into a finished work.

INTRODUCTION

In the early part of 1975 I spotted a poster in a local store which read......
"COME JOIN US, RELIVE HISTORY, JOIN THE FISHKILL MILITIA".

The local Historical Society was attempting to startup a "Militia" Company of sorts in time for the Bi-centennial. This Militia Company was to be similar to those raised in this area in 1774 - 1775. The Bi-centennial fever had started, and I've always loved history. So I joined up.

From 1975 through 1978, our little Militia Company, comprised of teachers, a School Bus driver, students and parents, participated in many parades, small mock-battles and ceremonies. But as 1978 began to wind down, many of the kids were growing up and looking at other interests, parents were tired and the older folks wanted something more and time had taken it's toll.

I wanted something different as well, so I joined a much larger organization called the "64th Regiment of Foot", they were based out of White Plains, New York, but scattered throughout New York, New England and down into Virginia.

I took on the role of "Pioneer" as there were none then in the 64th. Being rather independently minded, I wanted to be different. But as I was to learn, no one knew anything about "Pioneers" in general, nor what their role was within a British Infantry Regiment.

The 64th, as it was generally called was outfitted how it would have looked in Boston; according to the Royal Clothing Warrants of 1768; spending many long hours at the West Point Military Library; both in the basement section looking through *The Journal for the Army's Historical Research* to, and up in the rare book section. I gathered much information in addition I wrote many, many letters in my quest for information.

I want you to understand that the major part of my research covers what the Pioneer's did during the larger European Wars between 1745 through 1765.

Plus what I found very interesting is that the Pioneers and the terms used to describe their duties went back as far as the Roman Army.

This information as well as having a good imagination helped me to demonstrate what a Pioneer was and what he did. The longer you are in this role, the greater your knowledge becomes and helps to enrich your overall interpretation of this individual. It also helps develop your knowledge of the type of kit the Pioneer was required to have.

There were between 3 to 9 Pioneers per Regiment, or 1 per company. With an Orderly Corporal or Pioneer Corporal in charge. In Richard Todd's Diaries, I found mention of a Pioneer Sergeant.

The single largest turnout of Pioneers in any reenactment occurred during the 200th Anniversary of "The Siege of Yorktown, Virginia" in October 1981.

Here there were 22 present from both Regular British Line Regiments and from the Loyalists Regiment's as well. It was here that the "Pioneer" march was played and all the Pioneers marched out and they formed in front of the assembled British Regiments and led them out onto the field for the battle and the pass in review when President Regan was there. We at last had our fleeting moment of Fame and Glory, our moment in the sun.

The information contained herein will give the beginner a good idea of the varied tasks that were required of the Pioneer, his tools and various posts.

I also found terms, such as Quarter-Master (praefectusi castrorum), and the Color-Party, these are the individuals from each century (Roman) to move ahead of the main force, and use colored flags to mark the ground where the Army was to camp.

I also strayed a bit, covering the areas of Quarter-Master, Camp-Color-Man, and later in this book, covering our counter-parts in the French Army as well as the Canadians and a brief mention of our modern contemporizes.

Mention is also made of the evolution of the Miners and Sappers and the Royal Engineers. I did not wish to go too deep into their development as they have their own well written histories. The U.S. had for a brief time an organization known as the Miners and Sappers, which were organized in time for the Yorktown campaign and disbanded in 1783.

Again my intent of this book is to focus on the "Pioneer", beginning back in the Roman period and moving forward into the mid 1800's. Today many British Regiments maintain one or more individual soldiers to turnout as pioneers but for ceremonial purposes only.

In today's British Army you will still find soldiers trained as Sappers, so to in the U.S. Army. During the Gulf War, the British had Sappers as part of the 32nd Armored Regiment, as well as the Royal Pioneer Corps.

Above all else, I can only hope this information will be helpful to the next "Generation" of reenactor's who wish to portray a British Soldier/Pioneer and to turn out with the proper kit, good imagination, resourcefulness, to aid in your interpretation of the

For nearly 1500 plus years those who have served as Company-Regimental Pioneers, we indeed have a very long, proud and Honorable History.

CHAPTER ONE

IS

A BEGINNING

THE ROMAN ARMY

1856 IS THE APPARENT DATE THE BADGE OF CROSSED AXES FIRST APPEARED AND IS STILL WORN BY PIONEERS OF THE MODERN BRITISH ARMY

It would appear that the "Wreath" (without a bow), and in several styles, was the symbol of Roman Politics and Government. The wreath was also worn as a crown on many of the heads of Roman Emperors such as Caesar's and was also found on many Roman Legion Shields.

THE ROMAN ARMY

This is the overall makeup of the Roman Army[1] of for the Third Century A.D.

LEGION - This is the largest unit within the Army. Comprised of 6,000 men with Cavalry, Artillery and Headquarters. It was made up of 9 cohorts of 80 men each and one of 160 men.

COHORTS - This is 6 units of 80 men each - **CENTURY** - is a single unit of 80 men.

SECTION - (contubernium)[2] - is comprised of 8 men, with one pack animal to carry its tent, mill, kettle, with other items of kit and tools.

MARKING OUT THE CAMP - ARMY ON THE MARCH

A 10 man[3] team from each of the centuries was commanded by either a senior tribune or centurion.

The centurion was briefed by either the Army Commander or the "quaestor", this term broadly means a rank comparable to a Quartermaster General. These 10 man detachments moved ahead of the main Army, and with colored flags and markers laidout the ground on which the Army would camp.

This is where the modern term - "Color-Party" came from.

Josephus, Titus Flavius Josephus, 37 - c AD 100 was a law-observant Jew who believed in the compatibility of Judaism and Graeco-Roman thought, Commonly referred to as Hellenistic Judaism. His most important works were *THE JEWISH WAR (c75 AD)* recounts the Jewish revolt against Roman occupation (66-70). This is the source that Richard M Berthold drew his information from to write an article for the magazine *COMMAND, NOV./DEC.* the 1993 issue where he mentions Pioneers.

During the attack on Galilee it was noted that each Roman Soldier was generally issued an axe, saw, chain, sickle, spade, basket and rope. There is some evidence of that inscribed on "Trajans" column which shows that Roman Soldiers may not have carried many of these items, but transported them in a "Company" 2 wheeled cart.

What I found very interesting was Mr. Berthold's mention of **"Pioneers"**. I set out to locate his source as this is the earliest known mention of "Pioneers"

Mr. Berthold was a Professor, at the University of New Mexico, but I was unable to contact him to verify his comments; I'm not sure if Mr. Berthold is still at the University or even if he is still with us. I do thank him for his work.

On the left is a Preafectus of the Camp, generally a former retired Centurion responsible for the running of affairs of an encampment. Center and right are two Centurions with their distinctive crests. The fort in the back ground represents a generic Roman frontier fort which was common from the late Republic into the Imperial Period. It's located on private land in Lafe, Arkansas, north of Jonesboro, and is still a work in progress.

I found the source which was the full completed works of *"JOSEPHUS - complete works"*.[4] Mr. Berthold's article reads in part; *"But Vespasian, impatient to invade Galilee himself, now set out from Ptolemais, after drawing up his Army for the march in the customary Roman order. The auxiliary light-armed troops and archers were sent in advance, to repel any sudden incursions of the enemy and to explore suspected woodlands suited for the concealment of ambuscades. Next came a contingent of heavy armed Roman soldiers, infantry and cavalry. They were followed by a detachment of 10 men from each century, carrying their own kit and the necessary instruments for marking out the camp; after these came the pioneers to straighten curves on the route, to level the rough places and to cut down obstructing woods, to spare the army the fatigues of a toilsome march..."*

I found these passages in BOOK III; Chapter VI, part 2, on page 506 of the **Wars of the Jews** .... *"But as Vespasian had a great mind to fall upon Galilee, he marched out of Ptolemais, having put his army into that order wherein the Romans used to march. He ordered those auxiliaries which were lightly armed, and the archers, to march first, that they might prevent any sudden assaults from the enemy, and might search out the woods that looked suspiciously, and were capable of ambuscades. Next to these followed that part of the Romans who were most completely armed, both footmen and horsemen. Next to these followed ten out of every hundred, carrying along with them their arms, and what was necessary to measure out a camp withall; and after them, such as were to make the road even and straight, and if it were anywhere rough and hard to be passed over, to plane it, and to cut down the woods that hindered their march, that the army might not be in distress, or tired with their march..."*

First and foremost, the duties of the "Camp-color-men" are mentioned, but those duties were not labeled as such until after 1700. It would appear that in his article, Mr. Berthold took certain liberties in inserting the title "Pioneers", but the duties as described in both passages are in fact the duties of a pioneer but were defined much later in the 1700's. Berthold's mention of "10 men" is correct, as there were 10 Pioneers in each Regiment, one from each company.

The Headquarters of each Legion was a complicated organization. Comprised of various clerks and orderlies the H.Q kept a record of grain required by the Army, soldiers pay and properties of those killed in battle, among other things.

Among this group would be found the "Mensoris" or the "Surveyor", and the "Praecuris" or "Pioneer".

The Legions, once they setup a long term camp were required to build roads in their respective areas of command, thus the Surveyor's and his assistants were kept busy.

SIEGE WARFARE -"Polybius records that Philip of Macedonia, at the siege of Echinus in 211 BC, planned a two-pronged attack on the town and had two large siege towers built for that purpose".

"The two towers, 150 feet high, were slowly inched forward as the "Sappers"[5] beneath them leveled the surface of the ground to make their movement possible".

NOTE: I found no word for "Sappers" in the book *The New College Latin & English Dictionary by John C. Traupman, Ph.D.*

I also found mention of "Artificer's workshops"[6] being part of Caesar's Army in 56 B.C.

Also mentioned is a "Quaestor" - Army paymaster, personal aid to the Emperor.

Artisan's[7] - (faberbri) - **Skilled craftsman - faber aerarius** - coppersmith, **faber ferrarius** - blacksmith; **faber marmoris** - marble worker; **faber sandapilarum** - bier maker; **faber tignarius** - carpenter.

NOTE: A bier maker as best as I can determine is a "Liter Maker".

All photo's of Roman Soldier's were provided by a George Metz - *Legio XXIV* - from Newtown Square, Pa. They represent the Roman Army of the 1st Century A.D. , the Glory of Roman

A morning formation, most of the men have turned-out without their armor or helmets, but are wearing their "baltius" belts and tunics, which was the basic non-combat dress when they are not under threat of attack. Some are wearing ring-maile armor, which was adopted by Rome around 300 BC and was in use throughout the Roman period. Some have "segmentata" plate armor, which was in use from about 10 BC till 200 AD.

This formation is in marching order, the curved "Scuta" shields are typical of those used by Roman Soldiers during the Imperial Period. Each unit would have its own style designs and decoration, but the Eagles Wings, Lighting Bolts and Unicorn Horns were standard icons shown on most all Roman Legion Shields. Those that are shown represent **Legions XVII, XVIII and XIX,** the three Legions that were ambushed and destroyed in 9 AD in the Tueterburg Vald (forest) in Germany east of the Rhine.

On the left of the formation is the Aquilifer, Eagle Standard Bearer. The Eagle was the symbol for a Legion and each Legion would carry one before it on the march. To lose it, in battle would be similar to losing the Kings and Regimental Colors in Battle

A patrol returning to the Fort with a Celtic Chieftain, far left, Centurion, middle and Legatos, right, leader of a Legion. The Blue oval shield is an early Greek flat shield, also used by Rome during the Republic. Here it is being carried by an "auxiliary", who generally used this style of shield.

What follows is a series of sketches provided by a James Mathews of Gales Ferry, Ct. His notes are hand written, thus I decided to type out his notes for those of us with failing eye sight. These notes cover *A **list** of **Legionaries** **Tools**,* used to setup a marching camp, diagram of which also is included.

Jim's comments - *The Legionary was many things in wartime, he could be used as a fighter, builder, pioneer, etc. The **page** XXVII indicates the tools that each Legionary carried on Campaign.*

The Legionary tasks in the case of constructing siege defenses, if he was in the force perpetrating the siege, the Legionary would be tearing these things up, as he found them.

Page XXIV - *shows a sketch of a Roman Surveying Instrument. The Legionary Specialist who used the "Groma" and the "Hero's Staff " and Horbates were called "Gromaciti" and were relieved the fatigues of his Century (Company) He always worked under the direction of a Centurion, (Company Cdr).*

Looking through a partial list of Legion Specialists, I do not find a "Pioneer" specifically named. I think that those Legionaries being used in "Pioneer Tasks" were simple Legionaries working under the direction of a Centurion.

Jims area of specialty are maps and plans.

BLOGS: - HTTP://Living History Military Engineer - Blogspot.com
HTTP:// Roman Studies - Blogspot.com
HTTP:// Byzantium Novum Militarium. Blogspot.com

Early Roman Siege Defences

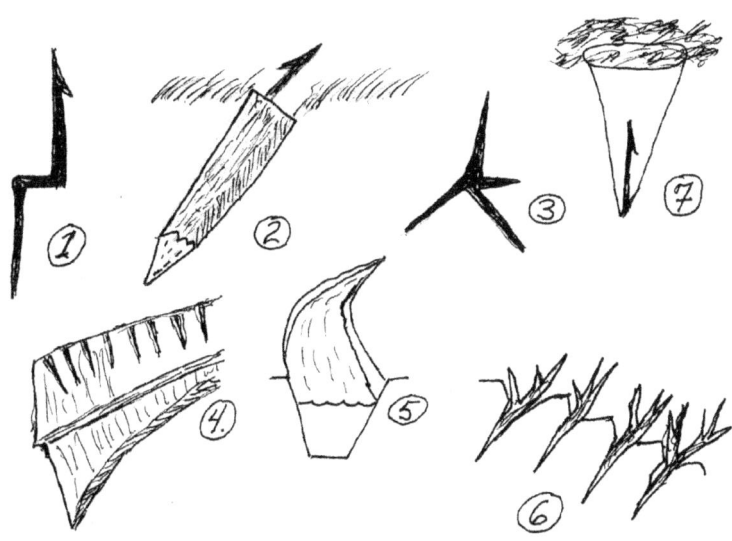

1. Iron Spike
2. Iron Spike in Buried Log
3. Caltrop
4. Dry Ditch + Wall with
5. Moat (Water Filled)
6. Five Rows or More of Sharped Obstacles in Front of the Defensive Rampart
7. "Tulips" - Holes 1 yard in circumference and at least 1 yard or more deep with a sharpened stake in the bottom, often smeared with human feces. The hole was then covered with light brush to hide it. These were dug in rows of three, alternating :-

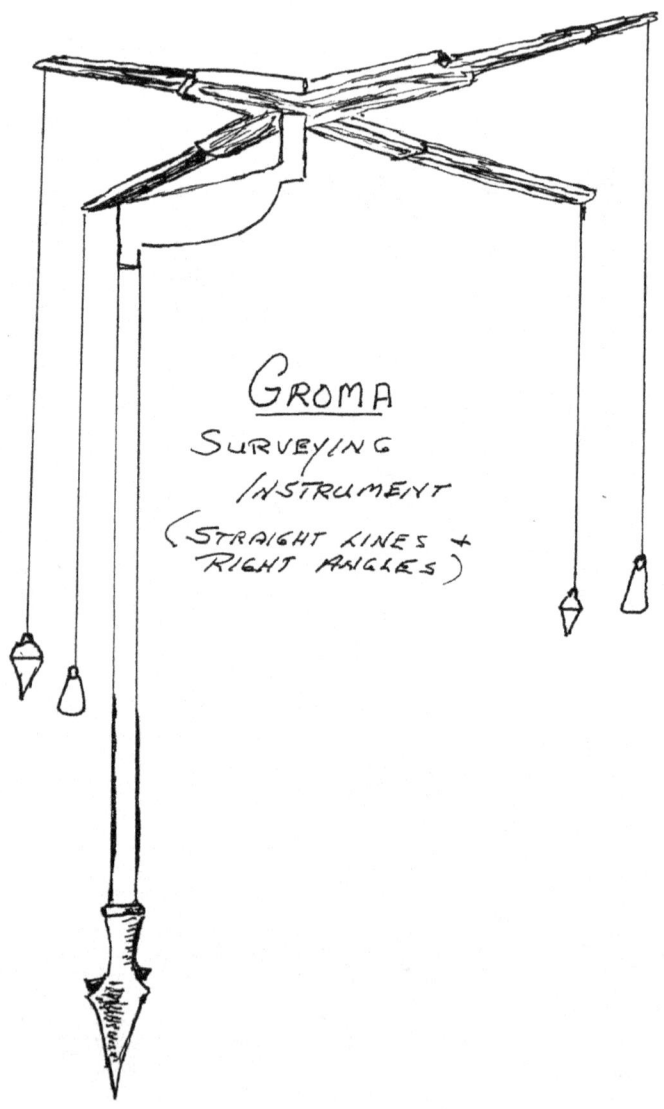

The Marching Camp

Jim's Notes : **(1)** - *The engineers and "Gromaciti" (Surveyors) rode ahead of the marching Legion, to select a place for the next marching camp. Once the area was selected and the layout of the camp was decided upon, them using the "Groma" (Survey instrument) and a measuring line (or chain) the out line of the ditch, parapet, and entrances were marked out with flags.*

(2) - *When the Legion arrives they begin to dig the ditch and build the parapet using the tools they carried with them. Meanwhile if there is an enemy threat, the Auxila would surround the work until it was finished.*

(3) - *Each Legionary carried two palesade stakes and a length of rope. The stakes were placed at the top of the parapet (Agger) and tied together.*

(4) - *Barriers formed from the palisade stakes closed off each of the four entrances. When the ditch (fossa) and parapet (Agger) are completed, then the officers tents are put up and then the Legion's tents. The Legion and Auxila are withdrawn into the fort and supper can be cooked.*

For further information - P. Connolly "Greece and Rome at War" Prentice-Hall Inc. 1984, pages 134 to 139.

THE MARCHING CAMP

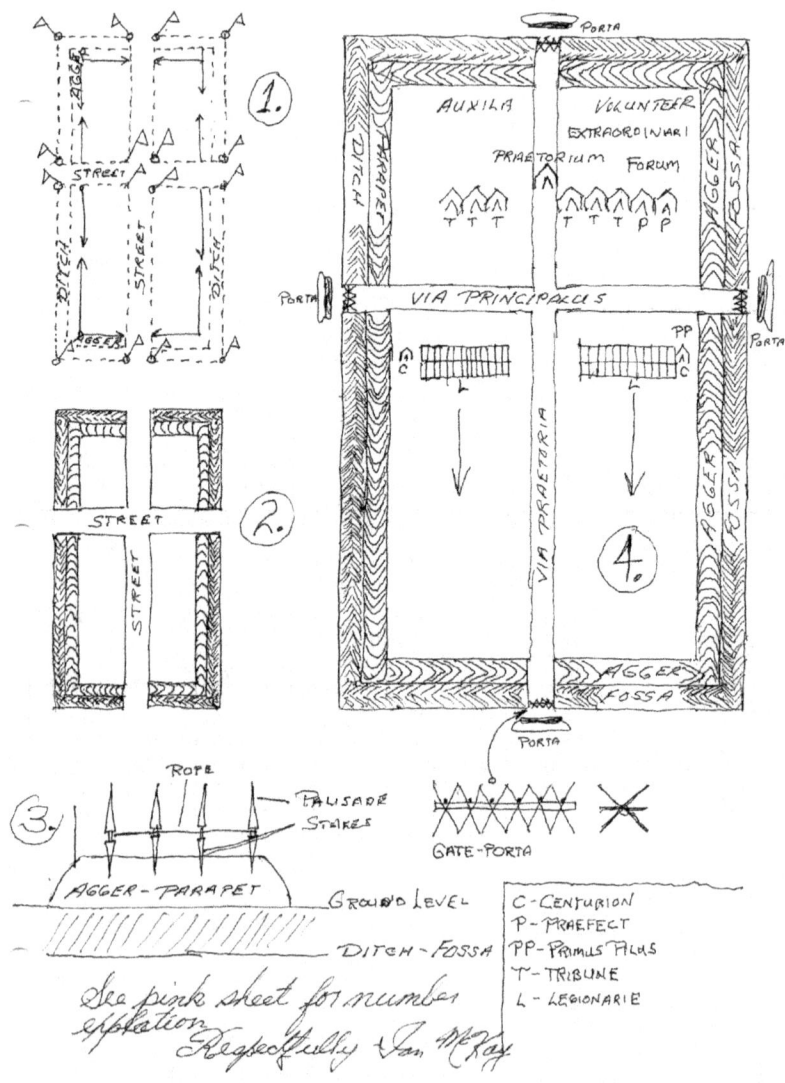

THE ROMAN ENCAMPENT

Legio III "Cyrenaics"

Currently near Webster, Mass

August 5, 6 & 7, 2006

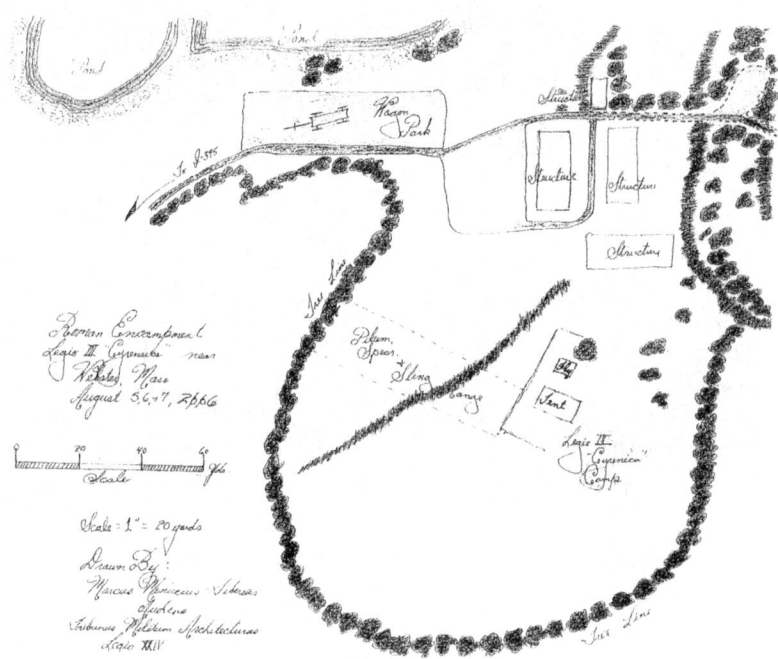

Another view of the morning formation preparing to go on patrol.

CHAPTER TWO

THE ENGLISH ARMY'S HANDMAN

A BRITISH ENSIGN c1750

My cotton 3 x 5 flag which I flew when I setup my full camp as a woodworker. I hand painted the design in the middle.

THE ENGLISH ARMY'S HANDYMAN
The early years 1066 to 1768

Miners, were skilled in the art of digging mines, which when used during a siege, drew pay above the average soldier/pioneer.

The French took the lead very early, and some years before the French Revolution, they had companies and regiments organized into what were called Miners and Sappers, or Soldier - Carpenters. The terms Carpenters or Artificers was also used, meaning skilled craftsmen. England[8] was very behind in engineer work in general but the United States followed the French doctrine.

Whenever Armies were raised, necessary craftsmen were always a part of the overall team. For either short term service or a major campaign, Pioneers or Sapeurs had a very mixed ancestry. Civilians, with special skills were drafted into service to provide the needed craftsmen for any field army. The term "Artificers" could also be found to identify a skilled workmen.

Many foreign armies maintained a detachment of workers (Pioneers) attached to their artillery regiments who were very skilled in building dirt emplacements to help shield their guns from return enemy fire. The Honorable Artillery Company of London had pioneers in 1727 if not earlier. You also had the special craftsmen who built the large siege engines of the Roman Army, and working with a few skilled engineers helped layout encampment's.

For the most part, local civilians were rounded up to do the roustabout work of building fortifications, clearing or mending roads, very little skill was really needed except how to use a spade or axe.

1066 - September 28th

Humphrey de Lilleul, the first recorded King's Engineer, who landed with William the Conqueror to supervise the construction of the MOTTE and BAILEY Castles. In his campaign to hold down Wales, *King Edward the 1st*, employed a thousand Fussatures, or Pioneers, accompanied by carpenters and woodcutters, to get his Army and siege train forward into the Welsh mountains

The Reign of KING EDWARD III - 1327 - 1377
1346 [9]

In a muster and pay roster of a British garrison at Calis, it indicated that miners and pioneers drew a higher pay then the average soldier. A Mounted Archer or Lancer also received a higher pay, but had to provide subsistence for himself, but fodder for his mount.

During siege work, pioneers and miners would creep forward to some part of the wall and begin digging a tunnel, shoring it up as it went deeper. They would burrow in quite deep and hollow out a chamber. Here more wood would be piled, then all timbers used to support the tunnel would be coated with tar, and set on fire. The theory was that once the supporting timbers used in this mining operation began to collapse, it would bring down a part of the fortification walls. This action of course was long before siege cannon's had reached a point that they alone were used to breach fortification walls.

The pioneer was an individual of courage and resolution, a specialist in this type of demolition work, which was accompanied by a very high degree of risk and peril.

This type of work, which demanded a high degree of technical skill as well as a great deal of danger. Especially so, when the defending garrison was busy sending out sorties or attempting counter-mining operations as well as tossing all forms of missiles or pouring boiling oil from the upper ramparts.

Reigns of KING HENRY IV - Henry V - Henry VI - Edward IV - Richard III - Henry VII - Henry VIII - 1399 to 1547

1400

Artillery in the early 1400's was setup to support the activities of the Pioneers and Miners, as they dug their approach trenches towards for walls. Another problem which had to be faced was the protection of the artillery from either return fire or sorties from the besieged in order to capture and spike these guns. Pioneers and Sappers were also charged with assembling "Great Watches", faggots and bundles of branches[10] to help construct raised earth banks, ditches and palisades.

1415

Henry V's Chief Engineer was made the first Master of Ordnance. This office was given Corporate existence by Henry VIII in 1518 and renamed the Board of Ordnance until it was abolished in 1855.

After the War of the Roses, little fighting was done, thus the term "Engineer" seems to have been considered not material enough to represent military duty, and a new term "Trench master" or Captain of Pioneers was introduced.

Reigns of Edward VI - Queen Mary I - Queen Elizabeth I - 1547 to 1603

1500 [11]

During the reign of Queen Elizabeth I, in 1559 when the Army for all intents and purposes had been drastically neglected, in 1559, a body of Pioneers were ordered to wear a uniform "A Cassock of Watchett" (pale blue), a white doublet, white hose, shoes, garters, points with a scull and cap, and a sword, dagger and girdle; for possible service in Ireland.

It was towards the end of Elizabeth's long reign and into the reign of her successors, that the high esteem so enjoyed by the pioneers under went a certain falling off.

During the siege of Leith in Scotland (1560), Mr. Pelham - (Trench master) was to approach the Citadel from the north west side of the town with his pioneers. The task was to determine the breadth and depth of the ditches around the town and measure the height of the walls to insure that the scaling ladders were built long enough.

Gun emplacements were built and tunnels driven for mines. the labors of the pioneers digging the trenches had to be constantly covered with musket and cannon fire for the French did everything they could to hamper the preparations.

May 7th - 1560, forces under Vaughan, Capt. Wood and Capt. Carvell began the final assault with Pelham, the trench-master, was given a roving commission to take his pioneers to sap any places that seemed particularly vulnerable.

Discipline - It was ordered that troops were to cover 10 miles a day when marching and content to have supper and breakfast in the place where they camped. Any horsemen who lost their horse were to be degraded to the pioneer corps.[12]

They were still to be employed by the Engineer Officer,[13] or by other exalted individuals such as, Surveyor of the Kings Works, The Master Mason, The Master Trench master, in doing such tasks as: repairing bridges, building fortifications, keeping road surfaces in order, and even in smaller tasks as cooperating, carpentering, wheel-Wright and coach building. However overall participation in combat had all but ended.

The increasing power of the Artillery and the ingenious use of gun powder made the use of pioneers unnecessary. the work of breaching the defenses now became the responsibility of the "Artillator", and his well trained gun crews. Thus the pioneers were off doing other chores for the Engineers.

So the pioneer lost his "Specialist" status as well as the higher rate of pay with which he had been rewarded.

1569

On the Administrative side, you have the "Master of Ordnance", he was responsible to issue stores to the troops through the individual Captains. He had his own company, which guarded the Train of Artillery, plus his own Pioneers - The Army Service Corps - to clear the way and entrench that part of the camp where the artillery was stationed. He also had charge of the armourers, smiths, carpenters, and wheelwrights, specialists who were becoming steadily more important as the artillery developed.[14]

1575

Out of a total of 183,000 able men recorded in the national musters in 37 counties, there were 12,000 selected for special training, and 63,000 equipped but untrained. The balance was made up of pioneers, able men who were neither trained nor provided with weapons; and about 3,000 cavalry. The figures for the county of Suffolk two years earlier were total number of males between the ages of 16 and 60, 19,000; able men, 9,000 selected for training, 2,600 carpenters, smiths and 1,500 labors; and just over 100 cavalry.[15]

Reigns of KING James I - Charles I - 1603 to 1649
1640

Before the days of Oliver Cromwell's "New model Army", there was no standardized "Sealed Pattern" uniform. The adoption of various badges or devices of either national or regional origin's did tend to give the garment's that were worn a sort of uniformity of appearance.

1645 [16]

A newspaper called "Perfect Passages" dated 7th May 1645 - states "The men are Redcoats all, the whole army only are distinguished by several facings of their coats" As Fairfax's own colors were blue, his regiment had blue facings. The contract for clothing in October 1649, for the army in Ireland, the coats were made of "Venice color red".

Reenactment - English Civil War period - Photo's provided by Mr. Jeff Elson

Battle reenactment of Hopton Heath, England

By this time, the title of pioneer had hit rock bottom, to be sent over to the pioneers was considered being degraded, a punishment inflicted on the most insubordinate offender in the Cavalry, Dragoons and Infantry.[17] This punishment applied to those troops based in England. You could also get this punishment for marrying an Irish girl without your CO's permission.[18]

1650 [19]

During Cromwell's siege and assault on Somersetshire, there were 4 Regiments assigned to storm 3 different places. 200 men in the middle, and 200 men on each side as forlorn hopes, these were to begin the storm. 20 ladders to each place, carried by 2 men each, with 2 Sergeants attending the service of the ladders, a musketeer to follow each ladder carrying a fagot, and a sergeant with them. 12 files of men with firearms and pikes to followed the ladders commanded by a Captain and a lieutenant. They were followed further by 7 more files of 200 men to finish the storm each party to have 20 pioneers who were to march in their rear.

Each group of Pioneers were commanded by a sergeant, pioneers were to throw down the line and make way for the horse.

It is true that there was one company of pioneers attached to the New Model, but they were laborers of the lowest class, not trained sappers or artificers as in the past. Pioneers, therefore were too few numerically and too unskilled individually to be of great service.

If mining operations were contemplated, skilled assistance was necessary, therefore at the siege of Sherborne Castle in 1645, Fairfax sent for a contingent of Mendip miners. (Pg 176 & 177)

Engineers were a neglected branch of service in the New Model Army, which influenced the character of Siege operations. As a rule the Chief Engineers were foreigners, especially in the earlier years of the war. The engineer-general of the New Model was a Peter Manteau Van Dalem, a Dutchmen or Walloon and in Scotland a Cornelius Van Bemmel seems to have been Cromwell's Chief engineer. (Pg 175 & 176)

Reign of KING CHARLES II - 1660 - 1685

When Charles the II was restored to the throne, in 1660. The New Model Army of England was formed in 1645 by the Parliamentarians in the English Civil War, and was disbanded in 1660 after Restoration. The lowly position of Pioneer was speedily re-elevated to the honorable position he once held.

The Standing army during King Charles reign was Comprised of: Infantry and Cavalry, and at the same time the Artillery and Engineers of the Board of Ordnance, which had been gradually reduced to nil under Fairfax; were revived.

In 1669 a Warrant was now issued which took steps to train young Engineers in the military art; studying such subjects as math, drawings and fortifications. Artillery had by now become its own branch of service, the lowly pioneer once now came onto his own.

Reign of KING JAMES II - 1685 - 1688
(14 October 1633 - 16 September 1701)

James the II was King of England and King of Scotland as James VII from 6 February 1685. During this time the siege train of Artillery contained it's own detachment of pioneers, under their own officers and NCOs'. Three years later, they had a uniform of "Red cloth coats, red kersey breeches, leather montreur caps(*), woolen stockings, shoes, with buckles and neck cloths."

(*) Montreur Caps are a peaked cap, generally of heavy leather; with side flaps which could be let down and fastened under the chin, refer to bottom of page 47 of this work.

Reign of KING WILLIAM III - 1688 - 1694

William the III's (1689) Regimental (*) Train of Artillery included a detachment of pioneers under a Lieutenant, 4 Sergeants and 54 Pioneer privates.[20] Represents 1 Company with 4-13 man sections; may have 4 corporals as well.

(*)The book source did not identify by number, the Regiment.

By this time the pioneer had become the army's handyman with small detachments assigned to the Artillery and infantry. Here the pioneer specialized in the particular sort of work regularly carried out by the unit they were assigned to.

(*) -Artillery - the pioneers would assist in building earthen embankments for the guns, and take charge of any demolitions which were required to open up fields of fire.

(*) - Infantry[21] - The pioneers took on the hazardous task of leading the assault parties, and cutting through the stronghold's outer works to give passage for the follow-up infantry. Both Artillery and Infantry were mentioned in an Article "*Nothing Barred*" (1944); for this time period.

Line of March - The Pioneer lead the battalion, axes at the ready to clear the way through tangled trees or underbrush. At the end of the march, they'd be making rough and ready shelter's in which to rest in.

So it was during this period that Pioneers were allowed to wear a full beard, which was regarded as protection against snatching, stinging tree branches, brush and briar's. In the same manner, heavy leather work aprons were also issued to help protect their limb and clothing from the harsh underbrush while forcing their way through heavy woods.

Reign of Queen Mary II - 1688 to 1702

Pioneer detachments were made a permanent part of the normal infantry battalion in 1700.

A plan was approved by Queen Mary that a Corps of Artificer's be enrolled with the basic regimental organization; with Companies comprised of 2 Captains, 2 Lt. Captain, 2 Engineer Officers, 2 Sergeants, 3 Corporals, 1 Drummer and 50 other ranks. The 1st Company (Training) would be responsible for training; it was from here officers and enlisted-men would pass through to their respective companies.[22]

The Companies:

No. 2 - Company - Miners
No. 4 - Company - Sappers
No. 6 - Company - Carpenters
No. 7 - Company - Smiths
No. 9 - Company - Pioneers

No. 3 Company - Pontoons
No. 5 - Company - Fasciners & Gaboniers
No. 8 - Company - Miners

This Corps as yet, had no permanent rank and file, and apparently only small provisional bodies of pioneers were raised locally. An Officer of Engineers drew up a complete scheme for forming companies of Artificer's and Pioneers together with drawings of uniforms, arms, equipment and colors.

The only Officer known to have done this layout was a Lt. Col. James Montressor, who at the time was serving with General Braddock in 1754. Lt. Col. James was in America serving as his Chief Engineer and served in that capacity in the attack on Fort Ticonderoga in 1758 and as Engineers in the Siege of Louisburg in late 1758.

This organizational layout would come to pass in later years as the Field Companies of the Royal Engineers. Additional staff would be made up of the Adjutant, Regimental

Quarter-Master, Commissary of Stores with an assistant, a Surgeon and his mate, 2 Draughtsman and their assistants and 2 Surveyors with assistants.[23]

THE PROPOSED UNIFORM[24]

UNIFORM - Coat Blue Faced buff, leather waistcoats and breeches, proper to perform their work in. the whole to wear a leather cap, lined with fur. the men were to have hats for full dress, buff canvas stocking for reviews and black leather leggings on a march.

ARMS - Rank and file, muskets no more then 2ft 8 inches in length in the barrel, to be rifled.

COLOURS - There shall be two - mounted on a staff 8ft. long, they shall be 2 feet square, on one side the Union and Crown, and the other the Ordnance Arms with a Phoenix underneath with the motto "EX FLAMINIS RESUREXI". The above color always to be at the head of the camp. The two sketches show a red ensign with the Union with White scrolls either side and crown above. the other is with a shield having the Ordnance Arms, 3 yellow guns on a blue field and 3 cannon balls on a White argent. the shield is edged with yellow and below a yellow ribbon with the motto and the Sphinx below.

Please note the sketches on the next page.

The proposed uniform was covered in C.P. Lawson's book *THE UNIFORMS OF THE BRITISH ARMY - Vol. II 1714 - 1760*. The uniform shown in the sketch is around this period.

Although this unit was actually never activated at the time, it's basic uniform layout was used in 1772 to form the Company of Soldier - Artificer's, pg. 129, and 130 of this work.

46

A. Officer.   B. Colours and Gorget of Artificer Corps.   D. Private.

From the Book
The Uniforms of the British Army
Page 196 & 197
Volumn 2 - by C.P. Lawson

FIG. 147. Artificer's Cap.

OUTLINE OF THE OFFICE OF ORDNANCE WITH SALARIES OF THE OFFICERS

Master-General of the Ordnance (£1,500)

Clerk or Secretary to the Master-General (£200)

Lieutenant-General of the Ordnance (£800)

- Treasurer or Paymaster (£500)
- Clerk of the Cheque (£94)
- Storekeeper of Fireworks
  - Chief Firemaster
  - Firemakers (£195)
  - Firemaster Mates (£80)
  - Firewokers (£59)
- Wagon-Master-General (£100)
  - Master of the Brass Foundry
  - Clerk of the Brass Foundry
- Purveyor (£60)
  - Agents at ports
- Master Gunner (£192)
- Master Gunners of Garrisons
- Clerk of the Ordnance¹
- Clerk of the Deliveries (£300)
- Artillery Train
- Deputy Keeper of the Armoury (£60)
- Armourer (£20)
  - Armourers at Whitehall (£20)
- Keeper of the Small Gunns Office (£80)
  - Furbishers (£50–£40)

Surveyor-General (£400)

- Storekeepers (£400)
- Clerk of the Survey
- Clerk of the Cheque
  - Principal Engineer of Great Britain (£300)
  - 2nd do. (£130)
  - 3rd do. (£136)
  - Engineers at Fortresses
- Storekeepers of Arsenals (£80–£146) with their Clerks of Survey and Clerks of the Cheque
- Assistant Surveyor (£250) (abolished 5 July 1709)
- Yeoworker (£170) (for building and repairing forts)
- Commissaries

- Armourer¹
- Labourers (£24)
- Messenger (£60)
- Proofmaster¹ (£20)
- Engineers (excluding pointers and miners) in states and garrisons

¹ I have shown the Clerk of the Ordnance under the Lieutenant-General since that officer was Deputy to the M.G.O., but in practice the clerk had a status approximating equal to the Surveyor with whom he jointly signed orders for receipt to the storekeeper.
² Carpenters, wheelwrights, smiths, collar makers, trimmers, &c.
³ The Proofmasters may have worked under the Comptroller of Fireworks; their task was to assist the surveyor in checking powder.

Time period 1701 to 1714
From the Book
The Armies of Queen Ann

Reign of QUEEN ANNE - 1702 - 1714

The first peace time train was formed in 1698. A typical train of 1703 carried 14 sakers (*), 10 three-pounders, 4 ten-inch and 6-eight-inch guns. It had two companies of gunners with engineers in the form of pioneers and pontoon men, as well as an Assistant Commissary of Stores, wheelwrights, collar men and tin (*) men.

The above comes from the Book, " *The Armies of Queen Anne*" pg 175, out of a foot note at the bottom, "History of the Corps of Royal Engineers" by a Whitworth Porter (London 1889) - Vol. 1 - pages 54 - 56 & 61

(*) The **saker** was a medium cannon slightly smaller than a culverin developed during the early 16th century and often used by the English. The **tin-men** maintain or made all forms of tin ware in a field army, good example of this trade can be found in Colonial Williamsburg, Virginia.

1706 [25] The present Corps of Royal Engineers was represented solely by officers, and the artisans were entirely civilian. There were no other ranks at this time. Artillery trains, of course, were not standard in size, but were designed for the expedition on which engaged. example - one was mentioned in "The Soldiers Accompt" in 1647, was commanded by a General of Ordnance, assisted by a Lieutenant-General. Very much like the combine arms of today's modern army, artillery, infantry, tanks and engineers.

There was a Chief Engineer, and six engineers "for ordering of trenches, fortifications, and approaches". For the guns and their transport and ammunition, there were twenty gentlemen of the ordnance, matrosses, a wagon-master, assistants, and conductors,(*) commissaries, and an ammunitionary. There are miners, and 600 pioneers with officers.

(*) - I have yet to determine what a Conductor was or what they did.

At the turn of the eighteenth century the engineers were, like the artillery, an arm of the Office of Ordnance only part military, and part civilian artisans. In the case of the engineers the civilian element was present throughout in all categories, and was not, as was largely the case in the artillery, restricted to specific tasks. (pg 183 - end note #25). Example: U.S. Government - part civilian and part military.

It would also appear that for Pioneers in general were attached to the various trains of artillery as needed and for the most part controlled by the Engineers. It doesn't appear that they had attachments to individual Infantry regiments at this time.

These appointments were all in the permanently established "Headquarters Staff"(*) of engineers. The engineers officers in the trains were drawn from line regiments, and commanded miners, pioneers, pontoon men and local laborers. (Pg 185- end note #25) (*) Headquarters was the Central Administration in all Military Units)

In the field a Captain of Pioneers drew 4s per day, Sergeants of Pioneers drew 2s per day and the pioneers themselves drew 1s per day.[26] (refer to page 48 for the pay scale in Queen Ann's Army).

Storming Parties and Mining [27]

During the siege of Lisle (Lille), **(1709)** there was a French garrison of 15,000 and 50 Allied Battalions who were detailed for the siege. Two storming parties were made up of 1,600 Grenadiers and 2,000 "Workmen and 30 Carpenters" assigned to remove the palisades. It's not clear if these "Workmen" were civilian or military, but it's safe to assume that due to the very hazardous nature of any assault, that the assault party would be comprised of disciplined troops.

During the siege of Tournai, it appears to have been the scene of a remarkable contest in mining, there being more mine galleries below than trenches above ground. A warren of tunnels extended for miles and counter-mining went on continuously. Often mines were found, after laborious digging, far outside the Citadel, and the powder was removed, before further mining. There were numerous fights with sword, pistol and bayonet, when opposing tunnellers met underground, and sometimes, owing to the darkness, men fought against their own side Frequently whole parties were asphyxiated by the gases from explosions, or drowned by undermining.

Reign of KING GEORGE I - 1714 - 1727

A Royal Warrant (**May 26, 1716**) was issued by King George I, thus the Royal Regiment of Artillery was born as well as a Corps of 28 Engineers was formed.[28]

The Guards Regiment (personal body guard to the King) was the first to have organized a detachment of Pioneers which were added to their establishment.[29] The COLD STREAM GUARDS raised in 1650, oldest regiment in continuous active service in the British Army.

Following close behind, many other regiments followed suit. When in 1739, the 42nd Regiment was established, (Royal Highlanders or Black Watch), they in turn had a detachment of pioneers attached, but not wearing kilts like the regular soldiers, but wearing Blue Cloth leggings and breeches made out of tent canvas; its possible that the entire Regiment worn this uniform in the field while in America. They became a permanent part of the Regiment. One must keep in mind, that the Highland Regiments were on a different Establishment than regular British line Regiments.

1720 - Duties of the Regimental Quarter-Master, Company Quarter-Master and the Camp-Color man[30]

In the History of the Regiment and Uniforms of the British Army, it mentions that there is a Sgt. of a regiment. and a man of a Company appointed to assist the Quarter-master during the campaign, in marking out and keeping the camp clean; as also for performing of all other things which appertain to their duty, such as receiving of ammunition, bread, or other provisions which shall be distributed to their regiments.; all ammunition, working tools, clothes, carriages and accoutrements"

Each Regiment[31] was responsible to transport its own baggage. Therefore, each Regiment had its own Wagon Master. Each Company had 2 wagons or carriages assigned for its Captains, 1 Wagon for the Subalterns, 2 Wagons for the Regiments Headquarters, and 2 wagons for each company to transport tents, poles, blankets, kettles and supplies.

Reign of KING GEORGE II - 1727 - 1760

In 1741 The Board of Ordnance made the necessary regulations to instruct those raw and inexperienced personnel belonging to the Military Branch of their Office.[32]

In Woolwich Warren, a room was setup for the purpose of instruction, thus the Royal Military Academy was formed. this became the only such established school in the United Kingdom setup to train officers of the Artillery & Engineer and in 1920 Signals, were also trained until 1939, when it was disbanded and moved to Sundhurst, and was thereby amalgamated with the Royal Military College.[33]

1745

Excerpts from the Diary of a Captain Philip Browne - 1737 - 1746[34] Browne had received a commission as Cornet in the King's Own Regiment of Horse, on July 17, 1737, of which Henry, 9th Earl of Pembroke, was at that time Col. Captain Browne purchased a commission as Exempt and Capt. in the 3rd Troop of Horse in 1745, until the troop was reduced, then he was placed on half pay. Capt. Browne's name appears on Army list in 1765 for the last time, probably died in 1764. (The term "Exempt", means he held a Commission but did no duty.) Capt. Browne was present for the Battles of Dettingen (1743) and Fentenoy (1745). His diary reflects operations where Pioneers and Carpenters were mentioned.

The Diary runs in 3 segments - Sept. 1737 to June 1743 - June 1743 to April 1745 - and April 1745 to February 1746[35]

April 23, 1745 - Soignies Camp - Every Regiment of Foot is to complete the tools they have from the train to 10 Pickaxes, 10 Spades, and 10 Shovels.

The Quarter-Master and Camp-Color man with the new guard shall assemble at the head of the Highlanders at 4pm.

April 25, 1745 - Monday - Canbron - The 2 Brigades of Guards march at 5, to fall in to the line. The Pioneers to be at the head of the column as usual with their wagons of tools and this is to be a standing order.

April 27, 1745 - Wednesday - Chateau de Moullbaix - The Quarter-Masters, Camp Color man, and Pioneers to be at the head of the Dutch Dragoon Guards on the left at 3 tomorrow morning. This was also mentioned in the Diaries of Lt. General the Hon. Charles Colville.[36]

April 29, 1745 - Friday - Brassoel - 6 Battalions and 12 squadrons from the right with 500 pioneers with their arms, and wagons with tools, are to parade at 10 o'clock at the head of Duroure's Regiment, (Later the 12th), with 6 - 3 pounders and 2 Howitzers of the English Train.

1st Battalion Guards Lt. General Thomas Howard's, Major General Richard Onslow's Regiment (Later the 8th), with Col. Robinson Sowle's Regiment, (Later the 11th), and 2 Battalion's of Hanoverians, comprise the 6 Battalions.

1748 [37]

FLANDERS - April - May 1748 - The Artillery train was proceeded by a strong body of infantry provided by the Army as "Guard". The first element of the train was a company of miners; "With their tumbrel of tools", drawn by 2 horses, and were followed by the forward part of the trains own escort, the Regts. of Artillery front Escort.

Every squadron had a forage cart and there are references to furrier's carts, which were presumably the traveling forges. Refer to the following sketches.

There are likewise some parties of pioneers interspersed here and there to mend the roads when they are spoiled by the forge carriages.[38]

The specialist vehicles included a "Trumbel", a two wheeled cart used to carry the tools of the pioneers and miners, and also the money for the Army.

This same cart was used in various ways, to transport powder for the Artillery, Bread and adapted as a traveling forge. Refer to pgs. 55 & 56 of this work.

The sketches on the following pages came from three sources. First an article found Vol. 61 of the Journal for the "*Society of Army Historical Research*", found at the West Point Military Library.

The second source came from the book "*Round Shot and Rammers*", by a Harold Peterson.

The third source came from Parks Canada, the Curator of the Louisburg Fortress Historic Site in Nova Scotia.

1756 [39]

So little importance was attached to target practice, that the allowance of ball ammunition for a regiment not on active service was limited to 4 balls for each man. In regiments that were keen on shooting, however, it was common to fix the butts (targets), against the bank so the lead could be collected and recast in moulds by the Regimental Pioneers.

1757 [40]

Officers of the Engineer Corps received military rank and the Chief Engineer, a William Skinner, (Chief of Royal engineers 1660-1802) was made Colonel. A William Green (1st Baronet 1786 - 1802) was appointed Captain-Lt. in 1757, and in 1759 served with General Wolf when he captured Quebec.

FIELD FORGES

A[41] later forge is illustrated in John Muller's *A TREATISE OF ARTILLERY,* first published in 1757. Although the system of contract supply was not much changed by that date, an Ordnance Wagon Train had been established, and this forge appears to be purpose built, rather than an adaptation of a civilian vehicle. It was, basically, a two wheeled cart, but the two main side members extended some distance to the rear to support a metal fireplace and hearth. Behind the fireplace a metal fire back protected the wooden superstructure from them flames.

A hole in the fire back gave access to the nozzle of the bellows, which were fixed to the superstructure behind, and worked by a handle called a rocking staff, suspended above. Boxes could be positioned around the bellows to contain tools and a water trough which was suspended at the rear of the cart.

A later edition of Muller's book, published in 1780, still shows the same forge and it can therefore, perhaps, be assumed that forges of this type were in service in the Austrian Succession War, The Seven Years War, The American Revolution and the early French Revolutionary War.

As this forge had two wheels only, some support was required to maintain it in the horizontal position when in use. This was provided by four swivel legs. These, however did not give a sufficient degree of stability in Muller's opinion, and he thought that a four wheeled wagon would be better. In the later edition of his work he mentioned that some four wheeled vehicles had, by then, been introduced and commented on the use of an artillery limber to provide an additional pair of wheels to what would otherwise be a two wheeled cart.

A scale model of the limber type of vehicle is on display in the Rotunda of the Museum. (exhibit 25/51)

The cart is of wooden construction with the body being 6 feet long and 4 feet wide; with wooden sides 2 feet high. The whole being covered by a rounded canvas roof.

Rolling Stock

In the field the British artillery was served by a well-organized system of rolling stock. There were wagons for carrying ammunition, powder carts for extra powder, two-wheeled tumbrels for general purposes, and travelling forges for field repairs.

From the book titled
Round Shot & Rammers

by Harold
L. Peterson

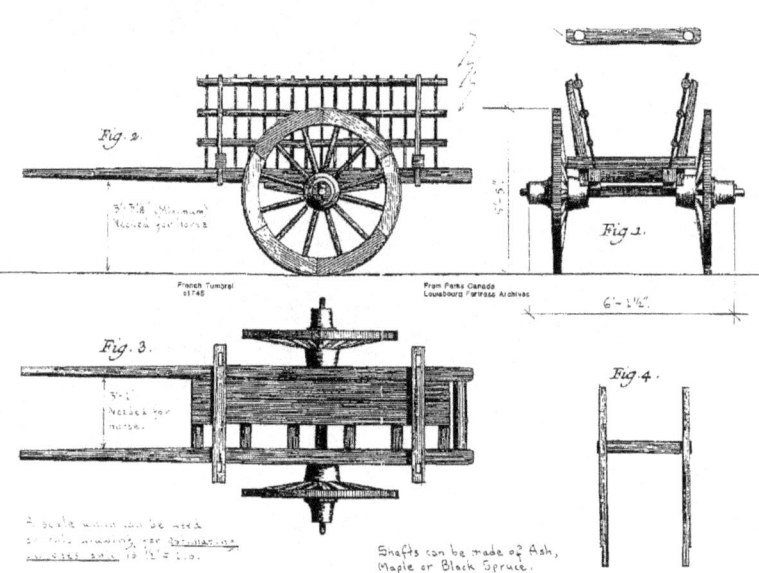

The above drawing was provided by Parks Canada Louisbourg Fortress Archives

FIELD FORGES

MARLBOROUGH'S CAMPAIGNS

MID TO LATE 18TH CENTURY

Journal for the Society of Army Historical Research - Vol. 61
Article by W. G. Child:
"FIELD FORGES OF THE BRITISH ARMY - 1700 - 1900"

In EXCERPS ONLY .....

..."An example of the kind of mobile forge that could have been seen in the Duke of Marlborough's military train is on show at the Rotunda Artillery Museum, Woolwich. There is a full scale model amoung the outside exhibits and a small version is on display inside. (Exhibit 25/12) This was a heavy four wheeled wagon, with billows mounted at the rear, and a metal fireplace sheltered by a metal hood, placed centrally. Under the fire there was an ash can, and forward of it a trough for water. a large box at the front presumbly contained tools."

It seems unlikely, therefore, that Marlborough's forge was part of the regular army establishment. It was probably a civilian wagon, hired to the army by contractors and adaped to its particular function. The museum catalogue indicates that it is of Dutch origin.

It is of inelegant construction and ill proportioned. Its general appearance, however, is in keeping with the ponderous, slow moving character of the armies of the period.

It has two wooden wheels 4 feet in diameter and a pair of shafts extending forward for a single horse. When the wheels are blocked, two short struts support the longer ones up front, but still looks unstable for a base for hard work.

The fireplace and metal hearth are mounted at the rear, and the bellows shaft is clearly shown, the anvil is on a large log, standing on the ground. Two furriers usually operate the forge. I suggest you refer to the sketches of the "Trumbles". Trumbles being as versatile as today's modern Army Humv's.

TREATISE OF MILITARY DISCIPLINE [42]
4th Edition c1720 and the 5th Edition of March 26, 1759
both by a Colonel Humphrey Bland, Esq.

Both books indicate that there were at least 10 Pioneers, in each Regiment (1 per company). There appears to be an evolution of drill which was used at Battalion formations to move the pioneers into their respective positions when the Battalion was either preparing to march out of camp or go on parade. There is also a tune played at this time called "The Pioneer March", which also might be known as the "English Pioneers March", titled "Round Heads and Cuckolds', Come dig".

Please take note of **DIAGRAM A - (Pg 58)** The basic movement or The Order of March by Regiments.

DIAGRAM "A"

THE BRITISH COLUMN * LINE OF MARCH * DEPLOYMENT OF THE PIQUETS
AND PIONEER DETAILS   c 1702 - 1761

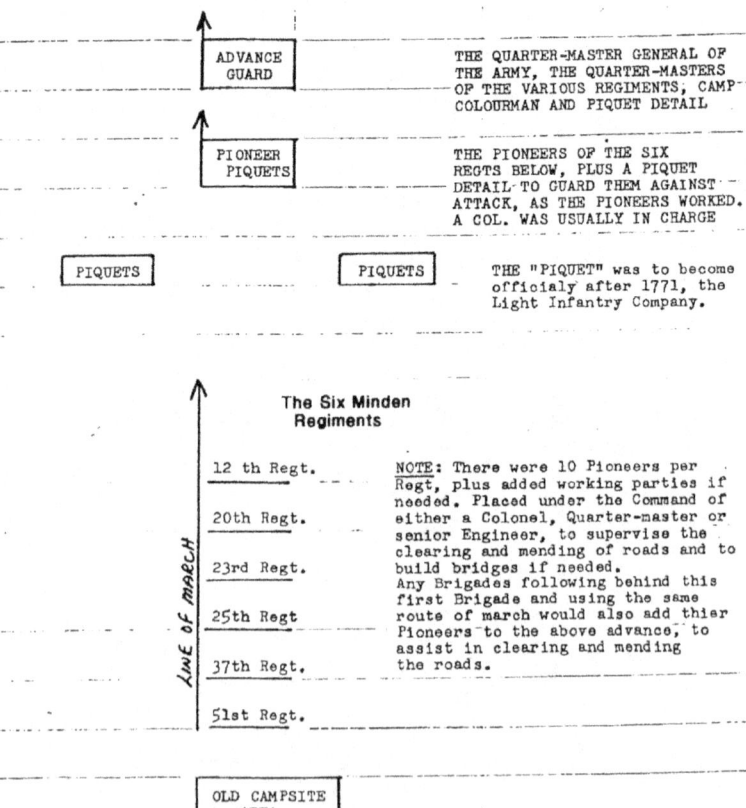

1702 - 1761 - The British Army of this period had few if any Engineers and no trained Engineer troops.

DIAGRAM "B"
(Pg. 60)

Taken from *"The Treatise of Military Discipline"* - 5th Edition 1759

In part goes as follows: Chapter 1; Art 1; Page 3

The pioneer, with his musket rested on his arm, marches at about 12 paces before his Captain, **(G)**. The officers are at **(A)**.

The Companies are to be formed as laid out in this diagram, when forming into a Battalion line.

DIAGRAM B - (Pg. 60)

The Drummers **(F)**, are to march about 12 paces in the front, where they face to the right-about, beating the TROOP, from the time they quit their respective companies, till the officers are at their posts.

The Pioneer advances 2 paces beyond the Drummers and then faces to the right about also.

Chapter 1; Art 2; Page 5

At the word of Command for it, all Pioneers face to the left as do, one half of the Drummers; excepting the two Drummers who are to beat orderly; and they face to the right about.

At the word of Command, MARCH, from the Major, the officers step off with their left foot, those who are to go to the left, marching on the outside.

When the Command of MARCH was given, the Pioneer march was played. Refer to Chapter on Music page 286.

DIAGRAM "B"

Depending on the direction of the march, say the regiments were moving to the left, the Pioneer from the furthest company or Regiment on the right, would turn and face left and begin marching down the front of the assembled companies or Regiments, picking up each pioneer as they passed each company and so on to the end, and take their respective position at the head of the column. the Grenadier company would then fall in behind the Pioneers.

If the Regiment wasn't moving into a column, but remaining in the Battalion line, the line of Pioneers and Drummers are marched down the line of Companies, each company Pioneer in turn, would join this procession until they reached the point where they then take their respective position to the right of the Grenadier company.

Chapter 17; Art 3; Page 247

When the Army marches, the Quarter-Masters and the Camp-Color men are ordered before to take up the ground on which they are to encamp; and as soon as the Quarter-Master General, or his Deputies have given them their ground, they are to mark out the encampment of their Regiment.

All of these exercise's were before the addition of the Light Infantry Company which came about in 1771

Reign of KING GEORGE III - 1760 - 1820

EXCERPTS: taken from the book titled:

THE MANUAL EXERCISE, *as ordered by His Majesty, in 1764*, together with plans and explanations of the methods generally practiced at reviews and field days.

POSITION OF THE PIONEERS IN THE RANKS [43]
DIAGRAM (C) - Figure (Pg 63)

From this station, they can lead the entire Battalion out, or move to the position of RESERVE, behind the Drummers and the colors at the center of the Battalion.

FIGURE 2

This is called the COLUMN, used to move the Battalion when marching from one place to another or a Pass in review formation. With the Pioneers and Grenadiers out in front.

FIGURE 3

This would be the Battalion's Battle formation, much like Figure 1, but the Colors, Drummers and Pioneers are to the rear of the line.

> From the Manual - Page 32 - **Fig 1** - "as the Regt. is drawn up for
> For a Battalion Formation"

Author's Collection

2001 British Brigade at Blue Bell, PA.

63

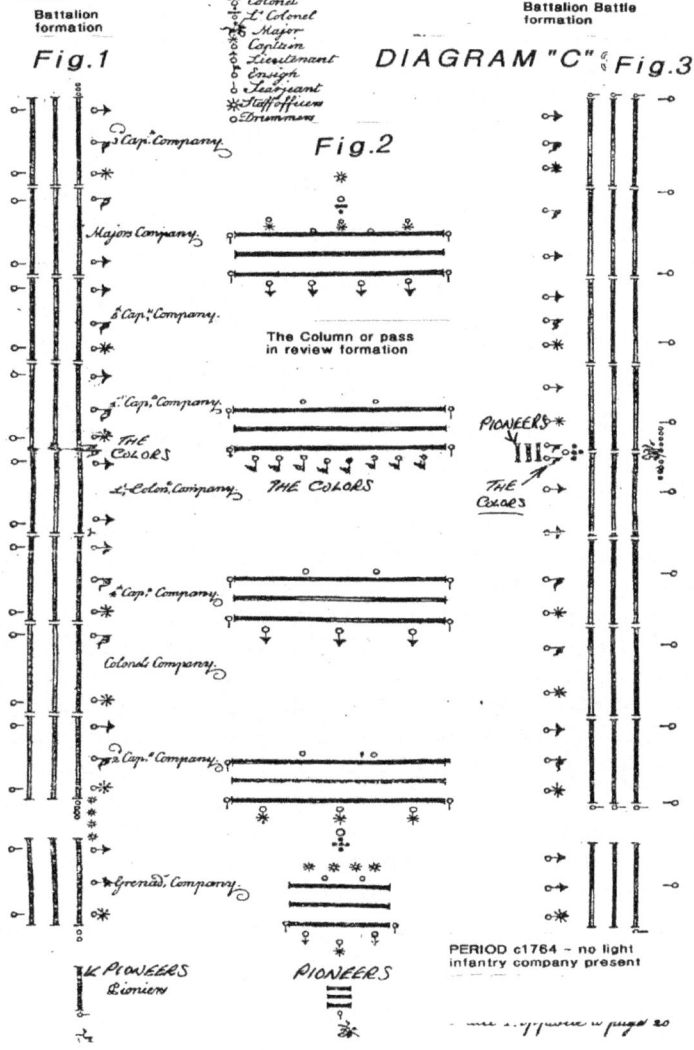

DIAGRAM "C"

Fig.1 Battalion formation
Fig.2 The Column or pass in review formation
Fig.3 Battalion Battle formation

PERIOD c1764 – no light infantry company present

The Grenadier company at 10 paces distance from the right of the battalion. The Grenadier Drummers and Fife's on the right of the Company.

The Pioneers in one rank on the right of the of the Grenadiers and at 10 paces.

FIGURE 2

Page 32 - "A pass in review by GRAND DIVISIONS"
The Regiment marches in the following order:
The Major
The Pioneers, in 3 ranks, with NCO in front.
The Grenadier Company, the Captain advanced 2 paces before the Lieutenants.

Chaplain, Quarter-Master, Surgeon and mate in one rank. The Colonel, advanced four paces before the 1st rank of officers, etc.

FIGURE 3 - PAGE 26
"Battalion Formed for Exercise"

The Regiment is then to go through the Manual and Platoon exercise as, after which the officers and N.C.O.'s return to their posts and by signal from the orderly drum the Battalion is then to prepare for firings in the following manner :

Grenadiers and Pioneers face to the left ...
Grenadiers and Pioneers march, the Pioneers follow the rear rank of the Grenadiers until they come to the rear of the colors when they stand fast.

The Command is given, for the Grenadiers to cover the flanks of the Battalion. This is before the addition of the Light Infantry Company, thus the grenadiers were divided into two sections, and each section therein covered a flank.

The pioneers in turn, faced to the front and are in position 4 paces in the rear of the Reserve. The Reserve - is made up as follows ...

The Colonel - The Lt. Colonel - The reserve for the colors is to be 6 files.

Lord Orkneys Regiment of Foot c1704

Photo taken from the collection of Sir Michael Grenier -Commander of the 64th Regiment of Foot in America
The Tercentenary Celebration at the Staffordshire's Regimental Museum Litchfield England in September 2005

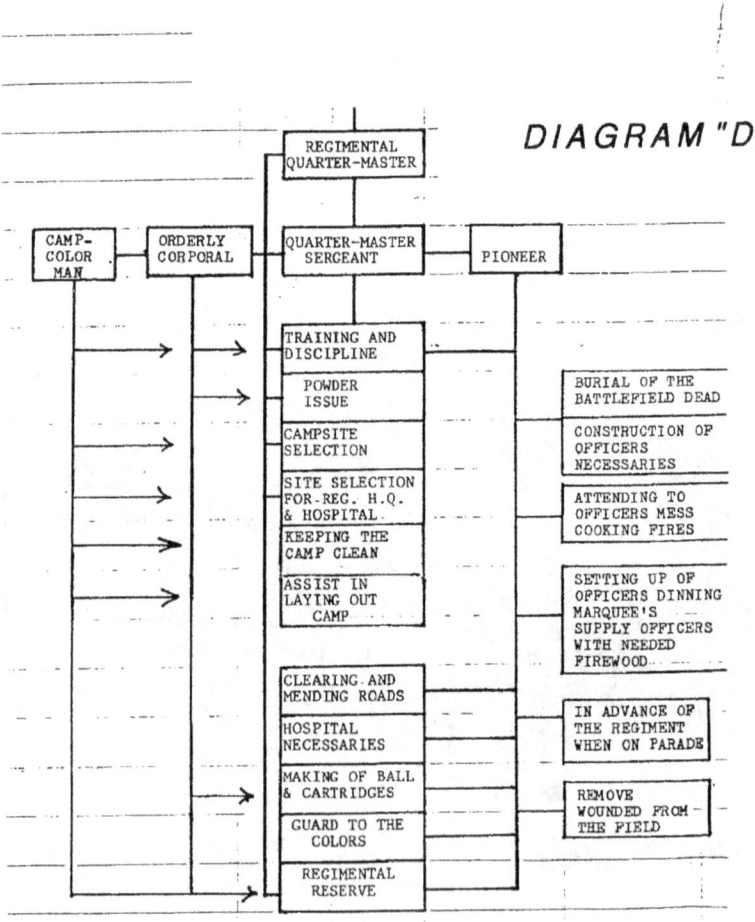

The Ensigns with the colors in the center rank with:
2 Sergeants to their front and 2 Sergeants to the rear.
The Basic make up of the British Infantry Regiments of that time were 9 Companies, 8 Hat Companies or Battalion Soldiers and 1 Company of Grenadiers.

It was after 1771 that the light Infantry Company was added bringing a Battalion up to 10 Companies of 477 Rank and file on the English Establishment.

DIAGRAM **(D)** **(Page 66)**

Shows in part the various assigned duties, for the Regimental Quarter-Master, Camp-Color man, Orderly Corporal and the Pioneers.

In general this information was collected from such books as: Art of Warfare in the Middle Ages, Treatise of Military Discipline 4th and 5th Editions, The Manual of Exercise - 1764, and the Soldiers Diary of the Seven Years War - Journal of Wm Todd, 12th Foot.

The locating of Todd's Journal was in fact my greatest find, and really opened up the entire realm of the British Pioneer. Found in the Journal for the Society of Army Research, Volumes 12 and 29 at the West Point Military Library. There are three known diaries, but only two have been found and reprinted.

1760 [44] Captain-Lt. William Green was appointed Chief Engineer and moved to Gibraltar, where he began the long job of improving the defenses of the fortress that were to bear fruit in the Great Siege.

Of a later period than Bishop[45] was William Todd who started his working life on the turnpike between Hull and Hedon. He enlisted in the Associated Companies of Militia of Yorkshire and served during the Jacobite Rebellion of 1745 -46.

When I found Todd's diary, in a foot note Bishops name had been mentioned, he had enlisted from the Royal Navy into Webb's Regt., which served under Marlborough in 1708.

From the Militia he enlisted in the 30th Foot. When that regiment was in Kilkenny in 1749, Todd started a journal. Early in 1755, war was appearing likely, the 30th and seven other "Irish" Regiments were transferred to England. In 1750; Todd having been prompted a Corporal, the 30th were in camp at Chatham with four other Regiments.

While in camp at Chatham, the Major issued orders - The Sergeants were not to drink with the Corporals, nor the Corporals with privates. Todd suggested that the Corporals form a club, to meet after roll call at the senior Corporals quarters. This excellent idea was followed up by the Sergeants, thus the beginning of the NCOs Mess in the Regiment's. This was all due to Todd's suggestion, which was followed up in other regiments[46]

EXCERPTS FROM " A SOLDIERS DIARY OF THE SEVEN YEARS WAR" [47]

The Journals of a Sgt. William Todd - Edited by C.T. Atkinson

PART II - Westphalla in 1761, with the 12th Regiment of Foot. Two parts of this Diary can be found in the J.S.A.H.R. - Vol. 12 and 29

Sometime in either 1760 or 61, Todd joined the 12th, which was operating near Warburg, Germany, as part of Lord Granby's Corps. He had been appointed to Corporal of Pioneers, and was constantly in the outpost line.

In camp near Lippstadt, he helped the men of his company, who he had first quartered with to plant beans, peas and carrots. He also stressed the frequency at which the Regiments drilled and went through the firings using blanks. He explained how the troops after receiving their new clothes, then converted last years coat into a waist coat.

Todd also mentions the high risks involved when out front to cut down wood, to make fascines or build roads or repair bridges through the woods. It was necessary that each battalion company provide at least one pioneer to assist the Regimental Quarter-master.

New tools, hatches and saws, were issued, with along with new aprons and special caps. The men were allowed to dispose of their old tools to the "Boars,"[48] on which money the pioneers had a very good drink; rum.

Several other duties were also mentioned in Todd's Diary in regards to various tasks:

    A. Responsible for cutting a wood supply for the officers and their mess, they were allowed to charge a small fee for these services.

    B. Construction of the officers necessaries (Toilets) and filling them in as needed.

    C. Setting up of the Officers Dinning Marquee and their cooking place.

    D. Construction of chimneys for the Officers Marquees when in winter quarters or when on campaign.

When reading Todd's Diary, it also became quite clear, that the use of pioneers was wide spread, they had the ability to move around at will. They operated ahead of the main army, keeping their arms with them but they also had their own Picquet[49] detail with them.

On at least one occasion, Todd mentions an attack by a rather large French Force; "drums beat to arms and the pioneers quit their work and took their places in the ranks. Granby's Picquets and pioneers together did not number 500 men."

They gave a good account of themselves before it became quite clear that their small force was going to be out flanked; but by this time Lt. Col. Lord Brome,[50] brought up a larger force and took on the fight.

Sandfords four Battalions and the Grenadiers performed wonders and maintained their ground against four times their numbers. The firing went on until night fall, when the troops lay upon the ground, covered by strong patrols.[51]

Understand that this type of warfare was on the main European Continent, where very large bodies of troops; upwards of 50 to 100,000 men; could readily move about.

In the Colonies there were large tacks of forest and few good roads which made movement into the interior nearly impossible Also add the very real possibility of enemy forces waiting in ambush to make travels a nightmare.

I doubt the Pioneers, if in fact any where used here during the American Revolution, had the same ability to move about so freely.

PIONEERS OF THE PRUSSIAN AND AUSTRIAN ARMIES

1754 to 1761

THE PRUSSIANS [52]

In 1740, Frederick the Great had a small but well regulated Corps of 45 military engineers.

There was a Dutch born Catholic, named Col. Gerhardt Cornelius v. Walrave (1692 - 1773), who had put the Prussian Engineers on an institutional basis in 1729 and virtually founded the "Prussian" style of fortress design. In May of 1741, Walrave was promoted to Major-General for his services and in 1742 was appointed to the head of the new Pioneer Regiment then in Neisse.

Unfortunately for Walrave, by 1745 he found himself in disfavor of the King and was placed under arrest and there after spent his days in Sternschanze Fortress where he died in 1773.

The King always complained about the lack of a trained body of Sappers, even though he did have 10 Companies of Pioneers who were repairing military roads. He failed to fully appreciate that valuable resource in Walrave's Pioneer-Regiment and even ignored the broad hint that was given to him after the failure of the siege of Olmutz. In November 1758, the King converted the ten musketeer companies of pioneers into an ordinary Regiment of Fusiliers (no. 49)

This left two companies of miners as a separate organization with a third company raised in 1761. Even with this, the miners still lacked proficiency. A fourth company was raised in 1783, with personnel drawn from the mining districts of the monarchy.

Pioneers of some sort must have had a rebirth, if to refer to the book by John Mollo and Malcolm Mc Greagor "Uniforms of the American Revolution", look for plate number 135, there you'll find a Pioneer belonging to a Garrison Regiment V. Stein

THE AUSTRIAN ARMY [53]
(*) see end notes for full officers names

The Corps of sappers was the child of Gribeauval (*) and the engineers, the Pioneers were the creation of the infantry. They met the specialized need of trained troops to move ahead of an army to clear and mend roads and build bridges if needed.

The first proposal was made in 1757, to raised enough pioneers to have detachments assigned to every force of 20,000 or so troops. By January 1758, the first battalion had been sanctioned by Maria Theresa, it had 4 companies of 111 officers and men, together with a company of Jager's to act as a covering force while the pioneers worked.

The pioneers and Jagers wore a common uniform of Hechtgrau with a black cap. Hechgrau is a fish gray color, very similar to today's modern German Army uniform.

The Jagers were recruited from Huntsmen and gamekeepers, the pioneers (Pioniere) came from men who worked with their hands and miners, boatmen and fishermen.

They were ready for service in March 1758 and were commanded by their founding father Lacy,(*) Austria's first Chief of Staff. They more then proved their worth in the hilly country of Southern Saxony, and by 1759 Lacy had built up the companies to 266 officers and men.

They should have been secure in their reputation, but by 1761 as the war ended, radical economies were undertaken, and Kaunitz (*) had singled them out to be disbanded.

(*) Full names and titles can be found in the end notes

Arguments against this disbanding were ignored and by December 25th, 1761, 200 personnel transferred to the Staff Infantry and another 200 to the Pontoniers.

By 1760, the average age of the pioneers was 25.

Members of the 64th Regiment of Foot (c1775) in America
Staffordshire Regimental Museum, Litchfield England
Photo from Sir Michael Grenier's Collection

Battalion Cpl.　　　Light Infantry　　　Battalion　　　Grenadiers

Please note the enlarged sketch of a Pioneer doing the manual of arms, not with a musket but with what appears to be an axe. From the Regulament 1749, the Company Zimmerleuth, or singular Zimmermann - Pioneer.

From the Book - **Instrument of War** - **The Austrian Army of the Seven Years**
By Christopher Duffy - Page 132   Company Zimmerleuth (Regulament of 1749)

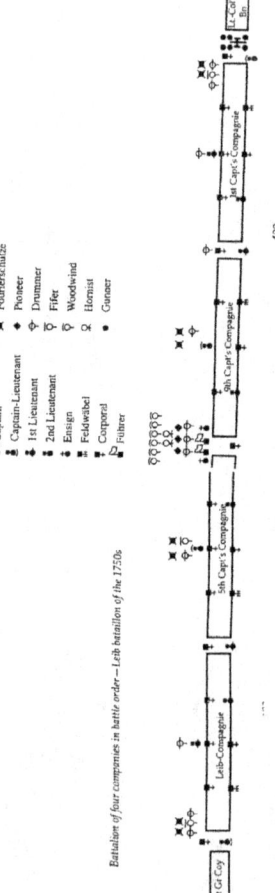

From the same book - The Austrian Army of the Seven Years War -
Note the position of the PIONEERS along with the music and behind the colors
Nearly the same arrangement as that of the British Line regiments

NATIONAL ARMY MUSEUM
Royal Hospital Road London SW3 4HT

Telephone Army Network Nam Military } ext 47
Civil Network 01-730 0717

Mr W Eisenhauer
Hyde Park Heights Apt 10 M
Hyde Park
New York 12538
USA

Your reference

Our reference
6415
Date
18 March 1983

Dear Mr Eisenhauer

Mrs Hopkins has asked me to reply to part of your letter of 27 February. I have identified the Lieutenant Colonels that you listed as follows:

Robert Dal. Horn, Elphinston   1st Foot
James Gisborne   10th Foot, Quarter Master General, Ireland
Alexander Mackay   39th Foot
John Pomeroy   18th Foot
Robert Cuninghame   Adjutant General, Ireland

As the 1st, 10th, 18th, and 39th were all stationed in Ireland in Nov 1761, it seems that the company was formed there, and hence Capt Steele had to go to Dubli to meet them.

Yours sincerely

P B BOYDEN
Department of Archives

The letter on the page 76, dated 18 March 1983 from the National Army Museum, names several Regiments and Commanders then in garrisoned Ireland. One of the officers named therein, Col. Pomeroy became an officer in the 64th Regiment of Foot[54]

Colonel John Pomeroy, age 40, 22 years of service; date of 1st commission was October 1745, Captain in 1749, and final Commission on March 19, 1762.

> Col. John Pomeroy, Commander, 64th Regiment of Foot, 1766 - 1790 (when he died) Also, commissioned as Major General in 1772, and Lt. General in 1777.

In early May 1981, I purchased photo copies of original letters from the Public Record Office in London. They are War Office Records dating back to 1762,[55] my only problem was to find someone to read this old 18th Century hand writing. So I contacted Col. John Elting, US Army (Ret), and he spent considerable time deciphering the many pages, which I found nearly impossible to read.

The photo copies themselves are quite large, too large to reduce them to a point where you could still read them.

The FIRST SERIES of letters, cover a period from August 7, 1762 to May 1763 and are in reference to the raising of a company of Pioneers. The Second Series of letters cover a period some 37 years later.

It's believed that the men to form this company of pioneers were drawn from these 4 regiments, letter dated 18 March 1983.

WAR OFFICE RECORDS - WO 1/982

SERIES I

Copies of letters and orders relative to Captain Steeles Company of Pioneers being appointed to march and embark for Portugal.

Whitehall, August 7, 1762

My Lord,
I am commanded to signify to your Excellency His Majesties pleasure that

you do forthwith give the proper orders for Draughting One Hundred private able bodied men, free from any infirmities, and fit for Pioneers, from some or all of the 5 regiments raised last in Ireland and commanded by Lieut. Colonels Commandant, Horne, Elphinstone, Grisborne, Mackay, Pomeroye and Cunningham, respectfully, in order to form a Company of Pioneers, to serve in Portugal, but which are to be placed on the Establishment of and paid by Great Britain, from the day of their embarkation in Ireland inclusive, and to be commanded by Capt. Richard Steele, to whom said Draughts are to be delivered without arms and accoutrements, at Dublin as soon as possible, and for which Draughts the said Capt. Steele is to pay, to the respective officers who shall deliver them, after the rate of five pounds English for each man.

To His Excellency the Earl greatest
of Halifax and etc. etc.
(?)

Eqrement

I am with

Truth

La

****

WO 1/982

TO Capt. Steele
London, Oct. 20, 1762

Sir,
I am Commanded by Lord Ligonier to acquaint you in consequence of a letter, received this morning from Sir Robert Wilmot, Secretary to the Lord Lieut. of Ireland, with an extract of a letter from Mr. Waite, Secretary to the Lords Justice of said Kingdom, who acquaints his Lordship that the Draughts which form your Company of Pioneers destined for Portugal, have been for a considerable time at Dublin. That you do obey such orders as you have already had communicated to (you?) by the Secretary of War.

I am, sir, obt & etc.
Richard Cox

NOTE:

Capt. Steele received verbal orders October 17th, 1762 from His Excellency Lord Ligonier, to march directly on his landing in England, for Portsmouth, there to embark in a vessel provided for Portugal by the Portuguese Minister, on which Capt. Steele and his officers provided horses & other camp necessaries, expecting to embark as soon as they could arrive at Portsmouth; but were afterwards directed by the route (marching orders) which they received on their arrival at Chester, to halt at Hempstead & Highgate until further orders.

****

This letter translated from French, of a sort ......

TO: Capt. Steele (TEAR ....icese Minister
(probable "Portuguese Minister)

Monsieur, the Corps of Pioneers which you raised by order, or with the permission of S.M.D. (undoubtedly "His Britannic Majesty") will be very useful, and do not doubt that we wish to also raise several companies in Portugal. I pray you, Monsieur, to provide the necessary tools for 300 Portuguese soldiers. I wish however to know in advance exactly the price of these tools, and you shall be repaid immediately after they are delivered. I also wish to know and this is the most important point, the time at which your Corps and tools will be ready, for if there is much delay they won't be of any service in Portugal. I hope, monsieur, that the activity with which you and Monsieur your brother proceed, to get yourselves as quickly as possible to Lisbon with the Corps which you command, shall be regarded by the King, my master, as (blurred - probably "proof") of your zeal, deserving to have your (blurred) that circumstances will present. For the rest I have the honor to be with much respect, Monsieur.

Your, etc.
De Mello

****

London the 17th of July 1762

White Church, Feb. 1st, 1763

Sir,

I have the honor to acquaint you the Royal Pioneers under my command have preformed their march hitter, with their arms, tools, tents and ordinary (?), baggage, with so much facility that I have not left a man behind. Therefore I humbly hope that it will be represented to His Majesty that the utility of this Corps & practicabilility proposed (by carrying about them all their requisitis for any expedition), is now fully proved by the experience of this march of 200 miles.

As it has been intimated to me that we may expect his Majesty will give orders for disbanding as, I will beg leave to represent that as I received his Majesty's commands to compose this Corps from Draughts & to furnish them with proper Arms, Tools & Tents, in order to ascertain the practicability of our plan by suitable experiment. I so little expected to be disbanded that I have in their clothing & equipment spared no coat, but have had a particular attention to have their arms & tools made for durability & in some parts of clothing have gone to an expense four times more than the ordinary, particularly in their helmets which I calculated to last three years; also besides the contingent expenses necessary incumed. the whole Corps (who have been marching six weeks during the very short time since their establishment) have got so deep in my debt per shoes & other unavoidable expenses on their private acct. that not less than 6 months strict can repay.

For which reason, Sir, I humbly hope, as I have fully accomplished & proved the utility of my undertaking and the practicability of our plan, that we may not be the first disbanded or that when it shall please His Majesty to give orders, such provision may be made as to preserve (?) me from being a loser.

May I also beg leave to add that my Brother the Capt. Lieutenant who has an equal share with me in the invention (if it is thought to have any merit), has had hitherto no reward, being only (?) from the same rank in another Corps.

I hope, sir, you will pardon me for troubling you with this detail, but as some things have touched, passed before you, entered upon your office, I think it my duty to submit it to your consideration. Cont.......

I am, sir, with great respect
Your Most Obedient &
Most Humble Servant

Richard Steele, Capt.

****

TO THE (badly faded) W. Ellis (?) esq., etc., etc., etc.

Chester, 2nd Feb. 1763

Sir,

I have the honor to acquaint you that the Company of Royal Pioneers under my Command arrived here this day, having performed the march with great facility and ease, without having one man behind, carrying all their arms, tents, tools and tent poles, etc.

I am with great respect, Sir
your most obedient and
most Humble Servant

Richard Steele, Capt.

****

To the Right Honorable
Wilbue Ellis, Esq.
etc., etc., etc.

Hamilton Street, Piccadilly
May 12, 1763

Sir,

My agent, having applied to your office in the usual form, for the proper power to receive my Contingent Expenses, together with the money I expended for the hire and victualing of a vessel from Ireland, which, to comply with orders for the immediate Embarkation of the Draughts, I was obligated to take upon myself, having applied to the Admiralty for the purpose in vain; and also for the allowance of Batt ("BAT"), baggage, forage, money, having provided horses & camp Equipage suitable for the Portuguese service, for which we were destined. The Gentlemen in your office alleging that they knew not that we were under orders for foreign service refuse to proceed herein without your particular orders; wherefore I am under the necessity of troubling you herein, wherein I enclose a copy of my Lord Eqsement letter, which I presume will put this matter beyond doubt. I can likewise produce Lord Legonier's orders to the same purpose, as also a copy of my application to the Lords of the Admiralty for a transport, but I do not chose to trouble you with so many papers unless you desire them, believing Lord Eqrements letter will be sufficient.

But I take the liberty to enclose the copy of the terms approved by His majesty for raising my company, though afterwards the appointment of the two Subalterns was taken from me, whereby I had L600 less towards defraying the expenses that I had expected. By Brother (equally concerned in the invention with myself), had no advance in Rank & the expense of the equipment (by failure our Contractors), exceeded every estimate we had made.

I fear, Sir, I have tried your patience, but beg your indulgence and that you'll be pleased to give the necessary orders for my reimbursement, which will greatly oblige Sir,

With great Respect, your
Most obedient, Humble Servant
Richard Steele

****

It's unclear from these letters if this idea if Company of Royal Pioneers saw service in Portugal, or any where else for that matter. It appears by the last letter, that the Company may in fact had been disbanded and that Captain Steele was trying as he might to recover some of his out of pocket expenses.

It's a very interesting, that men were draughted (drafted) from other Regiments to form such a company for service outside of England.

The Regiments involved in supplying these draughts are listed in the letter found at the beginning of this first series of letters. from National Army Museum Dated 18 March 1983. (page 76)

EXCERPTS FROM WARRANTS AND RETURNS OF 1768 [56]

CUTHBERTSON: As the pioneers are principally designed for clearing and mending of roads, for the convenient and speedy march of a
CHAP. 13 Battalion, the tools consisting only of a saw and hatchet for
ART. 34 each man, with which they are generally provided, must be often found very tedious and insufficient for that purpose, it would therefore be an improvement, and answer every design of their institution, if 3 pick-axes, 3 spades, 3 hatches, and 3 saws, with proper cases, and white leather slings for each, were to be established tools for the pioneers of a Regiment and to be distributed among them and a Corporal with a hatchet.

APPENDIX: IV
From the return of Necessaries, Arms and accoutrements for a Company of Foot
Page 169 - British Military Uniforms 1768 -96 by Hew Strachan

Listed are Hatches, Saws, Spades and pick-axes

6 January 1768 - C & C out letter to Major General Gage - W.O. 3/24, pg. 3
Number of arms and accoutrements for a Battalion of Foot:
Lists, Axes, Saws, and Aprons for 9 Pioneers

INSPECTION RETURN: 29 August 1768, indicated the following for the 1st Foot: "Grenadiers have cloth caps. Drummers, Fifers and Pioneers have fur caps. 0/13B

19 December 1768: - Misc. Book; regarding clothing, His Majesty's Warrant for regulation of Colors, Clothing, etc.,

PIONEERS[57] - Each to have an axe, a saw and an apron; a cap with a leather crown, and a black bear skin front, on which is to be the King's Crest in White, on a Red ground; also an axe and a saw. The number of the Regt. to be on the back part of the cap.

Returns from Regiments of Foot as listed from British Military Uniforms 1768 -1796

11 FEBRUARY 1770 - C & C out letter to Adj. General to 2nd Battalion of the 1st; 6th; 15th; 17th; 20th; 22nd; 33rd; 35th; 37th; Regiments of Foot. This RETURN, accounting for arms, clothing, etc.; including Axes, saws, and aprons for 9 Pioneers.

INSPECTION RETURN: 2 April 1770, indicated the following for the 48th Foot: "Caps for 43 Grenadiers, 6 Pioneers, etc." TREASURY OUT LETTERS: Ireland; supplies to the 48th Foot. T.14

INSPECTION RETURN: 10 June 1772, indicated the following for the 23rd Foot: "No Pioneer accoutrements in the Light Co."

INSPECTION RETURN: 13 June 1777, indicated the following for the 32nd Foot: "3 Pioneer caps, 3 Pioneer leather aprons, 3 axes, cases and slings, 3 saws, cases and slings".

TREASURY OUT LETTER, Ireland, Supplies to 32nd - T-14

INSPECTION RETURN: 22 Sept. 1778, indicated the following for the 77th (Highland) Foot: 24 Fusils for officers, Grenadier, Light Infantry and Pioneers completely equipped, except caps. T.14

Amherst Papers. W.O. 34 - 4 officer caps, 4 Grenadier officers caps, 10 Pioneer Caps.

TREASURY OUT LETTERS, Ireland. Supplies to the 77th Foot. T. 14

INSPECTION RETURN: 2 June 1792, indicated the following for the 30th Foot: "Pioneer caps wanting since 1781"

INSPECTION RETURN:[58] Oct 1810 - 2nd Battalion/ 3rd Foot, 40 grenadier caps in use, 20 wanting, 2 colours good.....Pioneers, 10 in number, were pointed out to me as idiots Inspection done by a Maj. Gen. Thewles, Berry Head - PRO, WO 27/100

THE COLONIAL WAR PERIOD - 1770 to 1785

The following comes from various sources, dates may be a bit scattered, but in general the information presented will fall within the Revolutionary War period.

Royal Highland Emigrants - 2nd Battalion - "Light Infantrymen had caps, the Grenadiers also as well as matches and rings, and match cases; Light infantry having hatches with cases and belts; Pioneers had caps, axes, saws and aprons. All this was probably sent to Halifax on board the Newcastle Jean in August 1776.[59]

Plans for winter Garrison - 1777 - 1778 - "Repairs were ordered for all houses used as barracks. As only a few chimney sweeps were available, the Pioneers were instructed to keep the chimneys of all quarters swept clean. As Stephen Popp "described, we were quartered in old empty houses on Front Street, the rooms were large, well papered, but very cold, having no stoves to heat them."[60] (The chimneys ran up the out side wall.)

Comments from Mr. Dennis Farmer on the ......8th Regiment of Foot at Niagara.

Mr. Dennis farmer is the curator of the Fort Niagara museum, he formed the 8th Foot, comprised of employees of the Fort; to turnout as British Soldiers to help give tours of the Fort.

In 1989 we were looking into background information for doing a Pioneer on site. After running down a number of returns, equipment lists, etc., we came to the conclusion that the 8th did not have assigned pioneers, and that ad hoc "Pioneers" referred to in the quote are simple labor or fatigue parties with hand tools, such as axes, shovels and picks.

In checking the returns, no man had been detailed as a Pioneer. The inventories of equipment also show no item detailed for Pioneers. However, many of the listed tools could be used. What we do know is that none are specialists items.

Thus it is believed that no "Pioneers" were assigned or used at the Great Lakes post during the war. The only "Pioneers" to appear were labor parties working on entrenchment's and fortifications or clearing fields of fire.[61] This work being done by either Provincial troops or hired civilians.

The Diary of Lieutenant John Baker, 4th Regiment of Foot
THE KINGS OWN
November 1774 to 1776 [62]

John Baker was born in 1750 into an old Suffolk family. He appears on the Army list in 1768 as a Junior Ensign in the 4th Foot, promoted to Lt. in the Regt. on December 3, 1771, and to Captain in the 10th Foot on 13 January 1776.

THURSDAY, 29 December 1774
"Nothing extra to-day but the Quarter-master and all the Pioneers ordered to clear the Grand Parade and the road to the magazine, from hence to the Officers Guard on the Common; that Officer has now the charge of the Magazine." (comment from Lt. John Baker's diary)

GIBRALTAR

March 6th, 1772 - Formation of a Company of Artificers, to serve in the garrison and Fortress of Gibraltar.[63]

The Captain, was the Chief Engineer of the garrison at the time; 1 Sergeant, as Adjutant; 3 Sergeants; 3 Corporals; 60 privates, 1 Drummer. [64]

March 25th, 1774 - An additional Warrant was issued to increase the company to 93 rank and file. Officers of the Corps. of Engineers were appointed to command this body, to which was given the name "The Soldier - Artificer Company".

The Continental Army under General Washington, copied the way the British Quarter-Masters did their jobs.

> 1775 - "At this stage of the war, Congress largely left the development of the logistical apparatus to the judgment of the local commanders, who relied on BRITISH PRECEDENTS. The most important official in the daily life of the troops was the Regimental Quartermaster. In the Continental Army his position was elevated from additional duty to permanent status. He was responsible for distributing rations, clothing, ammunition within the regiment, for assigning quarters, and for pitching

the camp. A daily duty detail of about 6 privates, known as the camp-color-men, assisted him. The Commissariat had numerous civilian functionaries. They included such specialists as conductors, storekeepers, clerks, labours, and skilled craftsmen[65]

For the British, the Infantry, Cavalry and Artillery constituted the three most important branches of the Army. There were in addition to these a Company of Military Artificers (the ancestors of the Royal Sappers and Miners), and a small but efficient Corps of Engineers. The Former saw no service in America.[66]

According to Brook Watson at New York, a number of Departments, or Branches, as they were sometimes called, were established as follows: [67] (W.O.) 60:12, June 1782)

COMMISSARY GENERALS OFFICE
Robert Ross - Comptroller of Transport Accounts
Frederick Hecht - Assist. Commissary and several assistants, clerks and porter.

PROVISION DEPARTMENT

Gregory Townsend and Robert Johnson, Assistant Commissaries and several coopers, carpenters, laborers, assistants and clerks.

Other Departments were: **FORAGE, CATTLE, FUEL** and of course **HIS MAJESTY'S BREWERY**.

Looking carefully through various sources I found the mention of Pioneers which came from the Regiments or even individual Companies to be far and few between. This entire time period between 1770 and 1783, what has already been mentioned is all I found reference to British Regulars being detailed as Pioneers.

Considering that England's military forces were scattered around the world guarding her vast Empire, and embroiled again in another War with France,

Believe that the British forces here in the Colonies were stretched woefully thin to allow for men to be detailed off to pioneers duties when others; (Provincials) could be found to do the same work.

It was still an on going practice, that the best men from the Battalion Companies were subject to being drained off to fill the ranks of the Grenadier and Light Infantry Companies. These standing orders had to be complied with

Dennis Farmer had sent me several letters in regards to Pioneers and where they were assigned during the campaigns in the field and garrison duty. Looking through my collection of letters, I found one letter dated 4 Sept. 1980 from Mr. Eric I. Manders which shed more light on the subject.

Mr. Manders had access to Volume I, of the Kemble Papers (NYHS Collections 1883); the papers and correspondence of John Mitchell Kemble (1807 - 1857). Within these collections were found the orderly books of Generals Howe, Clinton and Jones - 1775 - 1778.

Mr. Manders quotes ... " that while the British Army was in Garrison or in Camp - Boston, Halifax, Staten Island, Philadelphia or New York, no references to Pioneers can be found. but as soon as the Army moves into the field, they are there in force."

16 October 1776 - Throgg's Neck - (British Army's attempt to get around Washington's Army still on Manhattan Island). The pioneers of the Army are constantly to march at the head of each Brigade under the direction of an Engineer, to be appointed for that purpose by the Chief Engineer. Strangely, during the balance of the campaign, when the order of march were laid out, pioneers are referred to as 'carpenters". (Kemble Papers pg. 391)

24 October - New Rochelle - "A Division of carpenters at the head of each column". (pg. 396) (All part of the British attempt to out flank Washington's Army, which by now was moving into Westchester Country).

27 October - "The carpenters with the Engineers to be equally divided at the head of each column", (pg. 398.)

4 November 1776 - White Plains - "An Engineer, with a wagon of entrenching tools, and a Division of carpenters, will march at the head of each column of baggage". (pg 402) In White Plains, the British and American force finally meet in an extensive Battle.

19 November - "Two Engineers, with twelve carpenters and three guides were ordered to join a detachment under General Cornwallis". (Pg 411)

In 1777 - finds them as a distinct "Corps of Pioneers" - performing much the same assignments. They are mentioned on 25 through 30 June 1777. (Page 448)

July 8th, 1777 (pg. 466), 24 August (pg. 475), and on 27 August - Elf Ferry "The pioneers are to receive their orders from the Quarter-Master General". (p. 479) The titles of pioneers/carpenters are one in the same.

7 September 1777 - "The Corps of Pioneers to be divided into four Divisions, One Division at the head of the British Grenadiers, and one to each of the Brigades of Artillery". (p. 489)

One reference is found in 1778 for 20 June The order of march from Mount Holly to Black Horse, "60 Pioneers, with two wagons of the Pioneer entrenching tools. (pg. 596)

All the above suggest that pioneers were grouped into a single unit when operating in the field and generally under the overall command of either the Chief Engineer or the Quarter-Master General. Dennis Farmer pointed out there is no mention of them while in Garrison, (at Fort Niagara), so it likely they had returned to their respective companies.

It can't be determined if the fore mentioned Pioneers were British Regulars or Provincials, but they were not negroes. 24 August 1777, it was stated "All Negroes that may join any part of the Army are to be immediately conducted to Headquarters, where orders will be given for further disposal of them". (p.475)

On 27 August a McCrow was "appointed to the Command of a Black Company" (pg. 479)

Early, 1777 saw three Companies of Black Pioneers or Guides and Pioneers..

Manders goes on to say, that back in April 12th, 1776, there was a reference to "Armourers of different regiments", which suggests that there was a permanent function. (pg. 336)

There was even a call for men "who understands the axe and cutting down timber". This call went out to the 35th, 38th, 40th, and 43rd Regiments. (pg. 344)

The British Army was having an identity problem between Pioneers, Carpenters and Woodcutters, so it all fell on the Officer who was in charge, to make that determination. It wasn't until the Warrants of 1768; which continued the Warrant of 1802; that the term "Pioneer" became permanent.

Between 1776 and 1778 at least three individual "Pioneer" units were raised on the British side. Termed "Loyalists", or "Provincials" they were comprised of either free Negro's from the north or those set free from captured southern plantations.

The "UNIT RETURNS"[68] below cover a period from January 1st 1774 through September 1st, 1781. The Provincials are listed, throughout these returns, but this information shows the only times that formations known as "GUIDES" or "PIONEERS" are specifically mentioned.

March 24th, 1778 - Army at Philadelphia - pg. 12 & 13
Provincials: Penna. Dragoons (31 + 362); Guides (12 + 110)[69]

November 1st, 1778 - Army in New York - pg. 16
Provincials: Cavalry (157); Guides and Pioneers (122)

January 1st, 1780 - Army in Charleston - pg. 18 & 19
Provincials: Legion (part); Guides; Rangers

Before the end of the year (1780) most of the 17th had been exchanged, but Benedict Arnold had been detached from New York for a raid upon Virginia, with a detachment of Royal Artillery, 80th; Queens Rangers; Loyal Americans; detachments of the American Legion; Pioneers; Hessian Jagers.

Charleston, August 1780 - A field force at Cornwallis's disposal consisted of three companies of the 23rd Fusiliers, three companies of the 33rd Foot; five companies of the 71st Highlanders (which came from both battalions of the Regt. and were organized as two weak Btns). four companies of Lt. Infantry from various (64th being one of them) Regiments of the line, the British Legion, the Volunteers of Ireland, Hamilton's Corps. Bryan's Refugees, a detachment of Royal Artillery with 2-6 pounders and 2-3 pounders and a detachment of pioneers.[70]

It would appear that at least three individual "Pioneer" units were raised between 1776 and 1778[71], they were:

GUIDES AND PIONEERS - Raised in New York in 1776.

CAMPAIGNS - Philia, Forts Clinton and Montgomery, Siege of Newport. (Detachments operating with Cornwallis), General Benedict Arnold's raid on New London and Danbury, Conn.

DISBANDED - in Nova Scotia in 1783. UNIFORM - for the war, seems to be a short Red Coat, with black cuff and collar, White small clothes.
COMMANDERS - Major Simon Frazer and Major John Aldington

BLACK COMPANY OF PIONEERS - Raised in Philadelphia in 1777.

CAMPAIGNS - Apparently merged into the Guides and Pioneers in New York in 1778. UNIFORM - Green coat, each man received a great coat, hat, green sailor's jacket, white shirt and winter trousers. This uniform may have changed in the

later part of the war to something similar to that of the Guides and Pioneers.
COMMANDERS - Captain Allen Stewart and Captain Donald Mc Pherson.
DISBANDED - Port Roseway, Nova Scotia, which is on the south western tip of Nova Scotia; just south of Yarmouth.

HOLLAND'S PIONEER'S - Raised in the Spring of 1777. Very little is known of this unit, it may have been merged with the Guides and Pioneers. What is known, that their coats were red. It was commanded - by a Major Holland.

It would appear that the information on hand points to the fact that all three Pioneer Companies had been merged into one by 1778 and they were in turn attached to the Loyal American Regiment then commanded by Colonel Beverly Robinson. These units were disbanded in 1783 in Nova Scotia. It's unclear if the Pioneer unit remained the Company of Guides and Pioneers or changed to the title of Company of Black Pioneers. The muster list for the Loyal American Regt. and the Guides and Pioneers can be found on microfilm as part of the Ward Chipman Papers. The list may not be complete.[72]

With the southward shift of military operations, the British no longer tried to conceal their intention to make utmost use of Negroes.[73] Commander-in-Chief Clinton; on June 13, 1779; issued a policy statement from his Headquarters at Philipsburg in upper Westchester County, New York. He began by ordering a Proclamation to the Americans, that as they had adopted the practice of enrolling Negroes among their troops, he ordered that whenever captured by the British, Negro Soldiers or auxiliaries be enrolled for public service. The Philipsburg announcement then proceeded to forbid any person from selling or claiming any enemy owned slaves who had taken refuge in the British lines. And, finally, the proclamation promised every Negro who deserted from an enemy master full security to follow any occupation he wished while in the British lines.

The Americans, on the other hand, regarded slaves of Loyalists or British masters, as spoils of war. From the days of Dunmore, Virginians had appropriated slaves of "those unfriendly to the American cause" and put them to work mining lead and the always scarce salt. In Georgia in 1776 the Council of Safety ordered that 20 Negro axemen taken from the plantation of two Tory masters be employed in building a battery at Typee.

Many slaves who came into British hands were merely victims of Military force. By seizing slaves the British Army increased its resources and depleted those of the enemy.

When major campaigns shifted to the south after 1777, the loss of slaves in Virginia and South Carolina was severe. British depredations in Virginia, which had begun with the Lord Dunmore incident, were resumed on a larger scale. In late spring of 1778, the British took 500 Negroes in Norfolk County alone. Shortly afterwards, General Edwards left Virginia to rejoin Clinton in New York, taking with him 518 Negroes.

Many more slaves, however, voluntarily deserted to the British. They had no particular love for the England, but they believed that English officers would give them their freedom.

Military commanders were anxious to thwart the British aim of building up available black labor supply; civilian officials in the south were equally anxious to prevent the loss of a property which formed the base of individual wealth and regional prosperity. On the plantation the slave was not only a field hand working the crops; he was also the skilled labor, the carpenter blacksmith, shoemaker, weaver, spinner, and even the distiller. Hence both military and civilian authorities sought to prevent loss of Negroes to the British either by desertion or capture.

New York was occupied early by the British and their employment of Negroes extended to some 7 years. Most often Negroes worked as Teamsters; at one time most of the drivers in the city's Quartermaster Department were runaway slaves, working for wages and housed in separate barracks. In 1781 the British Commissary Department in New York counted 10 Negroes among its total of 102 personnel. On Long Island, at Flushing and Jamaica the British employed Negroes in the forage Service; the names of all eight workers in Jamaica being preceded by the word "Black".

At Fort Meadows there were 63 Negroes on the payroll of the 17th Regt. of light Dragoons. In Philadelphia the British had a "Company of Black Pioneers", consisting of 72 privates, under the command of Capt. Allen Stewart. This Corps performed whatever task was assigned to them.

Page 96 top shows a PRIVATE - GUIDES AND PIONEERS[74]- Raised in Philadelphia with the Loyal American Regt, and served largely with them. like their regular British counterparts they wore short brick-red jackets with black cuffs and collars and no lapels. the White linen gaiter trousers would have been convenient working pants.

At the bottom of page 95; is the BLACK COMPANY OF PIONEERS - Raised in Philadelphia. It was decided that Pioneer company was needed to build the fortifications, keep the streets clear and work on the docks. Each man was issued a greatcoat for winter wear, a hat, a green sailor's jacket, a white shirt and winter trousers. The winter trousers then in use by the British Army tended to be form fitting gaiter trousers of red, blue or brown wool.

By 1783, The Loyal American Regiment was in Red Coats, faced green, a further mention was made of GUIDES and PIONEERS as Red Coats with Cuff and Collar in Black.[75]

Various "RETURNS" (Rosters) from the William L. Clements Library in Ann Arbor, Michigan come from either the "Clinton" or "Wray" papers or a combination of both.[76] They show a Return dated 13 July 1777; Black Company of Pioneers; Signed by Capt. Martin and Capt. Allen Stewart lists 72 men present with 15 negro women.

Another return dated 17 Sept. 1778; was also signed by Captain Allen Stewart the location appears to be in New York. While its hard to read, it would appear to list, 1 Captain, 1 Ensign, 3 Sergeants, 3 Corporals and 30 fit for duty.

Refer to pages 147 & 148 for other de Loutherbourg prints

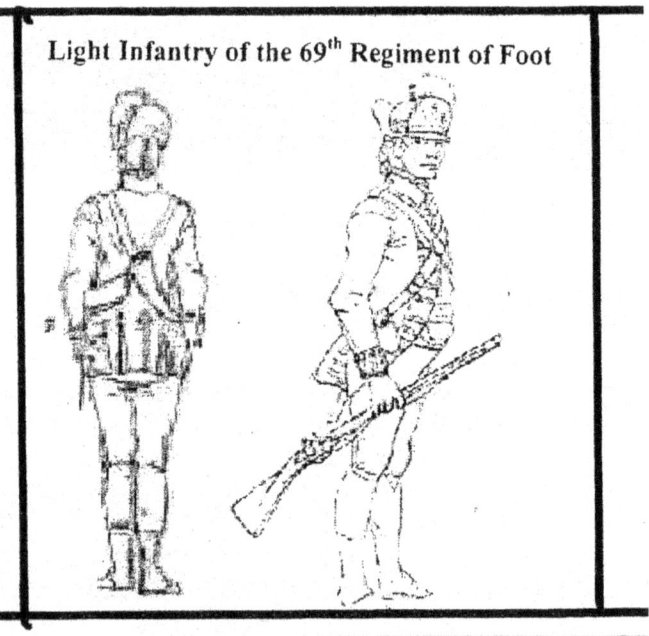

Sketch was made by de Loutherbourg of soldiers from one of the regiments at the camp on Warley Common, England c1778. This sketch was part of an article found in *The Black Knot* Journal - Vol. IX - No. 3 -

95

PVT. GUIDES AND PIONEERS
RAISED IN NEW YORK FALL OF 1776
SERVED WITH THE LOYAL
AMERICAN REGIMENT

Also shown is a request for 500 Indian Blankets, 35 pieces of Red Shouds for Jackets, 5 pieces of blue drills for cuffs and collar, 500 felt hats, and 2,000 yards of drill for breeches.

A Return for those employed by the Royal Artillery; then in Charleston, South Carolina dated 5 November 1782 lists carpenters, painters, sawyers and laborers.

From Bard College Library I obtained a copy of American Historical Review 1948 - 49, pgs. 315 to 325. "Negro Craftsmanship in Early America" by a Mr. Leonard P. Stavisky, assistant professor of History in N.Y. Teachers College in Oswego, N.Y. In the article describes many of the various trades the Negro's were taught while still in Africa, the Sudan; cobblers, tailors, carpenters, smiths. In 1751, Providence, Rhode Island, slave workers gave service as anchor makers, mast builders, rope makers and spinners. Interesting reading to say the least.

Likewise, the Royal Artillery tapped the pool of Blacks as in two returns dated under 4 January 1782. The Department listed 40 Laborers, 19 Servants, 10 Sawyers, 8 Carpenters, 2 Smiths, and 1 Teamster. A subsequent return for later in that year lists 67 Laborers, 35 Teamsters, 6 Carpenters, 2 Turn wheelers, 1 Painter, and 1 Wheeler. Muster rolls of the civilian branch of the train of Artillery in 1782 listed free Negroes as Carpenters, Wheelers, Smiths, sawyers, Coopers, Painters, Armoires and Turn wheelers.
(GPS. 139, 140)

Muster Rolls from the Royal Artillery Department in Charleston, 1780 - 1783, list Artificers, Laborers and Servants. (Wray Papers)

Generally, provincial troops were issued green regimental Coats with various facing colors. The first shipment brought over coats faced: Blue, White, Green, later buff, orange and black facings were added later. It was decided that starting with the campaign of 1778, Provincials would receive red, not Green Coats. Some units; in particular the 1st American Regiment (Queens Rangers) and the 4th American Regiment (British Legion) retained their green coats throughout the war.

Otherwise, the average Provincial unit received the same kit as worn by regular troops, although at times it may have been more out of date then the regular's. The information below came from a separate source.

The source was from "Some notes on the American Provincial Uniforms - 1776 - 1783 - by Albert W. Harman - J.S.A.H.R. Vol. 49 - 1971.

Listed: Black Company of Pioneers - considered a small unit, (100 men or less) raised in Pennsylvania.

Guides and Pioneers - considered a medium unit; 100 to 500 men; raised in various colonies

A listing of Officers and other ranks indicated the following: Black Pioneers - 6 Officers and 62 Rank and File Guides and Pioneers - 34 Officers and 165 rank and file

There is no listing for Holland's Pioneers. [77] This unit numbered less then 50 men, and had been raised in various colonies.

In the final campaigns of the war the British continued to employ Negroes on a large scale. Blacks accompanied the moving army as Cornwallis departed Charleston in the winter of 1781 and moved northward to meet his destiny at Yorktown.

During his complicated maneuvers across the state of North Carolina his Army lived off the country; Negroes were assigned the task of collecting provisions. Many of these forays degenerated into mere pillaging expeditions. To prevent Negro foragers from getting out of hand, Cornwallis on February 5, 1781, issued orders that no Negro was to be permitted to carry a firearm under any circumstances.

As Cornwallis moved into Virginia in May 1781 and took up positions, he and other British Commanders again pressed Negroes into labor service. General Benedict Arnold had already employed them to build dams and in the several public departments and for the works. A Black Corps; numbering 500; was soon busy with trench fortifications at Portsmouth, and in constructing the defenses at Yorktown and Gloucester (pg. 140)[78]

It should be obvious that to fill the overall manpower needs of the British Army, large groups of Negroes were employed. Considering they were with a large military force, they were more than likely enlisted into various "Provincial Corps" and subject to military orders and discipline. Along with Negroes who were either freemen or those who had escaped from southern masters, valuable trades came with them; Wheelwrights, Carpenters, Cobblers, Blacksmith's, Coopers, Teamsters and many, many other such trades, plus are raw unskilled labor force.

But as the war was reaching its climax, what was to happen to these Negroes. British military forces formally withdrew from Savannah in July of 1782, evacuating Loyalists with their slaves as well as troops. Between July 6th and December 23rd, nearly 5000 Negroes including family members had been evacuated.

During the same period, 5300 Negroes had left Charleston, half going to Jamaica, the others finding their way to St. Lucia, Halifax, England and New York.

By the end of November, 1783, an additional 3,000 from New York, 4,000 from Savannah, and 6,000 from Charleston had been evacuated. These figures represent those Negroes who were registered with the British for evacuation. It does not include the hundreds which had left by private vessels.[79]

Many of the Negroes evacuated from the U.S. did not go southwards; thousands went into Canada. One Thomas Peters who had fled from his master in 1776 and joined the British. During the war he served as a Sergeant in a Negro arms-bearing pioneer company, being twice wounded in battle. With the coming of peace, he and his wife settled at Annapolis in Nova Scotia, a Province to which many of the Canada-bound Negroes went.

The British had promised Peters and his comrades not only freedom but a farm. His Majesty's officers were slow in making good the promise of a farm, and the civilian authorities were likewise dilatory.

There were a number of Negroes at Port Roséway, and some expected at Halifax, "for whom lands are not yet located, nor other provisions made", wrote a Colonel Robert Morse to General H.E. Fox on August 23, 1783[80]

The black settlers in Nova Scotia felt cheated; either the surveyor was too busy to mark out their lands, or the plots they received were largely thick pine forest and hard to clear. Finding themselves landless, or holders of land that would produce little, many Negroes apprenticed themselves to farmers or congregated in Burch town, a nearly all Negro community. [81]

In Early 1791, Peters with the help of funds raised by his fellows, traveled to London to seek redress of the problems that he and many Negroes who served His Majesty during the late war, were having in getting the land promised them. The Secretary of State for Foreign Affairs, William W. Granville, received Peters.

A Corporation called "THE SIERRA LEONE COMPANY" had acquired a site and begun operations to develop a Community on the West Coast of Africa. On August 12, 1791 the Company authorized 2 agents Lawrence Hartshorn of Halifax and John Clarkson; to screen candidates for resettlement.

Peters helped Hartshorn and Clarkson in January 1792, carefully screen nearly 1200 Negroes to determine their character, sobriety and industry. They were in turn each granted 20 acres of land.   (pg.. 178, 179)

On January 15th they sailed from Halifax. The embarking Nova Scotians were not as happy as Clarkson had hoped. The Expedition ran into heavy squalls, temporarily separating one ship from the other. Some 65 of the voyagers died at sea, another 100 were too ill to be landed when the fleet pulled into Kru Bay in early March. When the remaining 1,000 stepped ashore they found that little preparation had seen made to receive them.

They knew they would have to work long hours if they were to succeed in throwing up enough shelters before the rainy season set in. But if at the moment their dwelling site lacked adequate housing, it bore a sweet sounding name: Freetown, West Africa. [82](pgs. 198, 199)

COAT of ARMS of SIERRA LEONE

200th Anniversary of Toronto at Fort York
Ontario, Canada.
Detachment of Grenadiers, Pioneers
and Battalion Soldiers
August 7 & 8th 1993

CHAPTER THREE - THE ROYAL MILITARY ACADEMY

From the humble beginnings (1066) when civilians were called either, woodworkers or carpenters; the actual term "Pioneer" didn't come about until the 1700's. The first attempt to organize an actual military unit came when the first company of Artificers were raised, trained and sent to Gibraltar in 1772.

The earliest academy started was the Royal Military Academy (RMA) at Woolwich, south-east of London; in 1741. Here the training of commissioned officers of the Royal Artillery and Royal Engineers took place. It was intended to provide an education and produce " good officers of Artillery and perfect Engineers". The RMA Woolwich was commonly known as "The Shop" because its first building was a converted workshop of the Woolwich Arsenal.

A second academy, known as the Royal Military College (RMC), was opened at Sandhurst, Bershire in 1799 to train officers for the Infantry and cavalry.

July 31, 1783 - The Soldier - Artificer Company stood as follows:
234 rank and file

1 Sergeant Major	4 Drummers	21 Sayers
10 Sergeants	38 Masons	32 Miners
10 Corporals	4 Nailers	6 Wheelers
5 File Cutters	3 Gardner's	38 Smith's
54 Carpenters	7 Lime Burners	3 Cooper's
1 Collar Maker	1 Painter	1 Brazier

October 10, 1787 - Warrants were issued with Pitt's help a second Corps (Soldier-Artificer's) was raised in England; similar to that which was stationed in Gibraltar. With the King's authority, the establishment of the Corps of Royal Military Artificer's was granted, to Charles, Duke of Richmond. They were to consist of 6 companies of 100 men each.[83]

1795 - Woolwich - becomes the Corps Headquarters[84]

1797 - June - The Soldier - Artificer Corps at Gibraltar was incorporated with the Royal Military Artificer's.

INFANTRY CLOTHING REGULATIONS - 1802[85] - Excerpts Only

A. - Pioneer Appointments

B. - Each Pioneer to have an axe, a saw, and an apron; a cap with a leather crown; and a black bear skin front; on which is to be the KINGS CREST in white; on a red ground; also a saw and an axe. The number of the Regiment to be on the back part of the cap

(D - No Alteration - C) - The pioneers to have an axe, a saw and apron; exclusive of accoutrements, and arms like the rank and file.

They are also to have caps with a leather crown and a black bear skin fronts on which are to be the Kings Crest in white (white deleted and brass inserted), on a red ground, also an axe and a saw. The number of the regiment to be on the back part of the cap.

The Pioneers are also to have felt caps similar to the Battalion.

The Letters and description below correspond with the letters and descriptions on this page and the next page; which come out of the regulations. It indicates if there had been any changes made.

(A) - ARTICLES
(B) - BY REGULATIONS OF 19 DECEMBER 1768
(C) - DATES OF ALTERATIONS AS MADE FROM TIME TO TIME
(D) - AS THE REGULATIONS ARE SUPPOSED TO STAND AT PRESENT.
(E) - FOR OBSERVATIONS AND IMPROVEMENTS
(Z) - INDICATES THAT COLUMN D (or Column A in Certain instances) IS REPRODUCED WITHOUT ANY FURTHER ALTERATION IN THE SECOND MS BOOK.[86]

In April 23, 1812 was the formation of a school at Chatham to instruct sapping, mining, bridge building, pontooning, the use of ropes, mechanical appliances, and other arts and contrivances which the Corps in its connection with the Engineer Department is likely to perform. (pg.30) [87]

March 5, 1813 - Title of Royal Military Artificer's officially changed to the Royal Miners and Sappers. The total strength of the Corps is 2,373 rank and file. [88]

May 25, 1855 - Board of Ordnance was abolished which controlled both the Royal Artillery and Engineers. Both came under the control of the Commander-in-Chief. pg.44

October 17, 1856 - The corps of Miners and Sappers were incorporated into the Royal Engineers. thus these two organizations became one. [89]

It should be mentioned, that during this early period, the Royal Engineers remained a completely separate organization, although they were required to furnish needed officers for the Royal Military Artificer Company in England. Any additional Sergeant-Major's came from Artillery,[90] while the other N.C.O.'s came from just the line regiments. Any privates that were recruited came from either line regiments or from civilian life but had to be tradesmen. Sergeant Major's need not be tradesmen, just good administrators and be able to handle proper training in military matters and discipline.

****

CHAPTER FOUR - April 3rd 1795 though December 31st, 1799

SERIES 2 - Letters covering a period from April 3, 1795 through December 31, 1799. Col. John Elting deciphered anything in French.

A series of letters (*all in French*) covering the fore mentioned time period indicated it was felt that some form of a Corps of Pioneers was needed. This one appeared to have a more formal organizational format then the one that Capt. Richard Steele tried to raise in August 1762. No doubt when it was raised, it was for a short duration and then possibly disbanded.

Col. Elting indicated that apparently this was a "French Corps of Pioneers", raised in 1794 in the Netherlands and was attached to the headquarters of the Duke of York. Supposedly it was disbanded in 1796. It had one Captain, two Lieutenants, and a Chaplain, but enlisted strength not given.

Col. Elton made further reference to the "French Corps of Pioneers", - Vicente Grouvel "Les Corps de Europe de Emigration" - Francaise (1789 - 1815), Tone I, pp. 37 and Enata for page 355, Sabretache, Paris 1957.

In June 1797, The Soldier Artificer's Corps at Gibraltar were incorporated with the larger Corps of Royal Military Artificer's, who were garrisoned in England, and there after discarded their scarlet uniforms. [91]

Still part of the 2nd series of letters that John Elton helped decipher.
Anything in French, John had to decipher

The messenger took Wm Dundas Dispatch to York House _____(?). I[92] should have had it about an hour sooner.

Henry Dundas, Secretary of State for War, Later he became 1st Viscount Melville

They were immediately under the Command of Quarter-Master General Fox, and seemed to have served capably.

In reference to the "French Corps of Pioneers" Vicente Grouvel **Les Corps de Europe de Emigration** Francaise (1789 - 1815), Tone I, p.37 and Enata for p.355 Sabretache, Paris, 1957.

WO 6/199   Downing Street 11 Dec.
                                                                   1798
Sir, Wm Lemon Bt
& Gentlemen
Fra S (?) Gregon Esq.

  In reply to your letter of the 18th Vttimo, requesting to be informed whether it is in the Contemplation of Government to raise any more miners in the County of Cornwall, I have the honor to inform you that there is not at present any intention to alter the provisions of the Act of Parliament which was lately passed for the purpose of raising a body of miners in the County of Devon and Cornwall.

I am, etc.
Henry Dundas
Secretary of State for War.

****

WO 6/199　　　　　　　　　　　　　　　　　　Downing Street
　　　　　　　　　　　　　　　　　　　　　　　9 march 1799
Sir, J Maishead, Bat (?)
　　　I have the honor to acknowledge the receipt of your letter of the 23rd ultimo, transmitting a muster roll of the Devonshire Miner Volunteers, together with a copy of a letter from Mr. Bostock, who offers to raise a Corps of Miners to serve as Pioneers without any expense to the Government, under the specifications of the Act of the 39th of His present Majesty, Cap 14, namely within the Military District in the case mentioned in the 1st (?) Section of that Act.
　　　In compliance with your recommendation I have laid Mr. Bsotocks proposal before the King, and I am commanded to communicate to you, His Majesty's gracious acceptance of this offer of service.

I have etc.,
Henry Dundas

2nd series of letters continued

MO 100/83 [93]

Plan of a Corps of Pioneers to be attached to the Quarter-master Generals Department.　　This Corps is to be composed of Three Companies, one for the South, the North and the Center of the Kingdom.

ESTABLISHMENT

This is very similar to today's modern Army's "Table of Organization" or TOA

Each Company is
to consist of:

1 Captain	4 Sergeants
1 1st Lient.	5 Corporals
2 2nd Lieut.	1 Drummer
1 Quarter-Master or Staff Sergeant *	100 Privates **

(*)The term Quarter-Master Sergeant or Staff Sergeant represents the Senior Sergeant. The terms as mentioned plus a Paymaster Sergeant were not part of the establishment for any unit until 1786. These ranks were placed on the establishment in addition to the sergeants on the strength of the companies.

** It appears that the Corps of Pioneers were raised nearly in the same strength per company as the existing Companies of the Royal Sappers and Miners, but operated independently.

OFFICERS

The Officers are to be composed of such persons as are known to be emmintly qualified for this service, or taken from the half pay, as best adapted to introduce military habits among the privates.

RANK

The rank of the Officers to be temporary

PAY AND ALLOWANCES

The Officers are to have the pay and allowance of their respective ranks, and when reduced are to receive half pay, without this prospect, it will be difficult to induce persons to enter into this species of service.

ENLISTMENTS

The Non-Commissioned Officers and privates are to be enlisted as soldiers, but are only to serve in Ireland, and as long as the War Lasts. *

* - War with France 1793 to March 1802

PAY OF NON-COM OFFICERS AND PRIVATES

Their pay is to be the same as their respective stations in the Line. (ie. - rest of Army)

BOUNTY

Three guineas will be allowed upon enlistment as Bounty to supply them with necessaries.

ARTIFICERS

It may be found necessary to induce some old soldiers among the N.C.O.'s, but as much as possible it will be attempted to form them of skillful artificers, and to attain this, it may be indicious to extend the Bounty to a few persons of this description.

ALLOWANCES

This corps is to be entitled to all allowances, privileges and to be under the same beneficial Regulations as the rest of the Army.

CLOTHING

The Government is to contract for their clothing in the same manner as that for the Invalids, and it is not to be of any Emolrement either to the Captains or Superior Officers at the Head of the Corps.

UNIFORM

The clothing is to consist of a round hat (*- 1) , Blue Jacket, with Red Cuff and collar (*- 2), (parsecs in Margin "or" of a Red Jacket"), Blue waistcoat and pantaloons, and is to be made up in such a manner as will be best adapted to the nature of their service, and at the same time not lose sight of their appearance as soldiers.

* - (1) - Black felt round hat superseded cocked hat in 1792. An attempt of sorts of another cocked hat was revived in 1797.

* - (2) - 1792, Winter Blue Jacket with Black Cuffs and Collar was worn by the Royal Sappers and Miners, precisely similar in cut and make to the duck jacket.

With the jacket a flannel waistcoat was worn, and serge trousers or pantaloons. Pg. 79, History of the Royal Saper and Miners

ENTRENCHING TOOLS

The necessary implements for their work will be supplied from the Ordnance apron the requisition of the Quarter-Master General, and such carriages for their preservation and convenience will be granted as may appear requisite.

DUTY OF THE CAPTAIN

The Captain is to be responsible for all articles delivered to the Company and upon his head, and all matter of account, Discipline, and interior Economy, the Quarter-Master or Staff sergeant is to be his principal assistant.

IF CALLED TOGETHER

From the nature of their service, it will be found so often necessary to divide the Companies that it appears better to consider them generally as independent, but should they be called together, they will blend into one Corps, under the Command of the oldest Captain, subject however at all times to the superior and immediate order of the Quarter-Master General.

SURGEON

It is proposed than an (sic) Hospital Mate should be appointed to each company when separated. the pay to these officers is but 2 s/6 d per day more than an assistant Surgeon and half pay will be saved, and these will be the added advantage than whenever these companies are assembled, one or two of the Hospital Mates may be disposed with.

AGENT

As the pay, allowance, etc., of this Corps are to be upon the same foundation and under the same regulations as the others of the line, it seems necessary that an Agent should be appointed to transact all their concerns to Dublin.

RETURNS

The Commanding Officers of each Company is to be responsible when detached for the returns of his Company. a Monthly one of each, will be sent to the Quarter-Master General, who can from them form a General State for the Adjutant General and War Office.

MASTER

What ever regulations as the Cheque and Master of the Army will be found to apply to this Corps can from time to time be adopted, until there is reason to hope that the same fidelity of returns will take place as in the rest of the Army.

QUARTER-MASTER GENERAL

Pursuant to his Excellency's orders, the quarter-Master General will direct the formation and attend to the progress of the Corps and upon the several, and at present unforeseen cases that must occur, he will resort to Government for all the instructions necessary to the accomplishment of the under taking.

Quarter-Master General office, May 18, 1799
To the lord Lieutenant, May 20, 1799, Dublin Castle.

Mradock
QM General

WO 40/12

Hoarse Guards
31 December 1799

Sir

I have it in Command from the commander in chief, to acquaint you for the information of the Secretary of War, that His majesty has been pleased to order, that from the 25th instant, A Corps of Pioneers shall placed upon the Establishment of the Army;

The Corps to be formed into four Companies, each company to consist of the under mentioned number of Officers, Non-Commissioned Officers and privates.

    1 Captain   1 Bugler
    2 Lieutenants   92 Privates
    4 Sergeants   8 Corporals

The said Corps to be commanded by a field officer with the following Staff;

    1 Lieutenant Col. or Major (Commandant)
    1 Adjutant   1 assistant Surgeon
    1 Quarter-Master   1 Sergeant Major
    1 Paymaster   1 Quarter-Master sergeant
    1 Surgeon   1 Pay Master sergeant

I have the Commander in Chiefs further commands to acquaint you, that it is intended that the Officers, N.C.O.'s and privates of the Corps of pioneers, that served with the Army in Holland, and whose numbers are stated with the enclosed return shall be incorporated into and form part of the pioneer corp. to be the same as that established for the Infantry of the Army.

To be clothed and appointed under the direction of the Quarter-Master General to whose Department it is His Majesty's pleasure, that the Corps shall immediately belong in. *continued.......*

> I have the honor to be Sir
> your most obedient, Humble
> Servant.
> Robt. Brownrigg *

* - General Robert Brownrigg, who was the Duke of York's "Military Secretary".

Lt. Browrigg was also mentioned in the book *History of the Royal Sappers and Miners*, by T.W. Connolly - London 1857 - page 117 in the Chapter covering 1798 to 1799

There does not seem to be any connection between the Corps of Pioneers raised and the overall operations of the Sappers and Miners from 1795 - 1799. Its entirely possible this Corps was raised for the necessary operations to serve in Ireland, thus freeing individual Companies of Sappers Miners for their operations outside of England, considering England was once again at War with France.

Photo from Sir Michael Grenier's Collection
Staffordshire Regimental Museum, Litchfield, England

Royal Artillery - One 3 pounder gun section

From Sir Michael Grenier's Photo Collection
Staffordshire Regimental Museum; Litchfield, Museum

80th Regiment of Foot c1879 - Zulu War Period
Closed order, battalion line volley firing

CHAPTER FIVE
THOSE ARMY HANDYMEN

LEFT to RIGHT

**60th Regt.   23rd Regt.   64th Regt.   Queens Rangers
Back Rank - Highlanders**

PIONEER, THE TRAIN OF ARTILLERY, KING JAME'S ARMY - 1688

During King James's reign, (*1685 - 1688*) special efforts were made to standardize the equipment used by the Army. These efforts are particularly well summarized in the regulations for musters of 21 February 1687:

" The Company of Miners to have long carbines, strapped; the barrels to be three foot 2 inches in length, cartouche boxes, bayonets, and extraordinary hammer hatches."

Pioneer - Train of Artillery [94]
From the Osprey Series #267 - The British Army - 1660 - 1704.

Pioneers were essential in an army that hoped to move heavy siege guns: roads had to be widened or improved, and bridges constructed or strengthened. When the destination was reached, pioneers were needed to construct gun positions and to dig trenches. The New Train of 1688 had its own pioneers dressed all in red.

Later in the same year, probably when William of Orange took command, the pioneers were issued with a cap embroidered with a shovel, a Blue coat lined orange, an Orange waistcoat, and Blue breeches and stockings

See the Chapter *(page 136)* which covers Helmet's, caps, and accoutrements, Mr. Dennis Knowe did a series of drawings showing the evolution of the pioneer caps.

PIONEER - TRAIN OF ARTILLERY - KING JAMES ARMY - 1688

Pioneer and Private man of the Battalion Company - 1742 - 1750 [95]

The detail for the pioneer is taken from Hogarth's picture (*William Hogarth, he was the leading English artist of the early 1700's, born in London, England on Nov. 1697. Died on October, 1764, in Chiswick, England*) of the "March of the Guards to Finchley". Though there are several references to pioneers at this period, in orders, clothing returns, etc; pictorial evidence is very scarce, so although no great reliance can be placed on Hogarth's regimental detail in his pictures, he was an artist concerned in depicting an over-all view of life as it was in his time, and did not concern himself with the very small details of regimental dress. An example of this is his rendering of the design upon the Grenadier caps of the Guards, which we know by existing evidence is incorrect. Even so, many artists both past and present, British and foreign, lacking the real background knowledge of uniform, have copied Hogarth's rendering of the design. But in the general appearance of the soldier of his time, his work is invaluable.

This book coupled with Hogarth's picture and the many regimental orders, endeavored to reconstruct the possible dress and equipment of the pioneer.

Head dress is red cloth, similar to the type of cap as worn by sailors of *Hogarth's* period: a kind of bag the end of which was a white tassel, a blue cloth turn-up, on which embroidered in white, a mattock and saw, white scroll embroidery at the sides and back. Hair is natural and appears to be turned up under the cap. The coat is the normal rank and file pattern, faced and laced exactly as described for the Private men. The coat is shown buttoned across in this case. The breeches and gaiters as for privates. The equipment is the same as the privates, and has a sword of normal dress. A buff leather apron hooked up on the left side.

Please note the print,[96] it depicts Soldier belonging to the 2nd Foot Guards.
According to the Clothing Regulations of 1742

PRIVATE and PIONEER - GUARDS BATTALION COMPANY - 1742 - 1750

PIONEER - 28th REGIMENT of FOOT - 1759 - BRAGGE [97]

The 28th was raised in 1694 and served in Louisburg, Cape Breton, Quebec, Montreal and Havana.

The uniform is based on the clothing regulations of 1751, as desired by King George II.

His cap is similar to that worn by the pioneer of the Guards, but here he only wears his waistcoat with work apron.

An Enlargement - Pioneer
28th Regiment of Foot
c1759

Gloucestershire
Regiment

Pioneer, Corporal William Todd - 12th Regt. of Foot - 1761 [98]

Uniform based on the clothing regulations of 1751, here he wears a russet leather apron, by the new Clothing Regulations of 1768, his cloth forage cap was ordered replaced by a leather cap trimmed with black bear fur, similar to that worn by the private of the 25th Highland Company, the figure to the lower right.

By 1790 these leather hats were replaced with a Grenadier cap, but with its own distinctive plate.

Sgt. Wm Todd
12th Regt of Foot

Pvt. Highland
Regt 1771

PIONEER - 29th REGIMENT of FOOT - 1768 [99]

The pioneer wears his distinctive cap, apron and accoutrements. His cap, though similar in shape to those of the Grenadiers and drummers actually had a leather crown. The front plate was of white metal with a red ground, above which was the bearskin trim which gave it its height.

In addition to the usual infantry weapons, he carried a saw and an axe, carried in special scabbards or pockets from narrow shoulder straps. The axe was carried on the left side.

The Artist and copyright owner Mr. Peter F. Copeland had done this piece for the Company of Military Historians Journal.

PIONEER - 29th REGIMENT of FOOT
An enlargement from a color plate, showing the 29th in Boston, from the Company of Military Historians

An approx. tracing of the face plate of the Pioneer Helmet

Sherwood Foresters

Worcestershire Regiment

PIONEER - 42nd ROYAL HIGHLAND REGIMENT - 1771

This rough sketch is done by a Richard Claydon, of a Pioneer belonging to the Light Infantry Company of the 42nd Highland Regiment. He has a small axe, cap with a red front, white apron, breeches and hose and half gaiters.

A different style of apron is shown here. Although white is mentioned, white wasn't used until the 1800's; and for dress parades only.

The musket has no sling, and no axe is shown. The Regimental number is shown on the front of the apron and the back of the cap. Three chains are specified around the crown of the helmet for Light Infantry for 1771 and appears to have a plume rather then a full bear skin trim.

23rd REGIMENT of FOOT
c1775

ROYAL WELCH FUSILERS

THE PIONEERS [100]

Another valuable asset to the Regiment is the Pioneer. This soldier has additional duties of clearing undergrowth along the line of march, cutting trees for firewood and abattis, and constructing palisades and other obstacles around camps and forts as well as cutting through those of the enemy.

His basic uniform and kit is the same as that of a private soldier. He wears a bearskin cap of Fusilier height (10 in.), a red coat with facings and Regimental lace and buttons, which indicate that he belongs to the 23rd Regiment of Foot. He also wears white linen small clothes, black full gaiters with horn buttons and white linen leg wraps, and black buckled shoes; and carries a musket, cartridge box with plate (The three feathers of the Prince of Wales), linen haversack, and whitened buff leather waist carriage for his bayonet.

The Pioneer has a very distinctive cap plate; rather than the black background found on the other bearskin caps in the Regiment, his is Red. The scrollwork beside the central helm and crown device is replaced with white metal saws and axes. A circular pewter ornament stamped with the numerals "23" is stitched to the hair portion of the rear of the cap.

He also wears a large russet leather apron to protect his uniform, and carries an axe and saw in a plain leather carriage slung on his back. The apron is normally worn under the coat, which is removed for heavy work.
The chief Pioneer is a Corporal and wears the white cord of his rank on the right shoulder. Another distinction is the wearing of two epaulette straps rather than one on the left shoulder worn by the other rankers.

Pioneer's cap plate, the ground painted red, with raised silver scroll and motifs, including axes and saws.

Pioneer, Pvt.
23rd Regt. of Foot
c1775

Front and rear views of the senior Pioneer, distinguished by a corporal's white shoulder knot. In addition to the normal haversack and canteen, pouch and bayonet frog, and musket, he has a leather apron, an axe and a saw — note black leather carriage for the tools slung behind him. In the 18th century a common soldier is most unlikely to have been able to afford spectacles, but in the re-created RWF£A some concessions must be made to modern needs, although frames must be of authentic 18th century shape.

The Pioneer pictured here, helped me make an apron pattern so I could make my leather work apron. Pattern copy of my own work apron.

SOLDIER ARTIFICER COMPANY - 1772 - 1789 [104]

Private in winter dress and soldier in working dress c1779. This Company had two uniforms; one similar to the ordinary dress of the Infantry Regiments, and the other a working dress, which was interesting as one of the first attempts to provide such an outfit for troops.

UNIFORM: Scarlet (1772 - 87). Lepels to waist (except working dress). Small round cuffs. FACINGS: Black (previously Orange).
LACE: Gold for officers, other ranks yellow, (Scalloped ends).
BUTTONS: Officers gilt, other ranks pewter (set regularly apart).
Breeches, waistcoat, and linings white. Long black gaiters with white tops (winter dress). Black leather stock. Hair not powdered on service. The below illustration shows the uniform of a private with bayonet and camp axe attached to his shoulder belt. It also shows the working dress; plain red jacket (winter dress), black gaiters, and a round white hat about 6 inches high, with a yellow band and a broad brim. - A.R. Cattley

104

126

PRIVATE - COMPANY OF SOLDIER - ARTICIFERS - c1772[105]

from a "Stadden" Uniform card by Stamp Publicity, Worthing Ltd.
Sussex, England

This is a series of notes, referring to the sketch of the pioneer, 27th foot, taken from the J.S.A.H.R. or as indicated.

PIONEER - 27th Regiment of Foot
1785

During the first half of the 18th Century, it is open to doubt whether pioneers carried a sword.

If they did it was doubtless a hanger (short sword) as carried by the infantry privates.

The Royal Warrants of 1768 - orders Pioneers to have an axe, saw and apron.

There is no mention of a sword. The sword was therefore abolished at that date or had not been in use for some time.

At the start of the 19th Century, Pioneers clearly did not carry swords.

British Regiments in service in the Colonies all but did away with the Sword by the late War period. The exception possibly the Grenadier Companies.

Gibraltar Standing Orders - 1803

From "Swords of the British Army" by C. Foulkes and Capt. E.C. Hopkinson

On this basis, the sword as shown can be questioned

From Journal for the Society of Army Historical Research - Volume 12 - Pg. 157

The Sketch shows the pioneer has his apron turned down at the top.

27th FOOT FACINGS: Pale Buff

REGIMENTAL LACE PATERN: 1 Blue and 1 Red Strip in 2's

The Lace Patterns

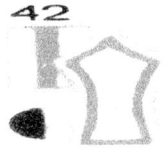 

42nd Regt. Of Foot   27th Regt. Of Foot
From *"British Infantry Uniforms - From Marlborough to Wellington"*
Liliane and Fred Funcken

PIONEER - 27th REGIMENT of FOOT 1785

The rough sketch at the bottom; A and B show an approx layout of the Pioneer helmet face plate

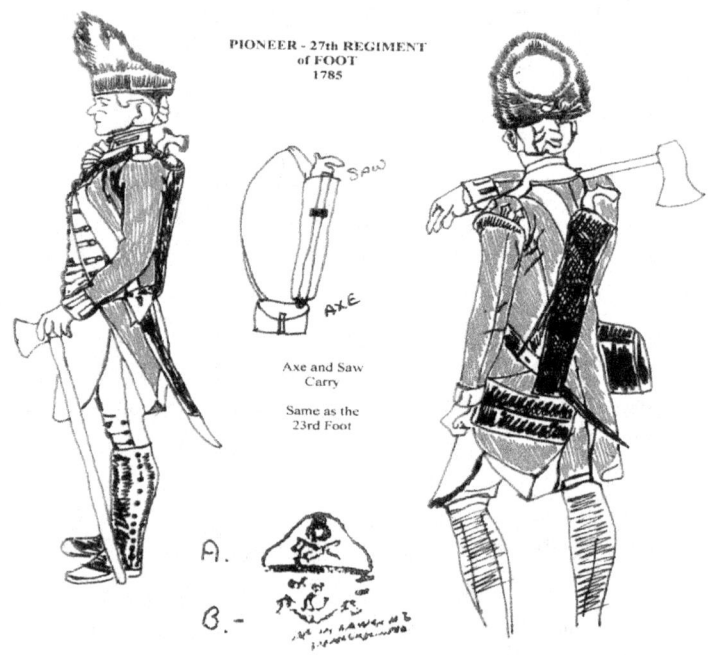

7th REGIMENT of FOOT (ROYAL FUSILIERS) - 1789 [106]

The source for this plate is a unique set of precisely draughted, highly finished contemporary watercolors in the possession of the Regiment. The paintings are neither signed nor dated; but the style, and the resemblance of the details of the uniforms depicted to those of the Regiment shown in a series by Edward Dayes, indicate that they were almost certainty executed in 1789 or 1790. Besides the figures shown in this plate, the set includes the Drum major, the fife Major, a Drummer, and a officer, a Sergeant, a corporal and a Fusilier of the Left Flank (or Light Infantry) Company.

Between 1789 and 1801, his Royal Highness Prince Edward Augustus, later the Duke of Kent, and destined to be the father of Queen Victoria, was Colonel of the Regiment. He took particular interest in the uniform of his regiment, and spent a great deal of money ensuring that its appointments were the best.

> "...The fiercely-whiskered Pioneer is obviously drawn from life. He is dressed according to regulations, his cap having a red-lacquered plate with white ornaments, and he is equipped with the authorized axe, saw and apron."

Looking back to the WARRANTS of 1768 and again at the INFANTRY CLOTHING REGULATIONS OF 1802. Both cases, mention is made that the Pioneer appointments are the same, no changes were made. Its very interesting to note the "Facial Hair".

PIONEERS - 60th REGIMENT of FOOT.

Author's photo collection taken in Charleston, S.C.

I met these two gentlemen at an event many years ago. We gathered with our wives for dinner after which we exchanged notes about our current units. So now I'm attempting to decipher those notes. THE 60th REGT. of FOOT was raised in 1755, later to be Brigaded with the 58th Foot (c1757) and the 48th Foot (c1751.) By 1881 all three were algamated into what is now called THE NORTHAMPTONSHIRE REGIMENT.

In 1960, after further algamations; Its new title became 2nd East Anglian Regt. (Duchess of Gloucester's own Royal Lincolnshire and Northamptonshire Regt.). In 1964 another algamation and the title now became 2nd Battalion the Royal Anglian Regiment (R ANGLIAN). I have no idea as to what the Regiments status is today.

Information points to 1783, when the 1st Battalion, had 2 Black Pioneers. In 1790 the 3rd Battalion was in Dominica. In 1792 the 1st Battalion was now in Longueil with the 2nd Battalion in Montreal

Mr. Reed, the one on the left is a trainer for Motel and Hotel managers. The two of them live in Florida; and generally only travel to events in Georgia and the Carolinas'.

PIONEER - 66th REGT. of FOOT - 1815

Col. John Elting notes. This is taken from one of
C. Hamilton Smith's colored plates in his famous
book on British uniforms of the Napoleonic Period.
"Costume of the British Army", possibly in the
rare book section of the West Point Military
Library.

It is considered a first rate reference

Collar and cuffs are green, lace is white.
Pioneer is wearing a Bearskin cap with
brass front plate, beard and moustache.
coat is red.

Trousers, with outer seam open,
correct for this period

He's wearing regular knee high
gaitors, worn under the pants - not spats

It would appear, that Officers and men had to
be clean shaven, while Pioneers were
allowed to cultivate luqiriant mustaches
and beards.

Pioneer of the 40th -c1815, supposedly from
a contemporary skitch, wears a "Waterloo"
Shako with oil skin cover. Clean Shaven.
Axe is carried in a black leather "holster"
on a narrow white belt over his right shoulder.
Haversack and canteen on his left hip.

Both have thier aprons pulled back on the
right leaving most of the right leg uncovered.
But, the Pioneer of the 40th clearly has his
lower right corner buttoned to bottom button
of his coat.

THE PIONEERS OF YORKTOWN, VIRGINIA - OCTOBER 1980

The two pioneers on the outside belong to the 23rd Royal Welch Fusiliers
in America - c1775
The two Pioneers in the middle wearing white leather aprons, belong to the modern
Royal Welch Fusiliers visiting from England

Photo from Sir Michael Grenier's Photo Collection
Staffordshire Regimental Museum; Litchfield, England
September 2005

Colour Sergeant Malcolm Bower with Watchman IV
Regimental Mascot.

42nd Regt. (Highlanders)   64th Foot   5th Regt. of Foot
(The Author)

A 2 man crosscut saw in a handmade leather carry case.

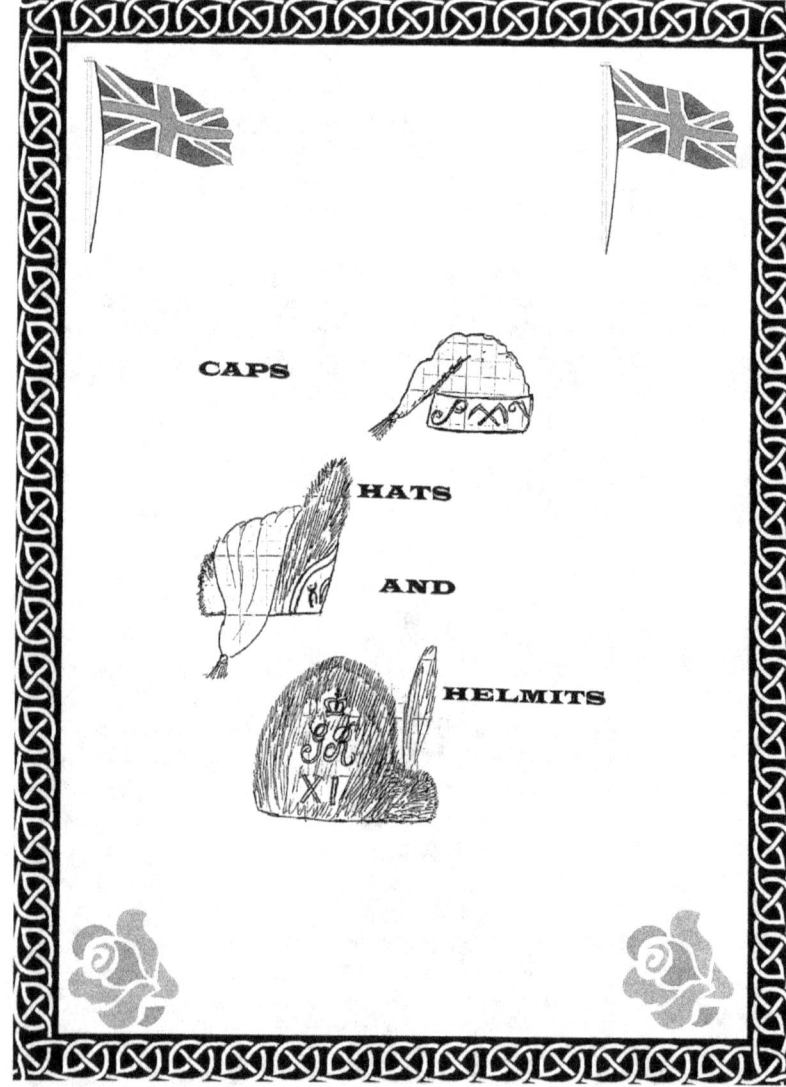

CAPS HATS AND HELMETS

Mr. Dennis Krowe provided several of the drawings which show the evolution of the pioneer headgear shown on the next few pages.

There isn't much reference material on such items before the Royal Warrants of 1768 and the Clothing Regulations of 1802.

Anyone who wishes to make such a helmet, if the recreated unit you belong to has no documentation on pioneer helmets, then there are three choices for helmets, the small leather cap, similar to a light Infantrymen's helmet, or the short version of the Grenadier helmet called a Fusiliers Helmet or go to the full sized Grenadier Helmet.

The face plate is generally made out of stamped metal. Refer back to the one worn by the pioneer of the 23rd Regt. of Foot, check in the Warrants chapter or look at the print from the P.J. de Loutherbourg collection.

The face plate design for my helmet isn't made of metal but hand tooled leather which was then painted and was used by the 25th Foot, 59th and the 64th Regiment of Foot. My face plate design can be found in the chapter of Hats, Caps and Helmets, page 149

By going to the design mentioned in the Warrants, is a rather safe bet.

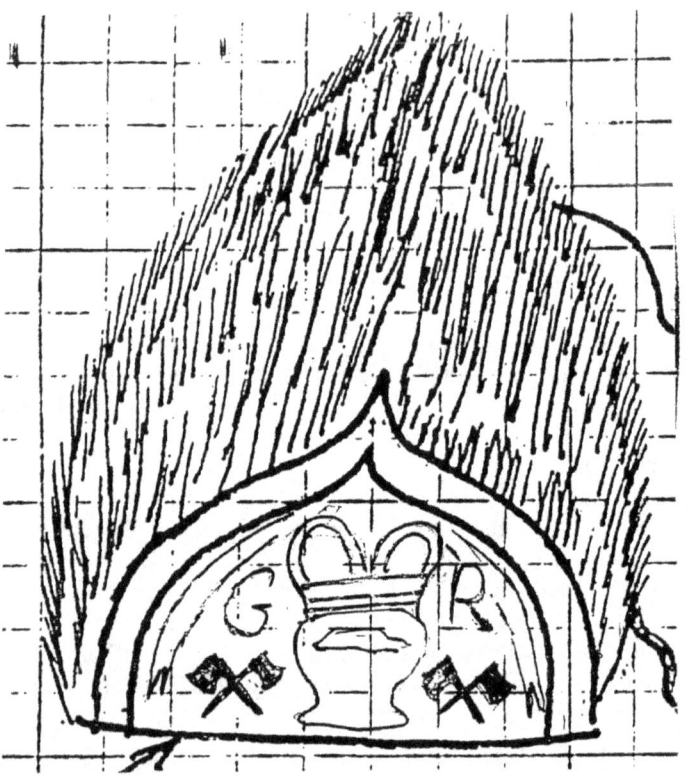

Using an enlargement of one of Mr. Krowes Pioneer/Furrier Helmets. It illustrates one other face plate design that I have seen, but at this time cannot locate.

You could have either crossed axes on either side of the Royal Crest or a crossed axe and saw design. If you refer to the Clothing Regulations of 1802, the Pioneer Helmet shown there is the same one found on page 99, (Yorkshire Buffs) and again the same in the sketch found in the 1802 Clothing Regs., and reference is also made to the Warrants of 1768

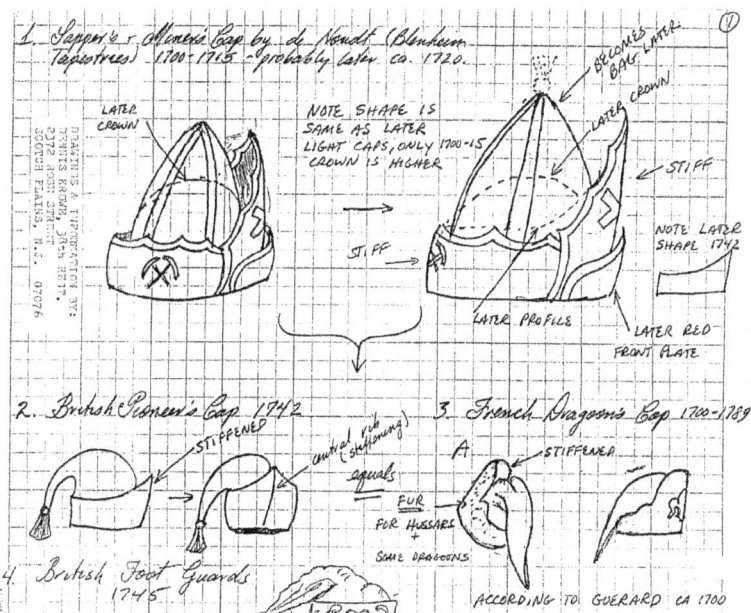

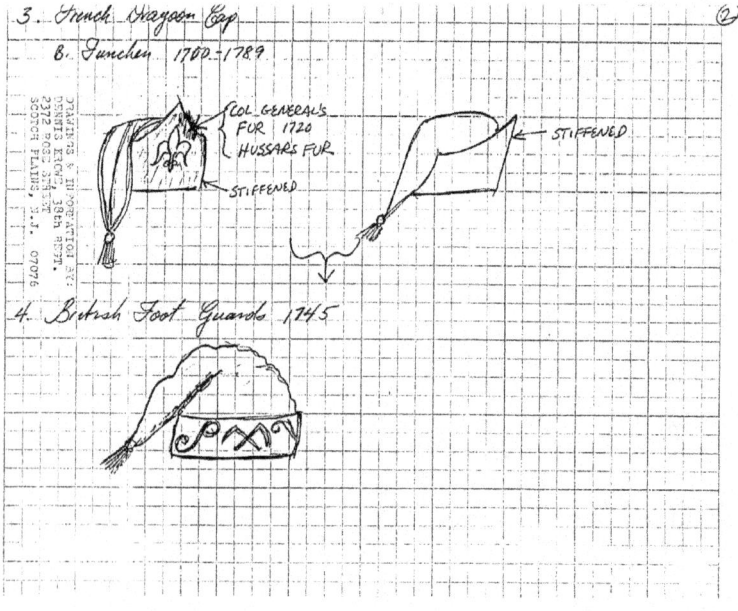

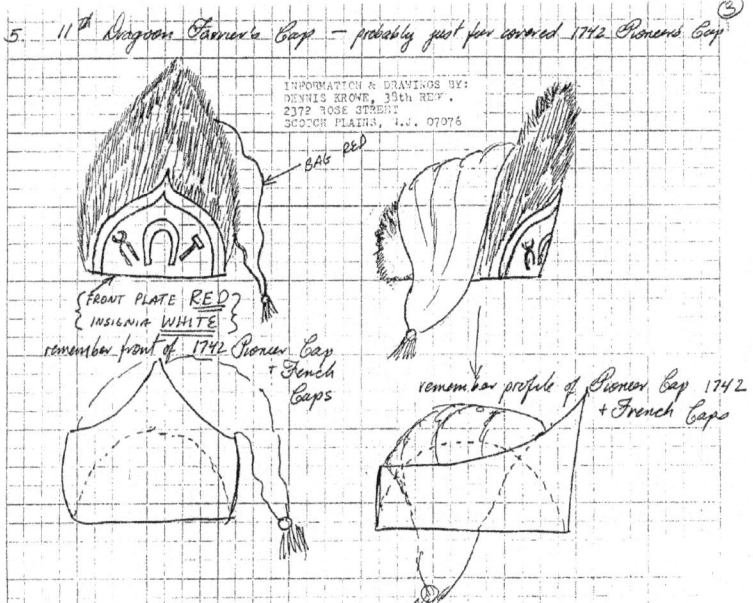

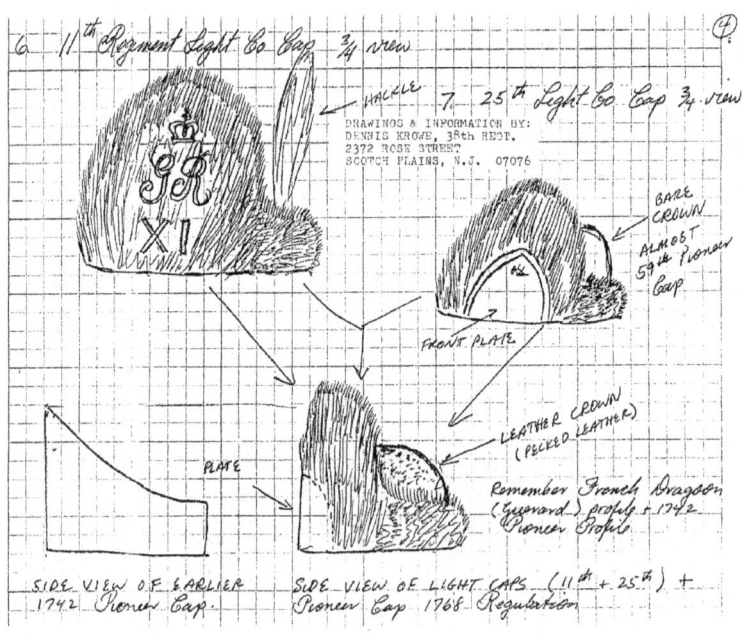

Conclusion: 1. We can see the basic profile and structure of the Pioneer-Miner's Cap in the de Hondt Miner's Cap 1700-1720 Figure 1.

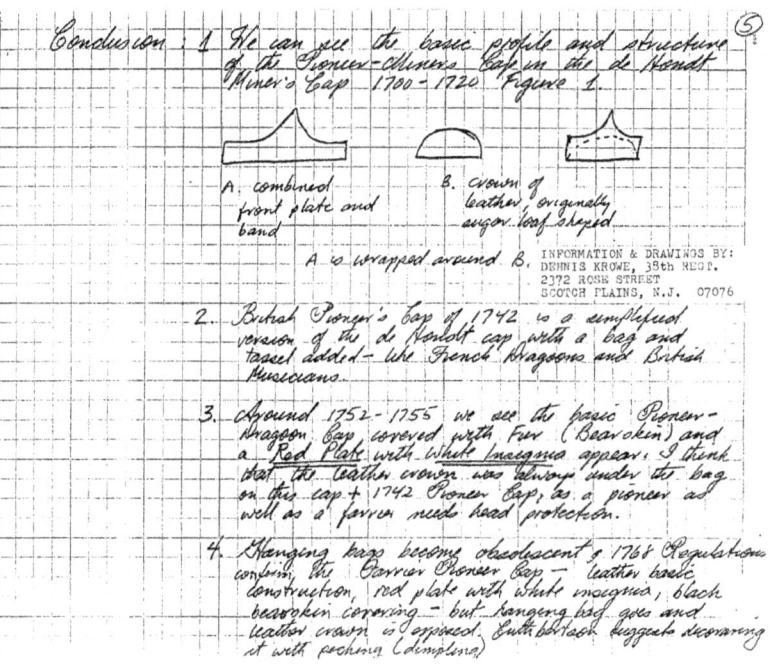

A. combined front plate and band

B. crown of leather originally sugar loaf shaped

A is wrapped around B.

INFORMATION & DRAWINGS BY:
DENNIS KROWE, 35th REGT.
2372 ROSE STREET
SCOTCH PLAINS, N.J. 07076

2. British Pioneer's Cap of 1742 is a simplified version of the de Hondt cap with a bag and tassel added — like French Dragoons and British Musicians.

3. Around 1752-1755 we see the basic Pioneer-Dragoon Cap covered with Fur (Bearskin) and a Red Plate with White Insignia appears. I think that the leather crown was always under the bag on this cap + 1742 Pioneer Cap, as a pioneer as well as a farrier needs head protection.

4. Hanging bag becomes obsolescent & 1768 Regulation confirm the Farrier Pioneer Cap — leather basic construction, red plate with white insignia, black bearskin covering — but hanging bag goes and leather crown is exposed. Sutherland suggests decorating it with pecking (dimpling)

(6)

5. We see that by 1770 - 1771 the Pioneer-Farrier Cap is widely accepted. The 4/11th Regiment LI, the 25th Regiment LI, and 59th Pioneers are using it. 11th & 25th watercolors however give us a good 3/4 view of the cap and show bearskin goes all the way around the cap, like the French Dragoons and Hussars.

6. 1772 Light Regulations are adopted and the Regiments' Light Boys seem to have abandoned the Pioneer-Farrier Cap - it falls into obscurity. However as it is sanctioned by the 1768 Regulations, which are generally agreed to have confirmed popular and desired usage we can assume that it, like the bearskin Grenadier Cap (until grenadiers), was fairly widely worn by British Pioneers.

7. As you can't paint Bearskin, evidently a badge of some sort was used to carry the Regiments Number, unless the number was painted on the exposed leather crown as the regimental designation was to be put on the red cloth part of the Grenadier Cap. ☆ TALKING ABOUT RED CLOTH ON GRENADIER CAP. IT SEEMS LIKELY, IN THE LIGHT OF THE FARRIER CAP HAVING A RED BAG, THE LEATHER CROWN OF THE PIONEER CAP MAY HAVE BEEN PAINTED RED WITH REGIMENTS NUMBER IN WHITE ON IT.

Therefore 59th Regiment Pioneer Cap seems correct for British Regular Regiments with full fur covering, no cockade and possibly a red leather crown with white regimental numbers on it.

DRAWINGS & INFORMATION BY:
DENNIS KROWE, 38th REGT.
2372 ROSE STREET
SCOTCH PLAINS, N.J. 07076

Mr. Dennis Krowe's Sources on Pioneer Helmets

Miners Cap - 1700 - 1720 - After De Glondt (Blenheem Tapestries)

Kemp, Anthony - "Weapons and Equipment of the Marlborough Wars" - (Dorset, 1980) Page 142

French Dragoon's Cap - on page 66 - Engraving cm. 1780 by N. Guerand
Funcken, Fred and Lelane - The Lace Wars Part II (London, 1977)
Page 22 - 28

British Pioneer's Cap - 1742 - 1745 - Lawson, Ceil C.P. *A History of the Uniforms of British Army - Vol. II* - (London, 1941) Pg. 208 - 209
Contemporary engraving of Lord Major's procession,
October 25, 1742

Shesgreen, Shaun - "Engravings by Hogarth (New York, 1973),
Page 74 - "The march to Finchley, 1745" - by William Hogarth

British Farrier's Cap - Painting of a Farrier of the 11th Light Dragoons by Moriar The Royal Collection

Funchan, op ut. page 56

British Light Infantry Caps - 25th and 11th Regiments of Foot
    Paintings, watercolors, of both Regiments Picket (Light) companies are in the Royal Collection, date 1770

May, Robin *The British Army in North America 1775 - 1783*
(Reading, 1974) Pg. 5, 15
And of course, the Regulations of 1768

The British Museum

Department of Prints and Drawings, London WC1B 3DG
Telephone 01-636 1555 ext

William E Eisenhauer
Hyde Park Hgts Apt 10M
Hyde Park, New York
12538   USA

PD/LS/JEM

28 March 1984

Dear Mr Eisenhauer

I have just received your letter of 19 March.

On checking through our drawings by P.J. de Loutherbourg, I have found four which are probably of interest to you: these are in a sketchbook. Page 8 - Royal Artillery; page 22 - Royal Artillery; plate 35 Glamorgan militia men (on your photocopy); and page 36 - Yorkshire Buffs (also on your photocopy).

I enclose a list giving details of our charges for photographs: I am extremely sorry that this was omitted from my previous letter to you. I fear that there is a delay of about six to eight weeks on photographic orders.

Yours sincerely

Lindsay Stainton

Lindsay Stainton
Assistant Keeper

Members of the staff of the British Museum cannot accept liability for the opinions they may express on objects submitted for identification or for information; neither can they give valuations

Inland and Overseas Telegrams: Britishmus London WC1

Drummer's cap of the Yorkshire buffs.   Pionier of the regiment
PRO ARIS. — ET. — FOCIS.   the same moto in rede letter

red ×
M
Y

Silver.

The cap and front very small
the tossels crimson. the front red lead.   pro — aris. et. — focis
ornaments. and crown silver. — letters black.   tossels crimson — the front red lead
officer of Grenadiers of   ornament silver. letters red.

the same moto. letters. & ground of the
front black. and the ornaments silver.   The grenade is silver with the initial letters
tossels according to the turn up of the Reg.t.   of the Reg.t. the tossels as mentioned before

Light inf.t of the 6.th.

These Sketches were drawn while the Yorkshire Buffs (3rd Regt.) were on Parade in England

A Closeup of the Pioneer and Helmet, the Yorkshire Buffs, can also be found as a sketch in the Clothing Regulations of 1802. Which are the same as mentioned "Without Changes", for the Warrents of 1768

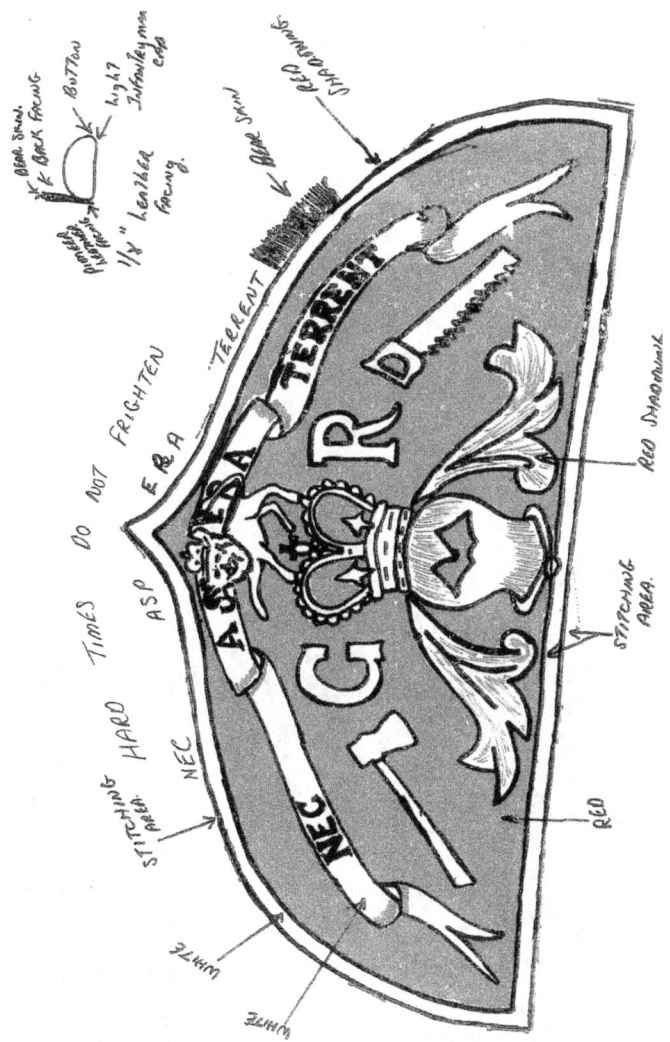

MARCH 23rd, 1980 - Saddlebrook, New Jersey - Reenactment of the British And Hessian Raids on Hackensack, New Jersey

The Author - Photo taken by a photographer from the Daily News

JULY 11/12, 1981 - Schraalenburg Raid - Dumont, New Jersey
Pioneer Pvt. Colonel's Company - 64th Regt. Of Foot
William Eisenhauer

NATIONAL ARMY MUSEUM
Royal Hospital Road London SW3 4HT

Telephone 01-730 0717 ext 25

Mr W Eisenhauer
1 Van Horn Circle
Beacon
New York 12508
U.S.A.

Your reference

Our reference
63(1326)XXXII

Date
27 March 1979

Dear Sir

I write in reply to your letter of 12 March concerning the uniform worn by Pioneers in the 64th Regiment of Foot 1775 to 1785.

There is not a great deal of contemporary material about pioneers for this period. There is however, a reasonable illustration of a pioneer in the 59th Regiment, fig 26, Uniforms of the American Revolution, John Mollo and Malcolm McGregor, Blandford Press Ltd, London 1975. The only difference between a pioneer of the 59th and one of the 64th would be the facing colour, lace and numeral on the back of the fur cap.

The Royal Warrant of 1768 describes the headdress as a cap with a leather crown, a black bearskin front 'on which is to be the king's crest in white, on a red ground; also an axe and saw. The number of the Regiment to be on the back part of the cap'. This description is repeated by Thomas Simes in 'The Military Guide for Young Officers', London 1772 and 1776. Bennett Cuthbertson in 'A System for the Compleat Interior Management and Oeconomy of a Battalion of Infantry' Dublin 1768 & 1776, recommended 'jack-leather caps, somewhat shaped like those worn by the Ligh Dragoons, answer best for Pioniers, as they are strong, and therefore suited to the kind of work they often are employed in; which being generally in the open air, and under the influence of the hottest sun, a contrivance should be made, to let the front flap down occasionally to shield the eyes'.

It is not known whether Cuthbertson's recommendations were adopted. Certainly his idea that the pioneer's equipment of an axe and saw, stated in the 1768 Royal Warra should be increased three spades, three pick axes, three hatchets and two saws all with 'proper cases and white leather slings for each' per regiment was not adopted in any great haste. He recommended that the tools be divided as follows: three me with axes, three with spades, two with hatchets and saws and a Corporal with a hatc only.

Cuthbertson goes on to describe the pioneer's apron as being of the 'best of thick brown leather' and that he should also carry 'a firelock without sling; small cartouch-box for 12 cartridges to fix upon the belt which carries their tools'.

It would appear that three pioneers were fairly general for each battalion. An out letter 11 February 1779, states that 'axes, saws and aprons 9' should be accounted for in the review returns. This probably means three of each item. A list of supplies made to the 32nd Foot, 13 June 1777 mentions 3 Pioneers caps, 3 leather aprons, 3 axes, cases and slings, 3 saws cases and slings.

cont d.

Mr W Eisenhauer
83(1326)XXXII
27 March 1979

The pioneers were generally privates, there certainly also being mention of corporals. The rank distinction for corporals at that period being a white shoulder knot on the right shoulder. They were part of the regiment and not 'on loan' from any other military department.

As regards the other information required, I have forwarded your letter to the appropriate departments within the museum from whom you will be hearing in due course.

Yours faithfully

S K. Hopkins

Mrs SK Hopkins
Research Assistant
Department of Uniform

NATIONAL ARMY MUSEUM
Royal Hospital Road London SW3 4HT

Telephone Army Network Nam Military } ext 25
Civil Network 01-730 0717

Mr J Eisenhauer
Hyde Park Heights Apt 10M
Hyde Park
New York 12538
U S A

Your reference

Our reference
83(1326)LIII

Date
26 August 1983

Dear Mr Eisenhauer

I write in reply to your letter of 14 August concerning the headdresses worn by Pioneers.

Your letter of 12 March 1979 specifically mentioned the period 1775 to 1785.

The information concerning the fact that the Pioneers of the 59th and 64th being similarly dressed except for certain regimental distinctions is based on contemporary (and I must stress this) evidence available to me.

The Royal Warrant of 1768 still applied. As you have a copy of Strachan's book you will see that this Warrant is produced in full, also that which remains of Inspection Returns etc for various regiments. This information plus the writings of Simes and Cuthbertson have led me to the conclusions of my letter of 27 March. To date I have found no evidence to suspect otherwise. Should I do so I will let you know.

The 124th Queen's Royal Irish was raised in 1762. In my letter of 8 April I referred to the Army Lists of 1763. The 124th was disbanded 1764/65.

Your query concerning cartridge box badges has been referred to my colleagues who will deal with this matter in due course.

I enclose a book list and have marked the volumes which may be of help to you with background reading.

Yours sincerely

S K Hopkins

Mrs S K Hopkins
Research Assistant
Department of Uniform

Enc:

64th Regiment of Foot, Ltd. - In America
Pioneer - Captain Stannis Battalion Company
♦♦♦

William Eisenhauer ♦ 107 E. Market St. - Apt. 10M ♦ Hyde Park, New York 12538 ♦ U. S.A.
Phone 914-229-0925 ♦ Email w.e.eisenhauer@worldnet.att.net

April 03, 1999

Staffordshire R.H.Q.
Whittington Barracks
Lichfield, Staffordshire
WS14 9PY ENGLAND

Atten; Museum Curator

Dear Sir;,

I'd like to introduce myself, I am Bill Eisenhauer, my friends generally call me IKE. I've been a member of the 64th Foot here in the State for nearly 20 years now. My primary interpretation is that of a Pioneer in a Battalion Company. I have, over the past 20 years collected quite a bit of research on the role of a Battalion Company Pioneer, and would like to share some of it with you.

In 1993, I stepped down as a Pioneer, Retired sort of. Due to various reasons, I found it hard to keep up with these younger kids coming in to the organization. But I took on the role as woodworker, and put on wood working and Camp life demonstrations at our various events.

I have enclosed some materials, documentation, from the National Army museum on my Pioneer Helmet, plus several photo's of the helmet and a drawing of the face plate, which by the way is not metal, but hand tooled leather.

The helmet was created over 20 years ago by Fred Wahl, I believe at the time there were about 10 of, now mine is the only one left.

One large photo of the members present in Williamsburg, VA., Sept. 1990, I'm on the far left. The photo of me clean shaven, was taken as the same time, but in camp. The other blank and white of me, with a beard, was taken in Tappen, N.Y., in 1978.

I would like to donate my helmet, with carry bag and leather work apron to your museum, if you are interested. I'm planning on retiring from my job in August of this year, I still have an interest in the hobby, but when you retire, your plans change. I don't want this helmet handed over to anyone else, nor do I want to see it get damaged or lost.

So, if you are interested, please let me know, and I'll gladly ship it over to you.

Thanks for your time and interest.

Sincerely,

William Eisenhauer
Pioneer - ret.

COLONEL IN CHIEF
His Royal Highness the Duke of York, CVO, ADC
COLONEL OF THE REGIMENT:
COLONEL T. R. COTTIS, MBE

Regimental Secretary:
MAJOR E GREEN

Assistant Secretary:
MAJOR H. M. TARBUCK, MBE

RHQ M202

Regimental Headquarters
The Staffordshire Regiment
(The Prince of Wales's)
Whittington Barracks
Lichfield, Staffordshire
WS14 9PY
Telephone:
Army Network: Ext 3240, 3263, 3229
Civil Network: 0121 311 3240, 3263, 3229
Fax: 0121 311 3205

William Eisenhauer
107 E Market St
Apt 10M
Hyde Park
New York 12538
USA

6 May 1999

Dear Bill

Thank you for your letter dated 3 April 99 and your very generous offer to donate your helmet with carry bag and leather work apron. My apologies in taking so long to respond, however the Museum has been closed down to enable a full refurbishment programme to be implemented. We relaunched with a grand re-opening on 29 April 99.

I, like yourself, have retired and have only just taken over the appointment as Secretary to the Regimental Association based in Regimental Headquarters in Lichfield. Your letter was one of the first to cross my desk, if I receive such interesting and informative correspondence in the future I shall find great satisfaction in my new employment.

I am sure you will be comforted to know that your prized possesions will be well looked after and much appreciated by Museum and visiting public alike.

I look forward to hearing from you in the near future.

Yours sincerely,

PC MULINGANI
Major (Retd)
Secretary
Regimental Association

THE STAFFORDSHIRE REGIMENT BENEVOLENT FUND IS A REGISTERED CHARITY   No. 268220

THE STAFFORDSHIRE REGIMENT
(The Prince of Wales's)

Curator:
MRS A S ELSOM, BA AMA

Regimental Secretary:
MAJOR E GREEN

RHQ M202

Whittington Barracks
Lichfield
Staffordshire
WS14 9PY
Tel: 0121-311 3240
Fax: 0121-311 3205

W Eisenhauer Esq
107e Market St
Apt 10M
Hyde Park
New York 12538
USA

5th July 1999

Dear Mr Eisenhauer

Further to your recent correspondence with Major Paul Mulingani. I would like to confirm the safe arrival of your 64th Foot pioneer helmet, its carrying bag and a leather apron.

Thank you very much indeed for presenting these to the Museum. We are delighted to be able to add them to the collection; they will be a great help in interpreting this early period of our Regiment's history to the public in general and to schools in particular. It is very useful to have all the associated documentation and photographs as well.

I am not sure that we will be able to come up with an answer to your query about a cartridge box badge but if we do turn anything up we will let you know. I imagine that this may take some time.

Again, many thanks for your very kind donation.

Our Best Wishes to the 64th of Foot in America. I enclose our new publicity leaflet. Any of your members who are travelling to the UK will always be made very welcome here.

Yours sincerely,

A S ELSOM
Curator

THE STAFFORDSHIRE REGIMENT MUSEUM IS A REGISTERED CHARITY.

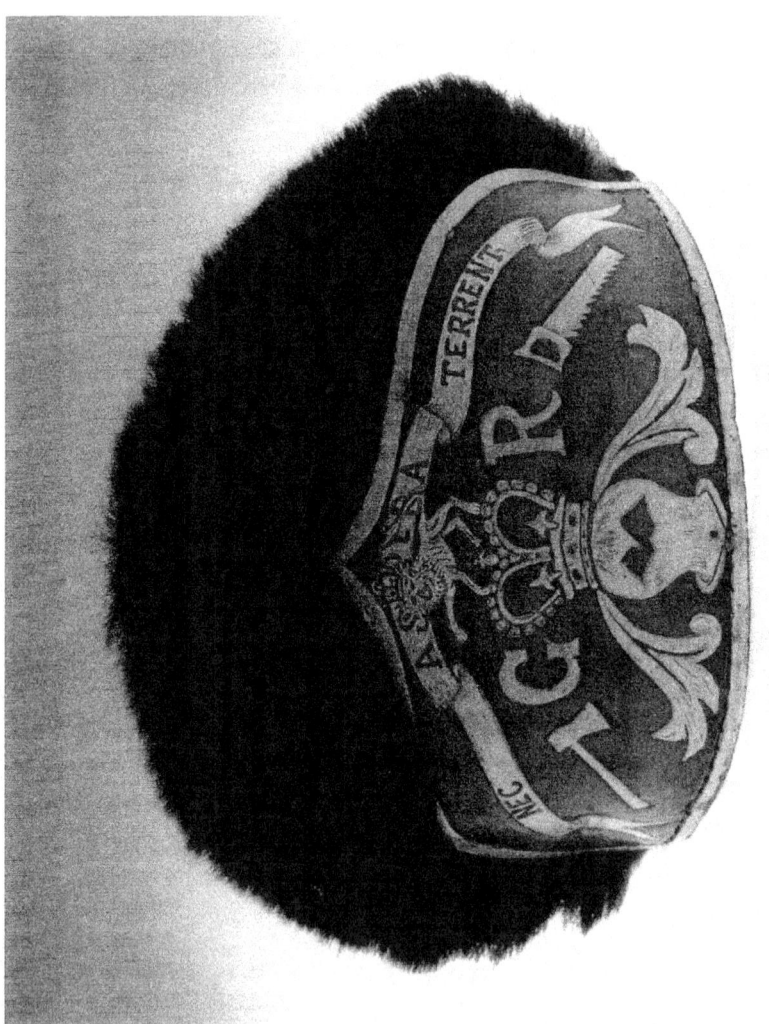

Helmet face plate is leather, then hand tooled to bear the present design and then painted.

Main body of the helmet is that of a Light Infantrymen's helmet, pioneer Face Plate added along with the fur trim according to the helmet design of the Pioneer of the 59th Regiment of Foot.

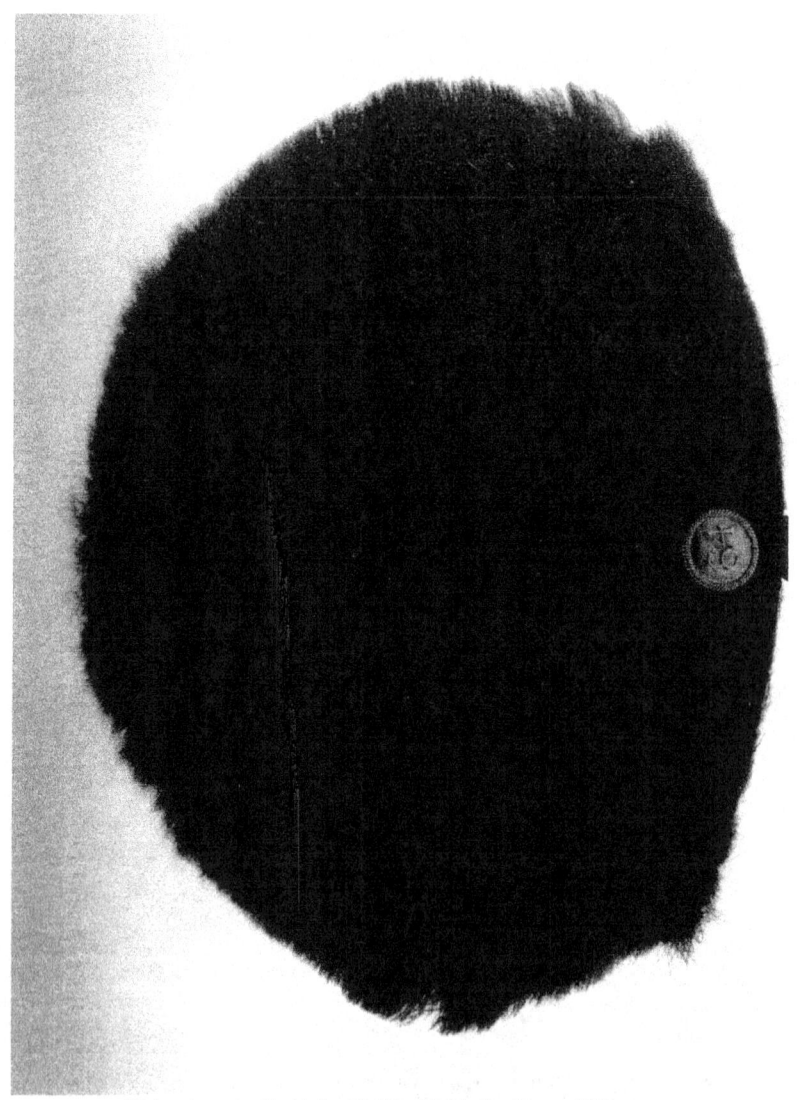
Helmet currently in the Staffordshire Regimental Museum.

YORKTOWN, VA.- OCT. 1981- BATTALION CO. BEING LEAD BY ENS. JACKIE BRADBURY BEARING THE REGIMENTAL COLORS OF THE 64TH REGIMENT OF FOOT

AUTHOR'S PHOTOS

PIONEER – FULL KIT
BATTALION COMPANY
64TH REGT. OF FOOT

CROWN POINT STATE STATE HISTORIC SITE, CROWN POINT, NEW YORK

AUTHOR'S PHOTOS

PIONEERS - 47TH & 64TH REGIMENTS OF FOOT

AXE HARNESS, HAVERSACK, CANTEEN, CARTRIDGE BOX; & REGT. COAT TO BE REMOVED FOR A WORK DETAIL

CAPT. STANNIS BATTALION COMPANY – 64™ REGT. OF FOOT
STE. JEANS, QUEBEC MILITARY ACADEMY – AUG. 10/11/91

AUTHOR'S PHOTOS

ANOTHER VIEW OF WORK APRON

BRITISH ENCAMPMENT – STE. JEANS, QUEBEC – AUGUST 10/11 1991

AUTHOR'S PHOTO'S

BROTHER'S IN ARMS
64TH REGT. OF FOOT

APRON UNFOLDED TO A
FULL OVER THE SHOULDER

Colonial Williamsburg Historic Area

The Crossed Axes - represent the current Badge of the Pioneers
c1856

September 1 - 3, 1990 - Market Days (c1770) in Colonial Williamsburg.

BRIGADED BRITISH PIONEERS AT YORKTOWN - OCTOBER 19, 1981
UNITS REPRESENTED: 4th Regiment of Foot (1)
23rd Regiment of Foot (2)   60th Regiment of Foot (2)
64th Regiment of Foot (3)   84th Highlander Regt. (3)
Queens Rangers   (1)   4th New Jersey Loyalist
Delancey's Loyalist   Battalion   (2)
    Battalion   (1)

The largest assembled detachment of Pioneers for any 18th Century event.

Photo Collection of Sir Michael Grenier
Staffordshire Regimental Museum; Litchfield, England
September 2005

64th Regt. of Foot ~ Light Infantry
c1775

Private
80th Regt. of Foot c1879

Battalion Soldier
64th Foot

**British Brigade Event at
Bordentown, New Jersey**

June 7 & 8 1997

BLACK KNOTS

64th Regiment of Foot
The Uniforms and Accoutrements of the Battalion Soldier and Company Pioneer - c1775

The color drawing of the Pioneer, 59th Foot, comes from the book titled *Uniforms of the American Revolution* by John Mollo and Malcom McGregor. The Regiment maintained the 59th title until July 1st, 1881, there after it became the 2nd Battalion - East Lancashire Regiment. On March 25th, 1970, its title was changed to:
The Queens Lancashire Regiment

The color photo, Author's Collection; is that of Sgt. Hiram Lyon of Captain Stannis Battalion Company, 64th Regiment of Foot in America.

The description of Uniforms, Accoutrements and equipment for a Battalion Soldier c1775 is based on information from the Royal Warrants of 1768; and other reference material such as from Cuthbertson and Thomas Simes, "The Military Guide for Young Officers, Hew Strachan's British Military Uniforms - 1768 - 96. Mr. Tom Brancellia helped with this information.

The basic uniform as described would also be the same for the Company or Regimental Pioneer for either the 25th Regiment of Foot; 59th Regiment of Foot or the 64th Regiment of Foot; the exception being the facing color and lace pattern used for each Regiment mentioned.

By (1778), many uniform items had in fact changed; the long Regimental coat was cut down into a jacket, the carrying of swords by Battalion troops were done away with.

UNIFORM AND ACCOUTERMENTS - PIONEER - BATTALION SOLDIER
64th REGIMENT of FOOT c1775

HELMET'S - Cuthbertson : Article 46
Jack-leather-caps, somewhat shaped like those worn by the Light-Dragoons, are best for the Pioneers, as they are strong, and therefore suited; which being generally in the open air, and under the influence of the hottest sun.

There has been some controversy over this helmet; especially the source from which it was derived, "Uniforms of the American Revolution" London 1975 by John Mollo and Malcolm McGregor; but the letters from the National Army Museum, dated March 27th 1979 pg 152 and August 26th 1983 pg 154, should pretty much put to rest, especially considering Pioneer helmet for the 64th is the same used by the 59th Foot, with the exception of the numbered button on the back.

Garrison cap or work cap, in the 1980's. No one had come up with a suitable one so I made one similar to that worn by William Todd, made from two old coat sleeves. Currently my portrayal of the Pioneer, 64th Foot closely resembles that of the Pioneer, 59th Foot. See Page 160 for color photo of my helmet.

The face plate is hand tooled leather, then carefully painted. Bear fur was placed across the top of the face plate as well as fur going around the base of the helmet ending at the back where the button is attached. Other Pioneer helmet designs can be found in helmet section as well. Currently my helmet is part of the display at the Staffordshire Regimental Museum in England. Currently the museum has no room for Rev War displays, but hope's to build an addition onto the current museum for these displays.
Author's Photo Collection.

Pioneers - 60th Regiment of Foot
Note the linen haversack, kidney shaped tin canteen and large cartridge box.

TOP: BORDENTOWN, N.J. - June 7/8 1997

Captain, with Battalion Company – 64th Regt. of Foot in camp

Pioneer –Pvt. Wm Eisenhauer - Battalion Co. 64th Foot

BOTTOM: MADISON, CT. - May 21st, 1987

HATS - BATTALION SOLDIER
Includes mention of White Worsted Hat Tape
Tassels for the hats.
CUTHBERTSON: Art.: 26 through 33, covers care and
maintenance of hats.

The hat is the standard military "Cock' of the period. The hat has a high rear brim plus a "short", sharp "cock" mentioned by Cuthbertson. The front of the hat does not have the sharp point of the "cocked" hats of the early 18th Century military. The front of the hat is flattened out so that the front "cock" is almost eliminated. Hat's of the 1790's showed both sides of the cocked hat almost flat and quite high. (this is shown by the Darves print of the 1790's, unfortunately not shown in this book); this print is not part of this book. Contemporary portrait's of the British military show a variety of styles of "cock". Suffice to say, nearly all Battalion Soldiers in the recreated 64th Foot are wearing the "cocked" hat's sold by a Mr. G. Gedney Godwin.

HORSEHAIR COCKADES

Cuthbertson and Simes both mention "Hair" cockades for the hats and the 1768 Warrants specify Black Cockades.

HAIR STYLE [107]

Clubbed: 27 July 1776 - Commander-in-Chief - out letter.
Adj. General to Lord George Lennox...
"... the King has lately expressed his intentions that the hair of all infantry should be tied in one uniform manner, and that the mode which is commonly called clubbed should be observed. I took the liberty of mentioning this to your Lordship as what His Majesty wishes, though no order has as yet, been given out."

See pages 147 & 148 for the de Louthberg painting of the maneuvers at Worley Common. 1778 which shows the Infantry all wearing their hair clubbed.

Post Revolutionary portraits and engravings show the "Clubbed" mode of hairstyle much in evidence. It would appear that the "wish" of the King must have eventually became standing orders.

Mr. George C. Neumann and Frank J. Kravic, also show hair clubbed on page 273. The book is Collector's Illustrated Encyclopedia of the American Revolution.

This book is a very good source of information for Uniforms, accoutrements, camp gear, tents, muskets.

I've found no reference to pioneers wearing wigs, but can assume, should they have hair to be long enough to "club" it probably would be. Although keeping things in perspective, long hair would present all sort's of problems considering the work they are required to do, least of these problems would be head lice. The main reason the wearing of wigs for all ranks was "head Lice", during the 18th century.

NECKSTOCKS

Cuthbertson and Simes mention black "Hair" stocks in "Necessaries to be furnished each soldier". Contemporary paintings all show the black stock (Horse Hair) for common use, the other of Manchester velvet for dress. Cuthbertson Article XXXV, pg 145 of British Military Uniforms 1768-96 By Hew Strachan

> Refer to Collector's Illustrated - pages 251, items 1 through 4. For another source on Neck Stocks.

SMALL CLOTHES LINNEN

The 64th Foot re-created, has adopted "Wool" for its breeches and waistcoats. Linnen is difficult to sew thus wool was adopted as its easier to sew and lasts much longer then linnen. The Patterns that we use do vary. In general we use B.A.R. patterns or the Williamsburg patterns. My pattern came from the B.A.R [108]

SHIRTS

Linen

REGIMENTAL COAT

The cut of the coat is a modified Williamsburg pattern, found upon comparison to originals in England to be the closest to the original cut. Most are copies of the 49th Regimental Officers coat found in the national Army Museum in London. There are some minor variations in style since the coats were all made by different people.

Over the passing years changes were made to both the coat and the arrangement of buttons and lace as additional research was completed in these areas. The weight, color of the wool has also gone through it's various changes all necessary to update what the private in the battalion Company of the 64th looked like when it first arrived in Boston in 1768.

COLOR OF THE COAT

According to contemporary sources, the red of the British Infantry privates coat was supposed to be "Madder Red", or "Brick Red". However, it does not state what shade of "Madder Red". Going further, the 18th century methods of dying were not capable of producing the uniformity which we have today. A good example is to see the various shades of blue in Police officers or Firemen uniforms.

There are many shades of "Madder Red", but in fact there are many shades of Blue as well. This shade of red is shown in the "Xavier Della Golta" paintings of the Philadelphia campaign, plus the 1st Foot Guards musicians coat in the National Army Museum in London is of a red quite close to our Regimental coats.

I refer you to the letter from the Victoria and Albert Museum dated 16 September 1981, on page 181.

FACINGS [109]

Facings are Black, according to the "Misc. Goods" of 19 December 1768: General view of facings, etc. of several marching Regiments of Foot, as fixed by His Majesty.

LACE

Mr. Hew Strachen's Book, pages 181 and 185, (*19th December 1768. Misc. Books: Clothing correspondence General view of the facings etc. of several marching Regts. Of Foot Regiments of Foot W.O. 30/13B)* plate number 36 - 39, show the lace and method of looping the buttonholes of each regiment of infantry as ordered by His Majesty, 1768. Lace is sold by *The Sutler of Mt. Misery - G. Gedney Goodwin - 610-783-0670 - www.gggodwin.com/*

BUTTONS

Buttons are cast from originals found in the Staffordshire Regimental museum in Litchfield, England. The present home of our parent organization.

Buttons are generally made of tin as they hold a shine better. Cuthbertson in Article XIII states, buttons should always made of a good metal and never of pewter.

STOCKINGS

White Wool yarn as prescribed by Simes in "The Military Guide to Young Officers"

GARTER STRAPS

1 inch wide leather, as prescribed by Cuthbertson. Gainsborough painting of 1770 "Officer" shows flank company officer of the 2nd foot, showing 1 inch wide straps.

(Cuthbertson; Art 18)

SHORT GAITORS

Cut from the '*Sketch Book 76'* pattern". Gaiter's polished as per Cuthbertson earlier photo's of unit personnel show short gaiter's but we have long since gone over to the long gaiter's as described by Cuthbertson in Art. 39. Mine are made out of canvas, painted black with a linen lining as a backing to stiffen them. The knee cap which is a separate item is made of heavy leather and painted black.

SHOES

Were the shoes are "Frye" 18th Century style, but as time went on the "Frye" type of shoe was hard to come by. Other suppliers made obtaining a pair easier, but more expensive. An individual in camp who took up the trade of making shoes, could take your measurements, and with a payment can make you a pair of period shoes. This arrangement would take several weeks depending on the number of orders taken.

CARTRIDGE BOX

As per Cuthbertson, Art. 21, and from contemporary paintings. Double flap with white leather sling.

In the early years we used a rather large battalion cartridge box, but addition research has found a more suitable box which is less cumbersome.

Refer to the "*Collector's Illustrated*" page 79 and check pages 76 and 77 to find a description of other different styles and time periods.

BAYONET BELT AND SCABBARD

One such belt can be found in the National Army Museum in London. Battalion soldiers carried along with the bayonet, a sword, Pioneers replaced this sword with a hatchet.

Cuthbertson, Art 34; indicates " the tools consisting only of a saw and hatchet for each man".

HAVERSACK

"Gray" - or natural linen; canvas has been used - B.A.R. Pattern

The Books titled "*The Book of the Continental Soldier*" by Harold L Peterson page 75, and "*The Collectors Illustrated*", pages 59 and 170, also show these item.

On the following pages there will be several sketches showing the "Back pack", "Haversack", "Canteens", "Waist belts" and "Cartridge Boxes". These were taken from the book "*The Book of The Continental Soldier*" by Harold Peterson.

Author's Photo Collection.

Battalion Soldiers - 29th Regiment of Foot

Photo shows the older type of wooden canteen and linen haversack

Victoria and Albert Museum

South Kensington London SW7 2RL

Tel: 01-589 6371

Mr. William E. Eisenhauer,
Hyde Park Heights apt 10M,
Hyde Park,
New York,
12538,
U.S.A.

16th September, 1981

Dear Mr. Eisenhauer,

In answer to your letter of 26th August, almost any book on dyeing or the printing of textiles will explain dyeing with madder, which was one of the more common dyes. It was particularly useful in the printing of textiles because different colours could be obtained from one dye bath by previously printing the cloth with different mordants such as alum, iron or tin. Perhaps this is the 'several shades' from one batch of which you have heard. Of course, when dyeing quantities of cloth for the same purpose the dyers would try to prevent variations in colour. In spite of their care, variations probably abounded because of minute differences in the quality of the madder root itself or of the strength of mordant used on different occasions, or even the trace elements of chemicals in the water used.

Particular details of dyeing with madder in the 1770's are given in contemporary dye-books. If you can, you should try to read "The Dyer's Assistant" by James Haigh, published at Leeds in 1778. In his chapter on dyeing with madder he mentions additions of Archil or Brazilwood to the madder in 'Reds for the Army'.

I do not know whether madder was used for the uniforms of Royal Regiments, though it seems likely. We do not collect uniforms, and I am afraid I must pass you back to the National Army Museum for this information

Yours sincerely,

Wendy Hefford

Miss Wendy Hefford.
Department of Textiles.

CANTEEN

The half-moon canteen, or kidney shaped canteen, can be found in the "*Book of the Continental Soldier*" or in "*The Collector's Illustrated*" on page 59. The book "*American Provincial Corps - 1775 - 1784*" by Philip R.N. Katcher, also shows this type of canteen.

KNAPSACK

White goatskin, preferably long hair to repel water. Good sources are: Book of the Continental Soldier pages 144 and 145; American Universal Military Dictionary by Capt. George Smith - London 1779; Paintings of the British Surrender at Yorktown by Blarenburgh eyewitness painting shows Grenadiers with blue blankets on top of brown goatskin packs; Xavier Della Gatto paintings of the Philadelphia Campaign; Cuthbertson, Art 43
Lefferts, pages 194 and 195

MUSKET SLINGS

Cuthbertson also mentions slings in Article 26.

Check source books - *Book of the Continental Soldier* - pg. 76 and *Collector's Illustrated*, page 35 item #3.

INFANTRY PACKS, HAVERSACKS AND CANTEENS [110]

1. A White Goatskin Knapsack, worn by British troops at the beginning of the war.

2. A Canvas knapsack, ofter painted the facing color of the uniform.

3. A back view, showing arrangement of the straps

4. A Brown goatskin knapsack worn by the British before the war

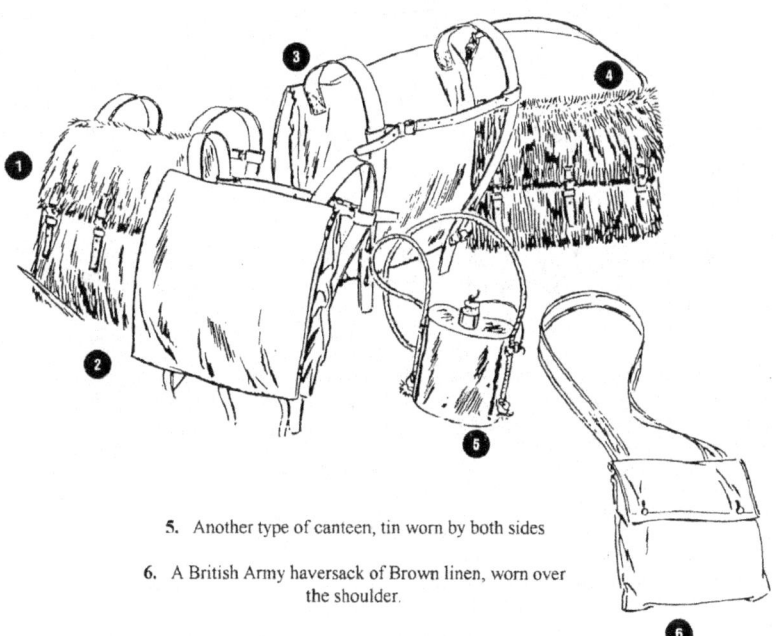

5. Another type of canteen, tin worn by both sides

6. A British Army haversack of Brown linen, worn over the shoulder.

ACCOUTREMENTS - PIONEER AND BATTALION SOLDIER

The sketches on the next two pages come from "*The Book of The Continental Soldier*", by Harold Perterson

1. The British old pattern cartridge box of the 1740's and 1750's. Despite its large size it held only 9 to 18 rounds

2. British pattern cartridge box in use from the mid-1750's through the Revolution.

3. Conventional type of cartridge box of the war with inner flap and holding 24 cartridges in 3 rows

The above 3 cartridge boxes were standard, throughout the British Army. The boxes in general did vary from unit to unit as the war went its course. The Pioneers did not carry such a box. The one they carried was attached to their tool belt and contained 12 cartridges. (Cuthbertson - Chapter 13; Art. 34)

4. Sword and bayonet frogs attached to the waist belt. Pioneers substituted the sword for the hatchet. by 1780 this arrangement was replaced by an over the shoulder carrying belt.

5. These are two of several designs of metal canteens, which were replaced by 1780 by wooden ones, because the metal rusted inside, and causing much illness among the troops. The metal canteen had cords to carry them.

6. The wooden canteen with carrying straps.

Sketches for the above descriptions are found on page 186

Both *THE BOOK OF THE CONTINENTAL SOLDIER* and the *COLLECTOR'S ILLUSTRATED ENCYCLOPEDIA OF THE AMERICAN REVOLUTION*, have many sketches and photo's of additional canteens used by both sides.

It is interesting to note, that the staff of the Brigade of the American Revolution, (B.A.R.) finally authorized the making of a kidney shaped canteen made using the dull side of Stainless Steel, as in fact many re-reinactors ran into the same rusting problems of tin canteens and wooden ones which forever leaked due to infrequent use.

AUTHOR'S COLLECTION

Light Infantry, 29th Regiment of foot.
Standard wooden canteen and linen haversack; but no large cartridge box, a belly box instead. A solid wood block drilled to hold 18 rounds, with a leather cover.
Note photo at bottom of pg 186

THE SKETCHES TAKEN FROM: *The Book of the Continental Soldier*

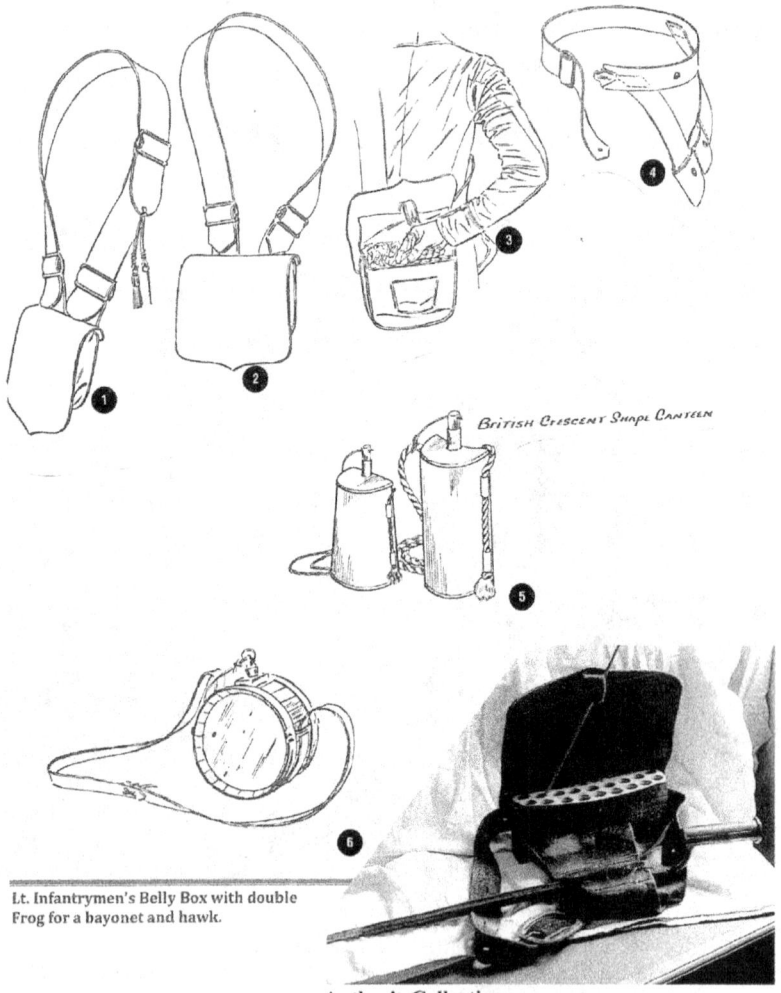

Lt. Infantrymen's Belly Box with double Frog for a bayonet and hawk.

Author's Collection

Author's Collection.

My camp was growing, from a privates tent to a wall tent with fly. So was my knowledge of woodworking tools and what I could make while in camp. Note the 2 individual cast iron bench grips, 2 draw knives on seat and a completed mallet

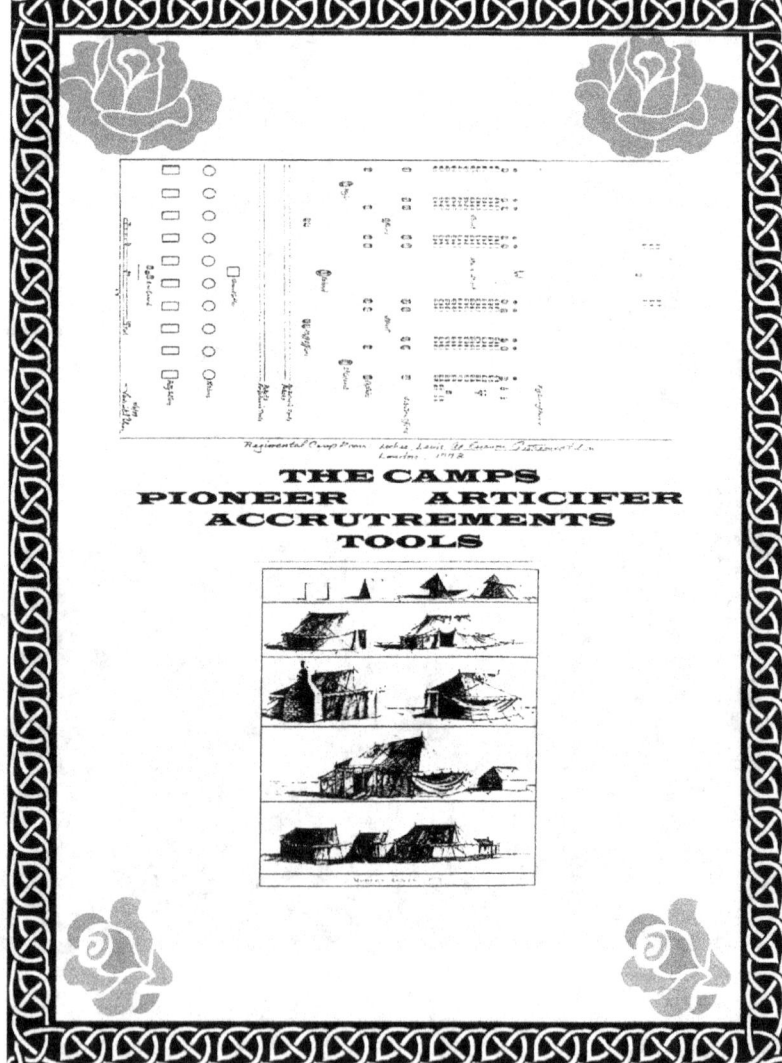

THE CAMPS
PIONEER ARTICIFER
ACCRUTREMENTS
TOOLS

DRAWING TAKEN FROM A REPRINT "AN ESSAY ON CASTRAMENTATION"
BY LEWIS LOCKIE'E MASTER AT THE MILITARY ACADEMY –
LITTLE CHELSEA –1778
PROVIDED BY A MR. JAMES CORBUT

This diagram represents a "Formal British" encampment where the Army would remain for a week or more. But on the march, soldiers would carry the basic equipment on their backs; and roll up in their blankets when it came time to set up camp & and lay on the ground, while officers would use a smaller wedge tent.

THE PIONEER CAMP

A regular Bell Backed Infantrymen's tent, along with a dinning fly to use as your work area. Depending on your unit, you may be required to set your tent up in the line, but your dinning fly might be set in the rear near the kitchen area. Always keep in mind the security of your tools. On the next page shows the setup with the dinning fly in front of my privates tent.

The shaving horse I had to design, much smaller then the one you find on a farm, as it had to fit into my small truck. A friend came up with the drawing, also made the clamping head for me as I had no way to glue it up. The average shaving horse was never meant to transport as it generally was just to big and heavy.

Once I retired as an active Pioneer I then became a civilian Articifer, thus I moved from the standard privates tent into a wall tent for more room and a larger dinning fly. I still did some limited wood working projects.

As time went on, my camp grew, with a table chairs and a fairly complete cooking mess so I could provide my own meals while in camp. Thus the area under my dinning fly had a dinning area, a cook area and my work area, plus I kept a set of fire irons that were used as a drying rack once my projects were finished.

Tools, collect only those you feel you can use, I started out with one chest, it grew to three later on. Make the tool chest's to fit a given area in your vehicle, and a size you can lift out of your vehicle vehicle. Weather you are 30 or 58, there is a difference.

I have a sizeable table, again designed to fit the space in my vehicle, with 2 ladder backed chairs. A personnel chest for my necessary items. Insure you have a large enough blanket to hide any modern items that may be inside your tent.

At the closer of this section you will find listings for various sources for wood working ideas, tools and suppliers. Best place to locate working tools are at Flea Markets, especially Farmers Flea markets or Actions.

THE APRON

Heavy brown leather, don't purchase shoe leather as it will be impossible to work with or wear as it will be to stiff. The following design is what I copied from the Pioneer of the 23rd Regiment of foot while doing the 200th Anniversary of the Battle of Monmouth in June of 1978.

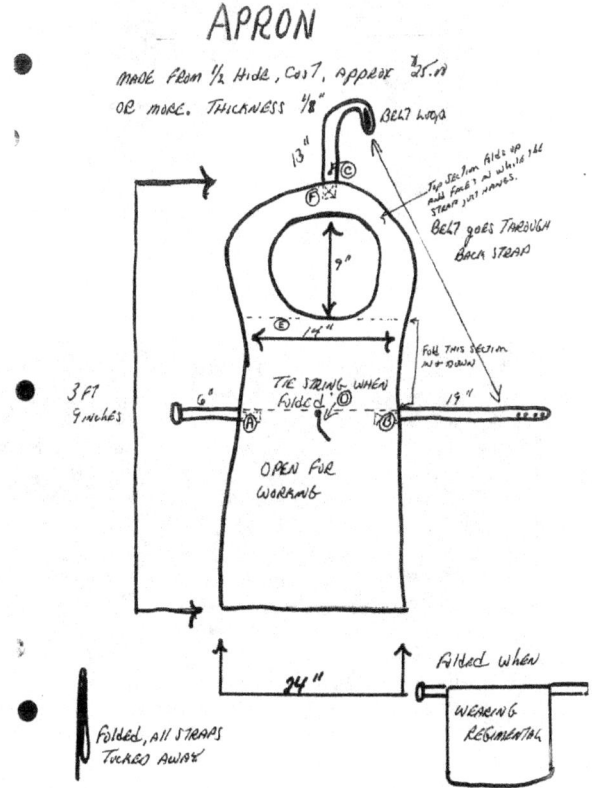

My Beginners Camp

The Pioneer Camp

This entire encampment would fit in the back of a Mazda Pickup, including a roof Luggage pod.

Another view of my camp while at Stony Point National Battlefield Park. Note another view at the bottom of the next page. While I was young and full of it, it would generally take about 3 hours to set up, hard work, since I was alone. The only thing I lacked here was a TV and Microwave. Time and age caught up with me and after I retired I was doing volunteer work at Fort Sisseton, SD; May through July 2003. It was here that I sold off nearly all of my camp with the exception on my shaving horse and wood working tools. The folks belonging to a group called *"The Army of the Dakota's* were happy to help me part with my camp. All I have now besides my woodworking tools is my possible box, Accrutrements chest, 2 ladder backed chairs and my table, all of which are in my RV.

By the time I had reached this size of camp, I had purchased an 4 x 8 cargo trailer.

Same camp that's on page 191 - Bare Bones - Note Mazda Pickup

The Civilian/Articifer Camp -Things were improving - note completed mallet drying on the fire irons. Assorted mallet handles on table.

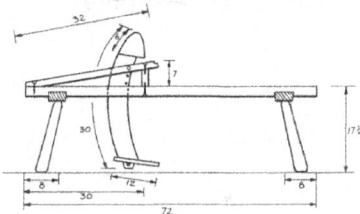

My shaving horse was built to fit inside of a Mazda Pickup.

THE BASIC WOOD WORKING TOOL CHEST ....

Hanging from the lid on the left is a work apron. To the right is a canvas case containing auger bits. Below which is a compartment holding wood chisels, small wood mallets, wood box containing assorted forged nails. Two hand saws.

FRONT LEFT, small hatchet, and a tack hammer, below which are secured two types of draw knives. To the right, rope, two rounders, a morticing gauge.

TOP TRAY, Auger bit handle, fascine knife with case, small framing square, folding ruler, scratch awl, screw driver, two skoke shaves, shop knife, penciles.

On the ground, felling axe, large mallett, used with the axe to hand split wood. The copper plate is used to layout the square hole that I set the wood handles into the mallet head.

AXES, SAWS, HATCHES AND KNIVES

Note drawings on page 198

1 The standard felling axe, carried by the Pioneers of both sides, for clearing trees, for paths or roads, while on the march or in camp. The broad axe was used for the squaring up of logs to build huts or log forts.

2 The axe carry harness is an over the shoulder carry. I've been able to stitch two additional straps on to it, so I can carry my shovel as well. This has added more weight to the harness. For a man 5ft 11 inches tall, with a chest of 43inches, the leather sling should be 70 inches long. It should hang at or about waist belt height. The carry harness for my two man cross cut saw has a brass bucket in the middle to allow for greater adjustments. The main part of each carry is black with the straps being white.

3. The saw, being a two man cross cut saw, with it's own carrying harness. The handles fit into their own pockets on the harness.

4 The hatchet or tomahawk, replaces the sword, and in the later part of the war, light infantryman were carrying the "Hawk"

5. The Fascine Knife, used by the Pioneers and other work parties to make fascines and Gabions, during Siege work if trenching is necessary. This was purchased along with the sheath, from Arrow Head Forge, Mr. Mike Quade

Please note the sketches of two axe heads on the following pages, the first on (pg 200) can be found at the West Point Museum, the second is mine, (pg 198 top sketch) which I purchased from Avalon Forge in Maryland.

The following sketches come from the book "_The Book of the Continental Soldier_" by Harold Peterson

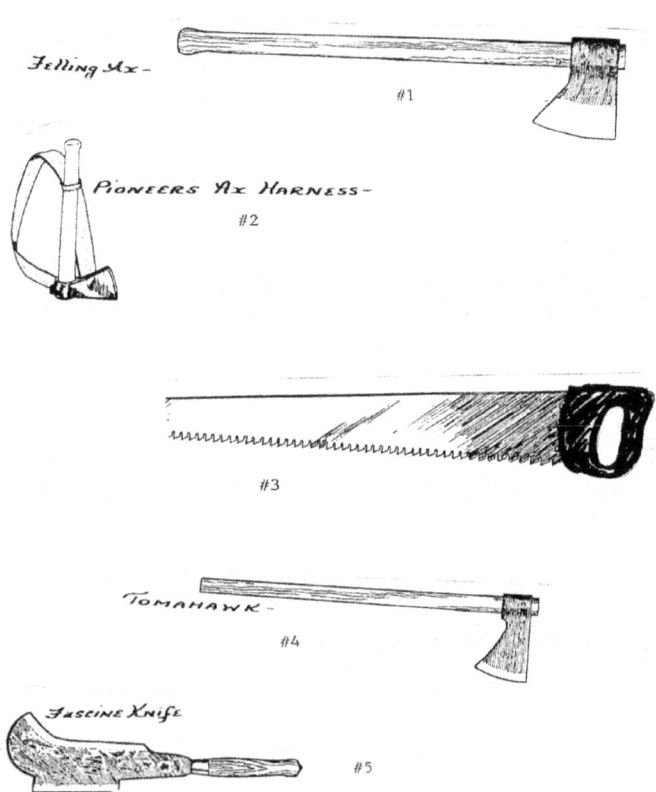

Sketches of item #1, 2, 4 & 5 came from the catalog of Avalon Forge. Refer to page 198. Sketch #1 is my felling axe and sketch of a second axe head is on page 201.

WILLIAM ↑
EISENHAUER

BRAD ↑
CHETWYND

ARLINGTON, MASS - BATTLE
ROAD APRIL 1981

April 18/19, 1981 - Arlington Mass - Event at the Jason Russell House.
Pioneers Wm Eisenhauer and Brad Chetwynd

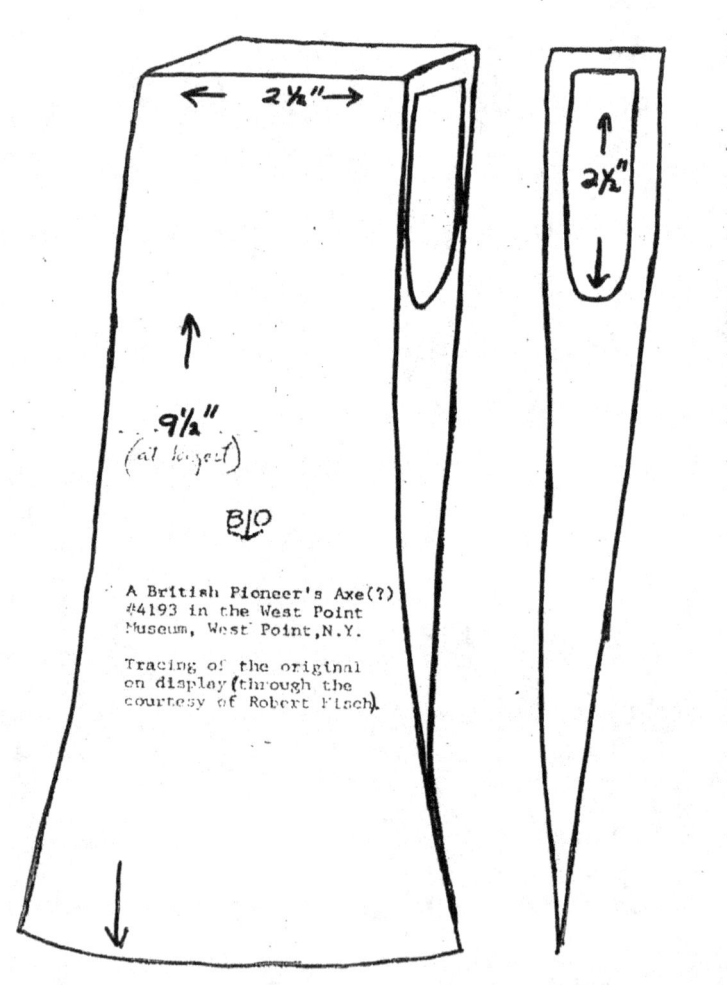

A British Pioneer's Axe (?) #4193 in the West Point Museum, West Point, N.Y.
Tracing of the original on display (through the courtesy of Robert Fisch)

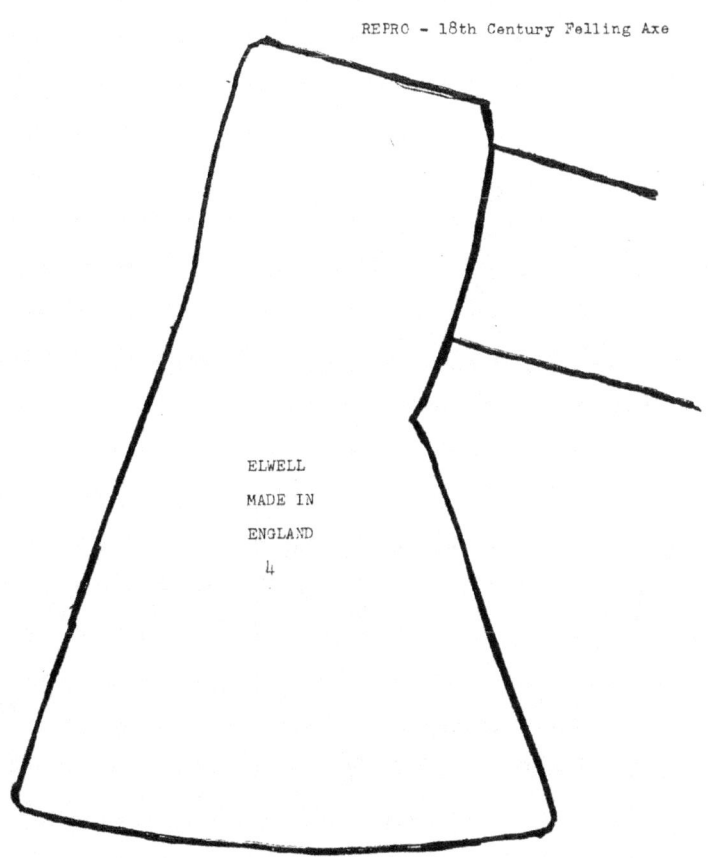

Tracing of the axe head carried by the Pioneers - 64th Regt.

**This is a tracing of my axe head,
once you sharpen the axe, you can cut down a house.**

ENTRENCHING TOOL ....

Taken from the *Book of the Continental Soldier* by Harold Peterson

1. Has a blade 8 inches wide and 11-3/4 inches long, with a widened flange at the top to support the foot and socket pierced with one hole for a rivet thought the handle.

2. Is an older variety, often found in the 17th century. Has a blade 7 ½ inches wide and 13 - 1/2 inches long of 2 piece construction designed as a shell around a wooden core. The pieces are welded together at the bottom and riveted through a wooden core at the top. These may be of American manufacture.

3. Is of modern appearance with a short wide blade 7 1/2 inches wide and 7 3/4 inches long. There is no flange at the top and no mark was found on the single specimen of this kind. Normally all 3 types of spade would have been fitted with straight wooden handles about 3 feet long with a short crosspiece forming a "T" at the top.

4. This specimen, 11 1/4 inches wide and 11 inches long, closely resembles those illustrated in Suirery de Saint Remy's "Memories d 'Artillerie", which appeared in various editions between 1697 and 1745, and since many of them bear still discernible French proof marks in addition to the maker's marks, it may be assumed that they are standard French Army issue.

5. These picks closely resemble modern picks, this specimen measures 23 1/2 inches from point to point and bears the French proof marks.

Sketches on following page.

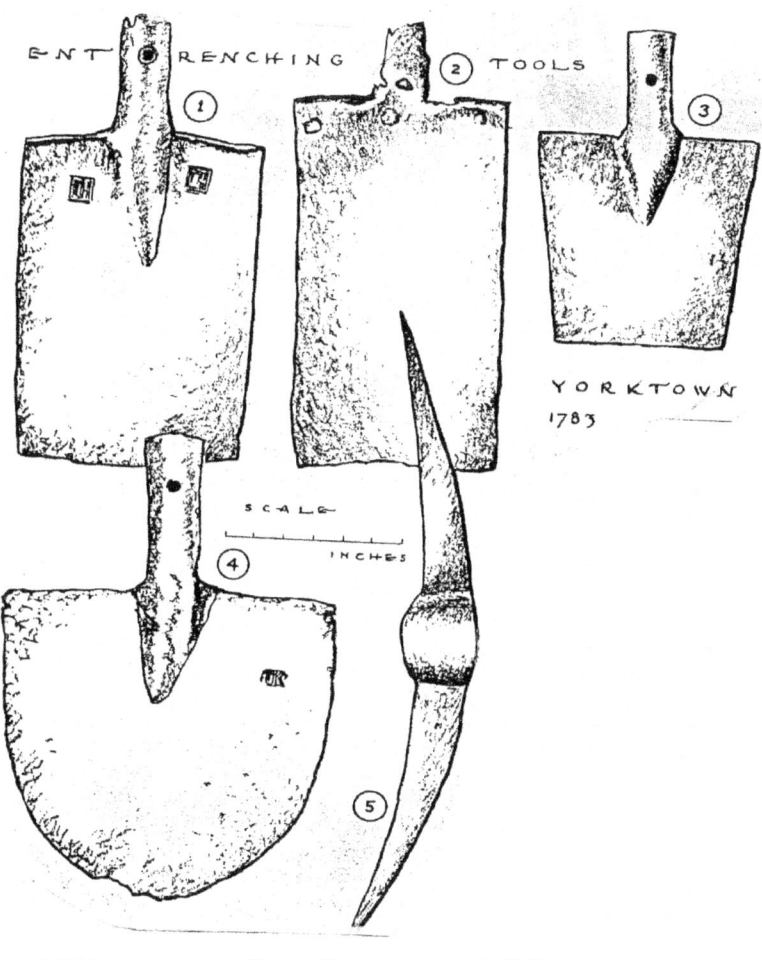

Shovels #1 and #2 are very close to mine as it's a common garden shovel, but I cut the upper metal handle off and glued a "T" handle atop it. Drawings from the "*Book of the Continental Soldier*" by Harold Peterson

23rd REGIMENT OF FOOT – COLOR DETAIL WITH PIONEER ESCORT
YORKTOWN, VIRGINIA – OCTOBER 1981

AUTHOR'S PHOTO'S

2 MAN CROSSCUT SAW; HANDLES ARE ATTACHED TO HARNESS WHEN NOT IN USE.

AXE HARNESS, SHOVEL ATTACHED. 7 LB FELLING AXE

Here you see my Axe Harness with attached shovel, using garters straps, sewn to my harness, it seemed a good idea, but weighed about 8 to 10 lbs. I didn't wear it very often. The 2 man cross cut saw I purchased it at a flea market

WOODWORKING TOOLS FOR CAMP DEMOSTRATIONS

From 1978 through 1998, I grew from a Pioneer to a Journeymen (*a worker qualified to work at a specified trade*) then an Articifer (*A skilled craftsman.*) My camp grew as did my collection of woodworking tools. Visiting Farmers Flea markets, Farm Auctions, and Flea markets. I learned what to watch for and bargained for a good price on what I wanted as a wood working tool. I designed my tool box by simply laying out the tools, so each had its own nitch to set in (pg 195), you'll notice next to the tool box is a supply of rough cut handles. I probably carried more then you would find in a British Army that marched through the Colonies. No doubt many of the tools mentioned would have been transported in the long wagon train, possibly as part of the Artillery Train of an Army on the move, in Europe, not here in America. Refer to pages 56 & 57 for the Army's rolling Stock. Many of these tools would be found in local woodworker shops on southern plantations or what was found in large city wood/carpenter shops.

I decided to make wooden mallets (*I got fairly good at*), generally from wood supplies that were "Free", (*firewood supplied by the host of the event, for camp fires; some of which made good mallet heads and handles*). Once the handle and head were finished, I coated them with boiled linseed oil, when dried, I gave them out in camp. Saturdays generally was a good day to make mallets. I'll make handles at one event, Mallet heads at another event and somewhere along the line I'd assemble them. My fire irons were very use-full as a drying rack.

I put on a limited camp life demonstration which allowed me time to socialize. Keeping in mind the time required to setup and breakdown my camp; weekends go fast.

In the Index the reader will find the listing of various reference books on woodworking, places which will sell good reproductions of woodworking or camp tools (hand forged), nearly all have catalogs available that you can call and request a copy.

Again I suggest farmers flea markets, or local flea markets as a good source for tools as well as auctions; the best markets would be in the New England area. Many tools you do purchase will be newer then the period you are in, and as long as you don't tell people who are watching you that they are not period but close examples of them, you should do fine. Always be aware that a person who might be watching could know more about woodworking then you do. Period tools are out there, but expensive.

Once I retired, I decided to do volunteer work at various historic sites, Fort Sisseton was my first such site. It also allowed me a location to offer for sale my encampment which proved to be no problem. Several folks with the organization known as *"The Army of the Dakotas"* offered to buy my camp, & camp mess, but I kept all my wood working tools. These I made full use of, now in the period *American Indian Frontier War Period - 1823 to 1890 - West of the Mississippi River*

OUR GANG
I had begun my first volunteer job at a historic site here at Fort Sisseton, (1864 to 1888), South Dakota. Restored in 1937 as part of a WPA Project. My volunteer time ran May to July 2002, and I worked 4 hours a day with a free RV Site. I had the opportunity to setup a working woodshop, the room itself had only the carpenters bench and a table, behind me. The Blacksmith's shop was to my left - across the breezeway and the Blacksmith himself is the fellow with the leather apron. He lived nearby, and operated a farm, and would come up on weekends to make things for the gift shop and put on blacksmithing displays for tours. There was a supply of rough cut wood, in the shop thus I made the shelf on the wall, note the shaving horse, set up to make a mallet handle. I enjoyed volunteering at Historic Sites, it put my limited knowledge as a Pioneer and I grew from there.

The Carpenters Bench All tools shown are what I had collected over the years as a pioneer. Bottom of bench top, a tack hammer, moving up a lathing hammer, next I was attempting to make a wood spatula, that narrow board is what I place against my chest when pulling a draw knife towards my chest, auger bit with ¼ in bit, there are 2 brass plates, the first one has 2 round holes for the part of the mallet handle going into the head, the 2nd one atop the wood head is square, this allows for that part of the handle, to be thicker and provide extra strength at the head. The handle will be drawn down enough to fit in your hand, two different sized draw knives, assorted wood chisels for light carving, a carpenters mallet, one mallet is ready for the handle. Note my shaving horse with another mallet head ready to work on.

THE CARPENTER'S SHOP
Another look at the bench, note additional mallet heads on bottom shelf. There are 4 large windows of Plexiglas within wood frames, you had to lift out and set aside the very heavy windows. I came up with the rope and pulley system to make it easier, the 4th window to the far right I sealed up as there were large cross cut saws hanging on the wall, didn't want anyone reaching in to cut themselves. To the left is that table mentioned earlier. One tool box (Mine) and the second setting atop the bench. Many of the tools and objects seen are mine including those on the shelving, except the broad axe heads, they belong to the Fort. Those signs hanging near the window are mine, they explain the manner in which mallets are made. You can see through the open door, a wagon. Once it was rolled out of the way, you could also see the side door that the blacksmith used, it generally had a chain across it; tours would enter in another door around the corner.

There's now a lap desk, that I made several years ago setting on the bench which I donated to the Fort. Next to it, I used that rough lumber to build an old fashioned carpenter's tool box and filled it with some of my tools. I now had a bottom shelf to that bench and there are 3 of my wooden block planes there, a large 22 inch jointer plane, and a 16 inch jack plane, a 8 inch rounder plane. I cleaned them up using a light wood cleaner. These I gave to the fort as well. You can see that light gravel on the floor, I covered the entire area with it as it brightened the room up and covered the darker, damp soil. You could not place anything on the floor as the dampness would damage it. The saw hanging there is a Carpenters Saw, which can be broken down into 4 pieces. At a Farm auction it cost me $10. No one there knew what it was used for; doing your research pays off.

Now I'm really getting into this thing, built another cabinet, another one of my tool boxes is on the ground. The lap desk now has several drawings on the top I had made. You can barely see a vice in the corner and a wood stove to the left. There's a curtain of sorts in the window, when the sun came in, it got a bit hot. There's a wooden vice attached to the end of my shaving horse. It became rather versatile over time. I made a wrought iron lantern hanger, the iron came from the blacksmiths shop, I made him one as well. That stuff hanging from the wall is tobacco that the blacksmith was attempting to dry. He did try to roll and smoke it, I think he said it damn near killed him.

The wood stove was donated by the blacksmith, I took it into Aberdeen, S.D. to have it completely restored; the Site paid for it. The wood stove was in fact fully operational, but the powers that be would not let me poke a hole in the roof for the stove pipe. I paid for that pipe, but by the time I reached this point it was already getting warmer. The bricks I found in and around the fort, so I laid them as such to make a stable platform for the stove. The wood shelf to the left of the stove top I made included additional iron for the supports, it was spaced enough so if you lit the stove off it would not burn the wood. That iron frying pan is mine, I donated it to the fort, the spatula I was working on was added. I even brought in some fire wood. Now this shop took on the appearance it was actually in use. I was still hopeful, about starting a fire, even the ash tray was new. Not sure about that vice, I think it belonged to the fort.

Tool Sharpening Bench; I requested to Forts Staff to build 2 additional benches, and I added the back boards. The broad axe heads on the bottom shelf belong to the fort. As I developed the shop, a group known as *"The Friends of Fort Sisseton"* took notice of what I was doing, and began donating all sorts of tools. The vice is for holding saws of all sorts for sharpening, the object in the corner is an up right hand drill, but it was missing some key parts.

During June a group called ' *The Army of the Dakota's"* come every year as part of Fort Sisseton Historical Festival, which began in 1978. There were many vendors, a band, and the reenactment units which comprised Artillery, Infantry and Cavalry (7th). The overall effort was to raise funds to continue restoration efforts on many buildings within the fort. One in particular was the Hospital (1887) which was in bad shape. What pleased me to no end was the arrival of the State Governor, who came into the wood and blacksmith shops and had a chat with those of us working there. Its my understanding that he's responsible for much state funding to keep this site open and running. The reenactment units would put on displays of horsemanship, infantry tactics and in the evening the range out back was available to us for shooting, even the Gatling gun was shot. The was also a Native American Camp and a Mountain man, Traders row out back.

Wheel Wright Shop, The remains of my wood supply hang from the ceiling. On the shelf are spokes for a wagon, many in different sizes. Bench top, left to right is a tool to bend the steel for a wagon wheel which rests to the left against the bench. Other tools on the bench and back board are all relayed to rebuilding wagon wheels. An old wheel hub is to the right, I found it in the barn, cleaned it up and put wood preserve on the hub. Against the wall is a completed wheel. So in nearly 2 months I turned a nearly empty room into something that looks as though someone is still working there, I even left my wood chips on the floor. I can only hope that its still being used for display. I purchased a book about wheel wrights and how to build wagon wheels and the tools needed, thus I identified those tools on the back board and left the book for future reference to the Forts museum.

The door you are looking through is where I can enter, behind it are various types of crosscut saws which belong to the fort. I built a large back board to so all can hang on display and off the floor.

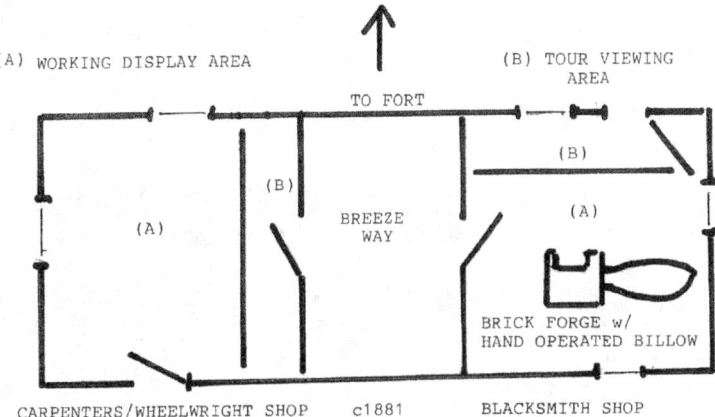

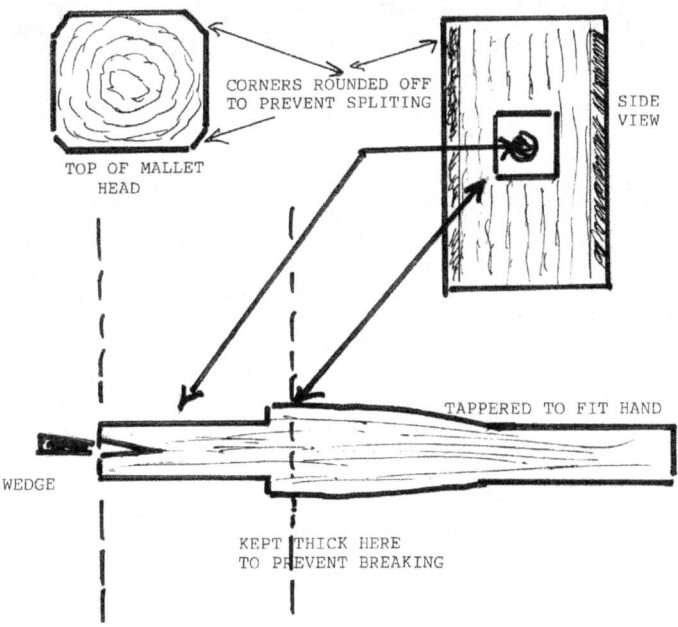

This camp setup is placed along the edge of the road leading into Fort Ticonderoga, or Sutler's Row (18th Century merchants). June 1994.

Here's a better look at how I setup my shaving horse - the large wooden blocks in front are from a large wood supply at an event; they are heart of oak about 20 inches long and I cut them in half. I loaded as many as I could into my small Mazda. You'll note the draw knife on the seat and the 2 forged vices, there were 4 sets of holes, and once in place you'd hit them with a mallet to set. The handle is in front of the head, the wood used for handles was generally red or white oak, the auger bit in place and about 4 wood shims under the bit, each was ¼ x 3 x 6 inches long with a center line marked on each one and varnished over, These I used to try to keep the auger bit straight and true so the hole would be nearly centered when it came out the other side. A small carpenters knife is on the table with an earlier mallet. It wasn't heavy enough, the ones I made were about 8 to 10 lbs. Generally I gave them to the camp followers, to help get the men folks attention. You will note the shaving horse head on the ground. The each leg set would have its own brace and a center brace and using turn buckles I could keep everything nice a tight.

BENT'S OLD FORT NATIONAL HISTORIC SITE. c 1830 to 1840

Carpenters/ wheelwrights shop - this is what you'd find at a garrison, such as Fort Ticonderoga, Fort Crown Point and Fort Niagara. I spent a weekend here as part of a seasonal Staff and Volunteer Interpretation program - May 28th and 29th, 2004.

The black Smith's shop - both photos are author's collection.

The Traders Rooms at Old Bents Fort

Author's collection

OLD BENT'S FORT

A GLOSSARY OF ARTISAN TITLES AND TERMS

Taken from Webster's New 20th Century Dictionary, 2nd Edition, and 'The Little Book of Early American Crafts and Trades" (18th Century) by Mr. Peter Stockham

ARTIFICER - an artist; a mechanic or manufacturer; especially, one whose occupation requires skill or knowledge of a particular kind, as a silversmith or saddler.

BRICK LAYER - is a Artificer who builds walls, and etc.; with brick. In London this business including titling, walling, chimney work and paving with Bricks and toles.

CARPENTER - those who perform the rough work in building of houses, such as hewing out, and putting in their places, the beams, rafters and joists.

COOPER - one who manufactures casks, tubs, of all sizes, pails, sundry other articles useful in domestic concerns

JOINERS - one who makes doors, wainscoting and sashes

JOURNEYMAN - originally, a man hired to work by the day. Formerly, a mechanic or workmen who has served his apprenticeship and thus qualified himself to work his trade.

LIME BURNER - one who burns limestone to make lime

LIME - a white substance, calcium oxide, Cao, obtained by the action of heat on limestone shell, and other materials containing calcium carbonate, and used in the making of mortar and cement.

MINERS - one who is knowledgeable in the construction of under ground mines, principally, coal mines.

PLUMBER - the art of casting and working of lead, and using it in buildings. He furnishes us with a cistern for water, a sink for the kitchen, covers the house with lead, and makes the gutters to carry away the rain water, makes pipes of all sorts. He is also employed in the making of coffins for those who are to be interned out of the common way.

SAPPERS - one who digs saps or trenches, refer to the chapter on Field Fortifications

SAWYERS - The Sawyer cuts the trunks of trees into beams and planks, fit for the use of carpenters. The timber is laid on a frame over an oblong pit called a "SAW PIT", and it is cut by means of a long saw fastened in a frame, which is worked up and down by two men, one standing on the wood to be cut, and the other in the pit.

SMITH - One who works with iron, and who from that metal manufactures a vast variety of articles useful in the arts of life, and of great importance to domestic comfort. there are several branches in this trade, some are called Black Smiths, others are called White-Smiths, or Bright-Smiths, these polish their work to a considerable degree, such as bell hangers. The black smith's make such things as horse shoes, iron chains, stoves, shovels, gridirons, trivets, nails, etc.

WHEELER - One who makes wheels

WHEEL WRIGHT - Man whose occupation is to make and repair wheels and wheeled vehicles, such as wagons, carriages and carts.

WOODCUTTERS - This term I found throughout much of my reference material. I believe this was a term used for a "Fatigue" work party to go out and collect wood for the camps or garrisons. Pioneers could have been part of this detail, but unless specifically mentioned, it is doubtful. This was one of those details that soldiers were routinely "VOLUNTEERED" for.

FORTIFICATIONS

FASCINES, GABIONS, PARAPET CONSTRUCTION AND FIELD WORKS

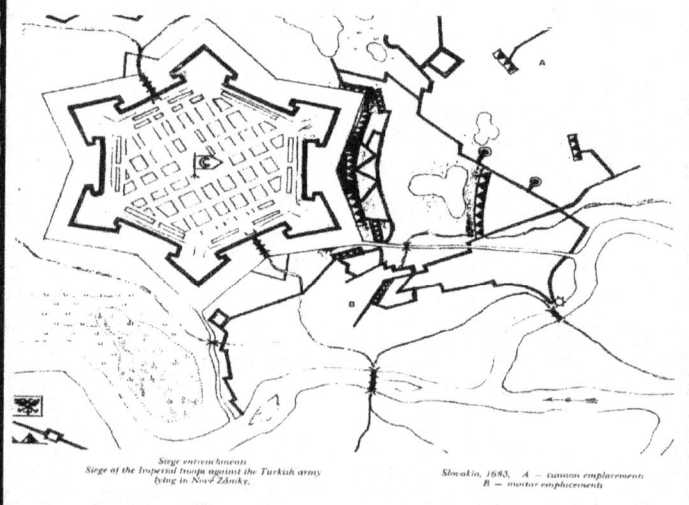

Siege entrenchments
Siege of the Imperial troops against the Turkish army lying in Nové Zámky, Slovakia, 1683. A — cannon emplacement; B — mortar emplacement

FORTIFICATIONS [110]

On the next few pages will be text, sketches and drawings on how to make Fascines, Gabions and construct earth works.

It is very doubtful that any reinactor (Pioneer) will ever be faced with such a task, unless one owns a modern back hoe.

If you are really ambitious you can make some in your backyard, that is if you can still find the type of trees that make up a fascine, and, if you have a back yard and the time.

The historic site at Fort Lee in New Jersey, has several redoubts made using fascines but out of cement, but you get an idea just how they were stacked to make a redoubt.

There is also an article from the _Company of Military Historians Journal_ which shows how to build a Chevaux-de-Frise (Pg 232 to 235 of this work). Now I have seen one of these made and brought to an event. It was quite a piece of work, a bit cumbersome to handle and no doubt difficult to pack along with all your other gear into a VW, bug, van or small truck.

The following information was provided by Mr. James V.T. McEnery, a Special Collections Library Technician at West Point Military Library.

A detailed description of fascines and gibbons as they pertain to the construction of earth works can be found on Pgs. 225 to 231 of this work. Taken from a book titled _"Military Dictionary Comprising Technical Definitions"_ by a Col. H.L. Scott - 1861 and reprinted by Greenwood Press, New York - 1968.

Several drawings; which detail field fortifications, wood shielding and implements used in parapet construction; from the book _" European Weapons and Warfare - 1618-1648"_ by Edward Wagner and printed by Octopus Books, London - 1979. Pages 226 and 227 of this work.

FIELD FORTIFICATIONS

Field fortifications were basically of two types: defensive and offensive. Defensive fortifications were built by every army whenever it interrupted its march. Their quality depended on the length of stay. Offensive field fortifications were systems of trenches and shelters built during a siege of an enemy stronghold.

When the marching column stopped, a suitable place for the camp was chosen, which would defend well and also provide water for the cavalry mounts and train teams.

For an overnight stay a simple wagon fort wall with tents and shelters would be whipped up. If a longer stay was planned, work on trenches and ditches would start first thing in the morning. The excavated earth was piled to form a protective parapet. For an extended stay the parapet and ditches were reinforced and the parapet was equipped with small bastions. The ground plan of such field works often followed the lay-out of permanent forts. It was quite common to incorporate into the encampment and its fortification any structures that existed in the place before the arrival of the troops. Chateauz, castles and citadels were used in this way because they offered lodging for the troops and their commanders and because of their strength. Whenever such structures had masonry fortification walls, these were incorporated into the field fortification system.

Quite often an army would stay encamped in such fortifications for a long time, using them as an operating base for sorties into the surrounding countryside.

When a Siege of an enemy-held fort or town was laid, the besieging arm tried to get as close to the fort ditch as possible. They also built permanent artillery emplacements there to enable the guns to fire at close range at the ramparts to so a breach for the assault troops to penetrate the besieged fort could be made.

To achieve this a system of inter-connecting trenches, called saps were dug in front of the besieged fort or city. These allowed movement of troops and equipment to the front lines immediately under the enemy's ramparts. To give enemy fire as few targets as possible the saps followed a zigzag course. Where the sap changed course, gabionage was erected, and the entire sap or at least some sections of it were covered with faggots or fascines.

To prevent the besieged seeing what was going on, the entrenchments, fences and screens were run along the works. Earth-filled gabions were thrown up to protect gun emplacements against enemy fire. Their manufacture was in the charge of the Work-Master or Chief Sapper. The gabions were five to seven feet around and six to ten feet high, with frame posts from two to four and a half inches thick. The frame was interwoven with wicker, the posts extending at least one foot at the bottom to allow the gabion to be firmly embedded in the ground. The baskets were then filled with earth packed with a hand hammer.

The besieged had usually ample means for repairing their defense works damaged by enemy artillery fire. If the attackers saw there was no chance of getting inside through a breach in the works, they would hire miners to dig galleries to undermine the ramparts. Underground saps leading from the attackers positions to under the besieged ramparts had at least one corner immediately before the target area to damp the blast wave from the explosion to prevent it blowing back through the galleries. At the gallery face beneath the walls of the besieged structure, a chamber was cut, to maximize the effect of the blast.

If the defenders realized that the attackers planned to mine their ramparts they would drive their own saps from inside the walls into enemy positions, and try to gas or blow up the enemy miners with antimony gases.

Life in military encampments was subject to the strictest discipline. Any mutiny or riot by the troops met with severe penalty. Leaving camp without permission, stabbings or shootings in brawls, etc., were often punishable by death. It was expressly forbidden to talk to enemy troops unless approved first by the supreme commander. Whenever both cavalry and infantry were laying in one camp, infantry were bound to clear space for the horses. No shooting or campfires were allowed without permission. Drunkenness and all felonies committed under influence of liquor were severely punished. If a spy was suspected in the encampment, an alarm was sounded upon which everybody was supposed to hasten to his tent so that the stranger's presence could be easily determined. Special care was paid to regular observation of picket and sentry duty.

Author's Collection

The sketches on pages 227 through 233 came from "Les Saps" found at the West Point Library Rare Book Section and Mr. Brian L. Dunnigan's book 'Siege 1759 - The Campaign against Niagara and Le - Blond "The Military Engineer" London 1759. The sketches on the following pages were copied from the original works and pasted on individual pages and placed in this manuscript. Thus you may notice some words misspelled.

What follows is a brief discription of various items used in the construction of field works. [111]

REVETMENTS - The interior slopes of the parapets of permenent and field works, as well as in some cases the sides of the ditches of the latter, require revetments to enable them to stand at that slope which is necessary, and to endure the action of the weather. The materials made use of in the construction of field-revetments are:
Fascines, gabions, hurdles, sod, sand-bags and timber.

FASCINES - are strong, close, regular fagots, carefully and compactly made, generally of green brushwood. They should be straight, cylindrical, and pliant; bound round with good think, unbroken gads or withes, of pliant wood, at equal distances, the knots well tied, and all in one line; no variation in girth exceeding 1 inch to be allowed.

Fascines are of several kinds and various dimensions, according to the purpose for which they are intended. The most common are the long fascines or saucissons, 18 feet long, 9 inches in diameter, about 140 lbs. in weight; such a fascine can be made by five men in one hour, including the cutting of the wood when at hand. **(figure 178)**

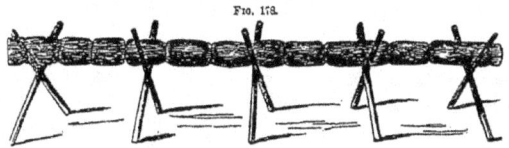
Fig. 178.

(figure 180) shows what is called "gad", which is used to keep the fascine together, rope or twine could also do the same if available. **(figure 181)** shows how completed bundles of fascines are stacked and secured to make a parapet.

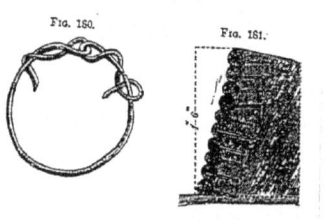
Fig. 180.   Fig. 181.

GABIONS - are stout, rough, cylindrical baskets, open at the top and bottom; they are made of various dimensions according to thier intended use. Those for revetting the interior slopes are usuallyee feet high and two feet in diameter; strongly and somewhat coarsely made. Those used in sapping (called sap gabions) have about the same dimensions, but are carefully finished. To construct a gabion, a circle of 22 inches diameter must be traced on a clean, hard, level piece of ground, each quarter of this circle is then divided into four or five equal parts, and small holes made at the points of division, to receive straight up rights of 3 1/2 feet in length, around which the withes are interwoven. Gabions may be made with one, two, or three rods woven together about the uprights; when two rods are woven together, the work is called pairing, when three, waling. the last gives the strongest gabions. The method of working will be best understood by reference to **(Figure 182)**. Each rod passes outside two, and inside one, upright, and the three are twisted together like rope.

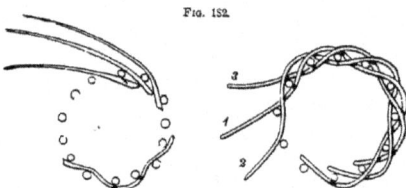

Fig. 182.

HURDLES - **(Figure 184)** - are the common course wicker hurdles made for farming, and other purposes, usually 3 or 4 feet high and 6 to 9 feet long. they are useful in temporary works, to retain earth at a steep slope, for a short time. When thus used, they should be surcured by anchoring pickets. Hurdles are moreover useful, to form a dry footing in trenches, during wet weather; in the passage of wet ditches, and for many similar purposes.

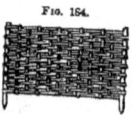

Fig. 184.

SAND-BAGS - are coarse canvas bags, of a capacity sufficient to hold about a bushel of earth; when empty they occupy only a small space, and are frequently of great use. A good field-revetment can be built with sand-bags, laid as sods; such a revetment, however, is only fit for temporary purposes, as the sand-bags soon rot; they are unfit for lining the cheeks of gun embrasures, as the flash of the guns speedily destroys them. In rocky positions, it is sometimes necessary to construct entire batteries and parallels with filled sand-bags. **(Figures 187 and 188),** are shown a section of a parapet revetted with sandbags, and an enlarged plan of the same.

SAND-BAGS SHOULD BE TARRED, AND HOLD ONE CUBIC FOOT OF EARTH.

TIMBER - is used for revetments, in particular case only, as where it may be considered advisable, in important field works, to retain the escarp of the ditch at a steep slope. In this case, a revetment is necessary, which may be constructed of beams or trunks of small trees, planted 3 or 4 feet deep, vertically in the ground and touching each other, or by lining the surface of the slope with planks secured by stout posts, 3 or 4 feet apart, planted several feet in the ground, and fastened to heavy horizontal beams.

What follows are a series of drawings showing the Saps and trench works around Fort Niagara during the british Siege in 1759. They give a very good idea just how the use of Gabions and fascines were used. [112]

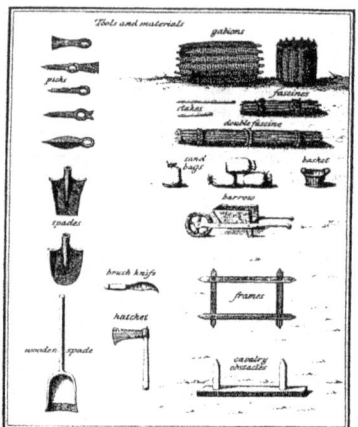

The basic tools of siegecraft. From Vauban. *Courtesy, The University of Michigan Press.*

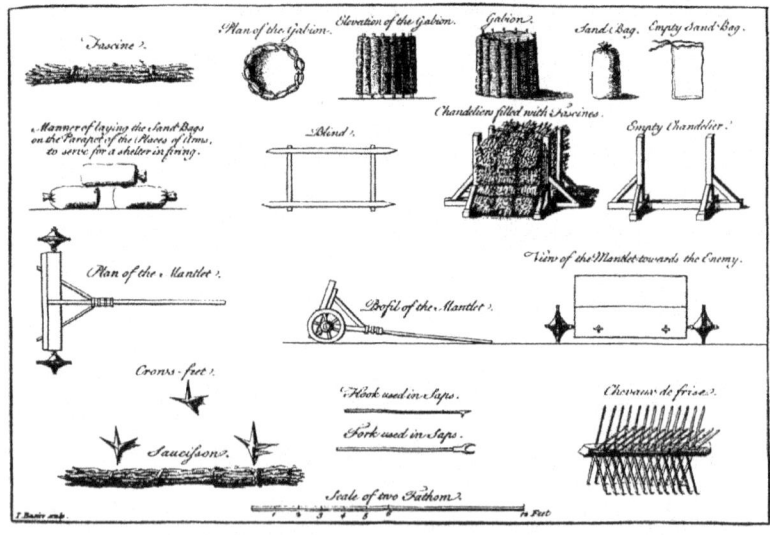

The equipment of siegecraft. "Saucissons" were used at Niagara to provide cover for snipers in the trenches. From Le Blond, *The Military Engineer ...* (London, 1759).

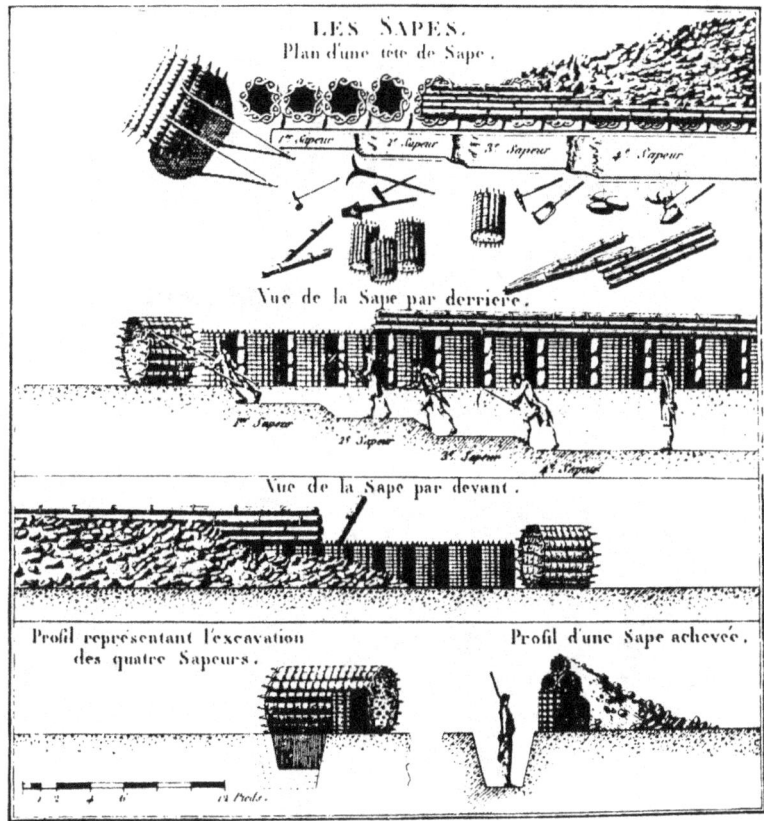

Vauban's drawing illustrates the manner of digging a sap. From top, the plan of a sap showing the work of four men; a view of the sap from behind; a defenders' view of the advancing sap; a section of the sap with the work of the four men; and a completed sap safely sheltering its occupant.

113

Page 232 to 233 - covered in end note #113

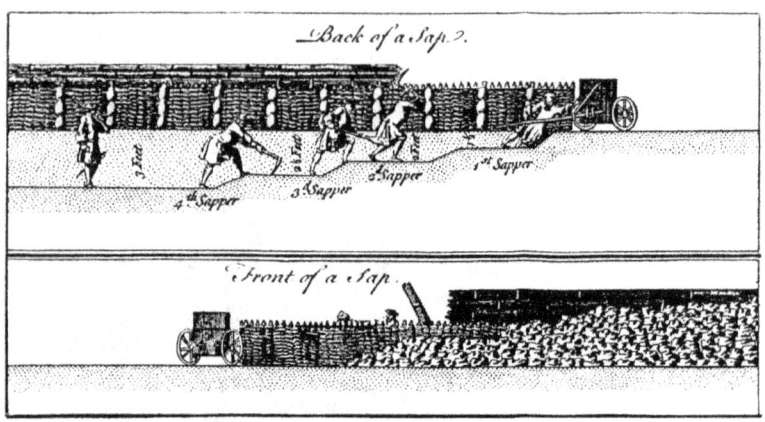

The front and back of an advancing sap. From Le Blond, *The Military Engineer* ... (London, 1759).

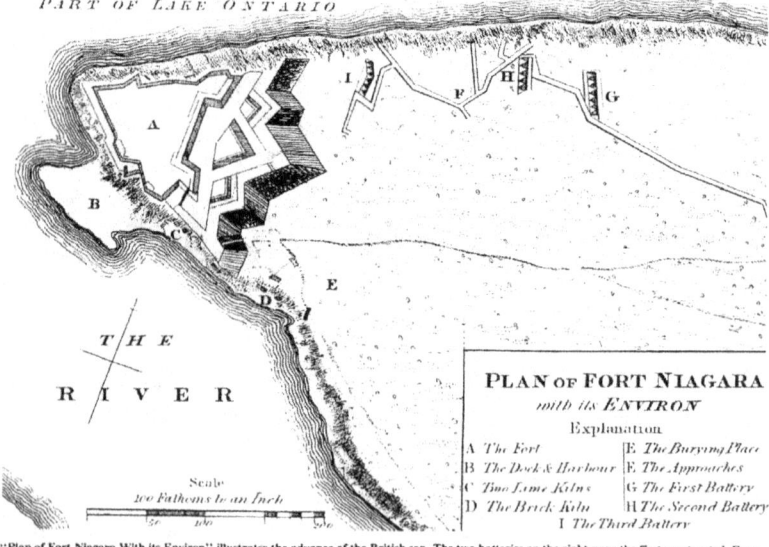

"Plan of Fort Niagara With its Environ" illustrates the advance of the British sap. The two batteries on the right were the first constructed. From Rocque, *A Set of Plans and Forts* ... (London, 1763).

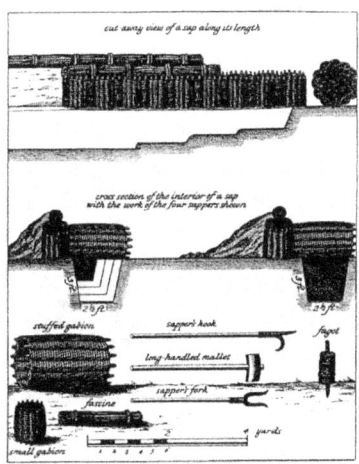

Another technical plate showing Vauban's recommended method for advancing a sap and some of the tools used in the process. *Courtesy, The University of Michigan Press.*

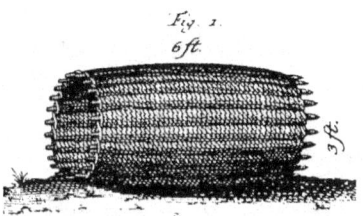

The indispensable gabions were to be made 2 1/2 feet in diameter and 3 1/2 feet high. From Vauban. *Courtesy, The University of Michigan Press.*

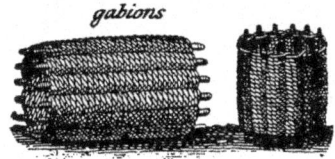

Courtesy, The University of Michigan Press.

A properly finished trench provided nearly complete shelter for its occupants. From Le Blond, *The Military Engineer* ... (London, 1759).

CHEVAUX-DE-FRISE: HARDWARE AND CONSTRUCTION

by

Joseph M. Thatcher

"Chevaux-de-frise, in fortification, a large joist or piece of timber, about 5 or 6 inches square, and 10 or 12 feet in length; into the sides whereof are driven a great number of wooden pins, about 6 feet long, and 1½ inches diameter, crossing one another at right angles, and pointed with iron. They are used on numerous occasions as to stop up the breaches, to secure the avenues of a camp from the inroads both of horse and foot . . . . ."[1] This entry from *Smith's Universal Military Dictionary* of 1779, describes chevaux-de-frise as used by both British and American forces during the Revolutionary War. These portable, spiked barriers were used in permanent and field fortifications and in camps to block openings or roadways into the works and could take the place of abatis, the intertwined tree tops which were the 18th century predecessor to barbed wire. Chevaux-de-frise were used well into the 19th century, although they were considered less effective by D. H. Mahan, in his *A Complete Treatise on Field Fortification* of 1836. Mahan provided a drawing (FIG. 1) and a more detailed description:

Chevaux-de-frise. A cheval-de-frise consists of a horizontal piece of scantling of a square, or hexagonal form, termed the body, about nine feet long, which is perforated by holes two inches in diameter, and five inches apart; round staffs, ten feet long and two inches in diameter, termed lances, shod with iron points, are inserted into the body, so as to project equally from it. At one end of the body a ring and chain are attached; at the other, a hook and chain; for the purpose of attaching several together, forming a chevaux-de-frise.[2]

Although these comments illustrate the general appearance of chevaux, little has been known about how they were made. Recent examination of hardware excavated at several New York sites has offered an opportunity to reconstruct a British example from the Revolutionary War and to better understand the method of construction.

The hardware, consisting of an end band with a ring and toggle, tips or points for the lances, or projecting spikes and reinforcing or key plates was excavated from Stony Point State Historic Site, and the site of Fort Independence, in the Bronx. Individually the objects had been identified in a variety of ways, and it was not until they were compared that their use was clarified.

Thirteen of the lance points were found at Fort Independence, and were originally identified as "polearm sockets",[3]. Additional examples were known from Stony Point, Ticonderoga, and Fort Montgomery[4]. These points (FIG 2) range in size from 6 to 6 ½ inches in length, and 1 ⅛ inches in diameter. They are in the shape of a cone, with two tangs or side straps and two rivets to attach them to a wooden shaft. They are made from one piece of iron folded in half and forge welded together, with the side seam left partially open. The tip or point has been hammered into a four-sided chisel point. Although the condition of the examples varies, it is apparent that there is a great deal of uniformity in size and manufacture.

The reinforcing or key plates (FIG 3) and 3 ½ inches long and 2 ⅝ inches wide. Each corner has a

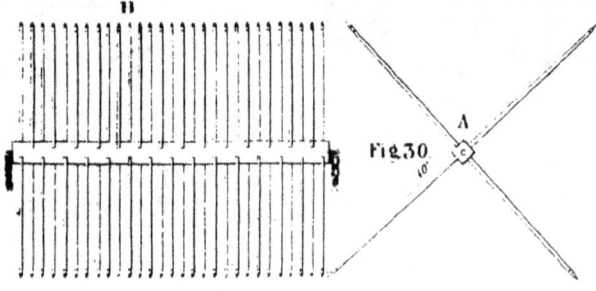

FIG 1
A chevaux-de-frise as drawn by Mahan in 1836.

235

FIG 2
Iron lance tip showing rivets and weld seam.

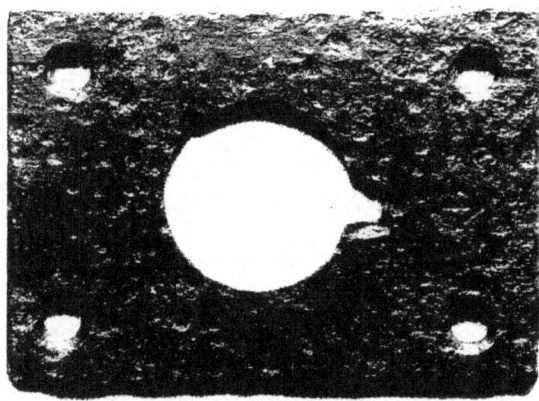

FIG 3
Reinforcing plate with keyway
broad arrow stamp.

FIG 4
Endband with ring and toggle.

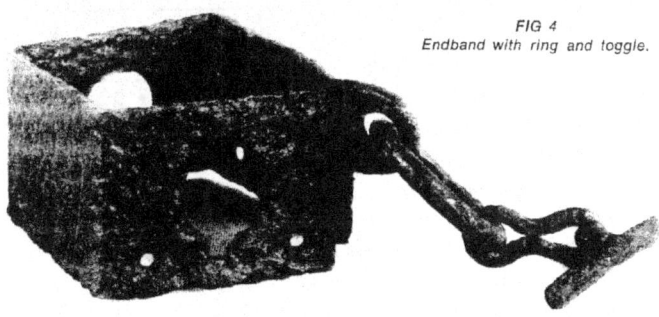

"countersunk hole for a fastener, and the center hole is 1 ¼ inches in diameter, with a ¼ inch square keyway or slot. The example pictured is also clearly marked with the British broad arrow, although most were not marked. Some of these plates were also reported as found at the Van Oblienis Farm by Reginald P. Bolton[5].

The final clue to the puzzle of these various objects was the end band (FIG. 4), also found at Fort Independence. In addition to this complete band, fragments of two others were also found.[6] The band is of iron, 2 ½ inches wide, bent into a square 3 ½ inches on a side. The two adjoining ends have ears 1 ⅜ inches wide welded together and pierced with a hole containing an iron ring 2 ¼ inches in diameter, with a figure 8 shaped link and toggle attached. Two adjacent faces have countersunk holes for attachment, and the two opposite faces have holes 1 ½ inches in diameter, identical to those in the key plates. Only one of these holes has the keyway however. It became clear that the band, key plates and points represented the metallic components of a chevaux-de-frise which could be readily disassembled for storage or shipment.

The following description presents the author's proposal for the fabrication of chevaux-de-frise using the examples of hardware as found. A piece of timber, hewn to 3 ½ inches square, could have been relieved slightly at each end and the end bands slipped on and nailed in place. Holes were bored through the beam on alternate faces to accept the lances which were made with a point on each end. Each hole was counterbored or slightly enlarged on one face of the beam and the rectangular key plates nailed over each one. If each lance had a small projecting pin inserted near the center, it could then be slipped through the hole and keyway and rotated, locking the lance into the beam in the manner of a bayonet mount. This would allow for a secure mounting, but which could be easily taken apart and packed for re-use at another location. The drawing (FIG. 5) shows details of the proposed system. The only piece not located to date through archeology is the locking pin, but these would probably resemble nails, or other small bits of iron rod, and would be impossible to identify. The toggle and ring seem to be an improvement on the hook and ring as described in Mahan, since individual units could be fastened together without matching proper ends. The toggle and ring on the example excavated are readily interchangeable, allowing flexibility in assembly.

The size of the chevaux indicated by this hardware is slightly smaller than that mentioned in Smith, but is consistent with the portable nature of these barriers. A scale model, constructed by the author for display at Stony Point State Historic Site, used lances

TYPICAL DETAILS
(not to scale)

FIG 5
Drawing of typical details.

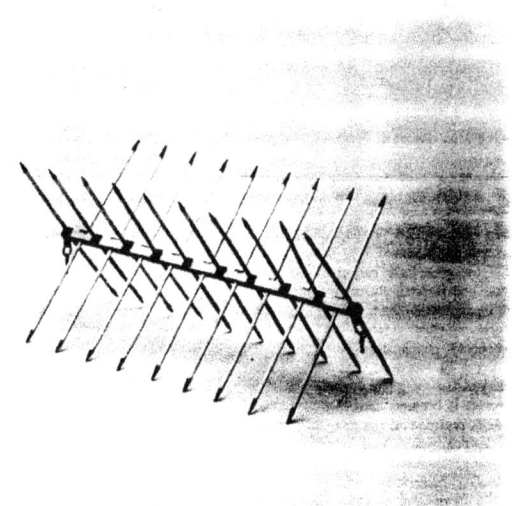

FIG 6
Scale model of a chevaux-de-frise showing the hardware in place.

6 feet in length, set into a beam 9 feet long. The lances were spaced on 12 inch centers, alternating on two sides of the beam, thus making the lances 6 inches apart. The hardware is well-made, and extremely consistent in size, no matter on what site it is found. It is not known if American examples followed the same construction techniques, but the ability to easily re-use and transport the chevaux must have been recognized as desireable. It is hoped that further examples of this type of hardware may be identified in other collections, expanding our knowledge of the use of the chevaux-de-frise in this country.

NOTES

1.—Captain George Smith, *An Universal/Military Dictionar* (London, 1779), p. 63.
2.—D. H. Mahan, *A Complete Treatise on Field Fortificatio*, (New York, 1968 reprint), Plate 4.
3.—Julius Lopez, "The History and Archeology of Fort In dependence on Tetards Hill, Bronx County, N.Y.", *Th Bulletin*, Number 73, p. 17.
4.—*Ibid.* p. 18.
5.—*Ibid*, p. 18
6.—*Ibid*, p. 20

The author wishes to thank Heidi Miksch, Joseph McEvoy Jon Jameson, William Stevenson and Thomas Ciampa ,fo their help in preparing the artifacts, photographs and drawin for this article.

 **PIONEERS BRITISH - 1856**

 **FRENCH SAPEURS 1866—1875**

AND A FEW MODERN CONTEMPORIZES

THE BRITISH IN NORTH AMERICA [114]

A demand was soon made for a Company of the new Royal Military Artificers. Colonel John Graves Simcoe, appointed as the first Lieutenant-Governor of the newly created province of Upper Canada (Now Ontario), had visions of his province becoming the very "Bulwark of the British Empire in America". *(British Military Artificer in Canada 1760 - 1815)* Sincoe's plans for transforming the backwoods included the employment of Military Artificers on public works of benefit to the whole community.

Before leaving England in the fall of 1791, Simcoe had succeeded in securing authorization for a new corps of military pioneers, to be raised in Britain and sent out for service in Upper Canada in the spring of 1792. In addition to this new corps of Queens Ranger's, Simcoe also hoped that one of the Duke of Richmond's companies of the Royal military Artificers would be dispatched for duty in Upper Canada. Richmond himself was sympathetic to Simcoe's request, but an artificer company was only to be sent if a replacement could be raised in England. With the expense being charged to Upper Canada. As an alternative Simcoe suggested that an artificer company be formed "on the original plan for Canada by Captain Twiss", to be drawn from the British regiments, but placed under his own control, not that of the engineers.

In the end the eruption of war with France intervened and though the Duke of Richmond did obtain a Warrant in September 1793 for the formation of four more artificer companies, to be posted abroad; Two for Flanders, one for the West Indies, and one for Upper Canada. The Corps for Upper Canada was never embodied.

Although Simcoe failed to obtain one of Richmond's artificer companies, the newly authorized Queens Rangers were raised and dispatched to North America in good time. The establishment of the new corps consisted of two companies, each of 213 officers and men, with a small staff.

Indeed the services to be performed by the Queens Rangers were varied and extensive. Nor was the corps worth to be found only in the value of its labor.

In building of bridges, erecting of barracks, clearing lands, navigating of craft, and in short, on any military of Civil Service which may occur.

Reality, however, produced rather different results. After an initial period of employment as military pioneers the temptation to use the rangers as ordinary soldiers grew strong and Lord Dorchester, commanding the forces, insisted that the first duties of all troops were to be those of the garrison and communications.

Although the idea of posting the Royal Military Artificers to Upper Canada persisted until the end of 1798, it was never brought to fruition.

To obtain the necessary laborers, local militiamen were embodied but the results pleased neither the Duke nor those citizens called upon to provide military work parties.

Prince Edward, Duke of Kent and Strathearn. Fourth Son of King George III and father of Queen Victory, became the commander-in chief in North America in April 1799. Was ordered to Canada in 1791. For most of this period he lived in Halifax, NS and was instrumental in shaping that port's military defenses.

In order to correct the situation the Duke of wanted more regulars and in September 1796 he also received a small detachment of the Royal Military Artificers; 1 Sgt., 2 Corporals and 20 artificers; to alleviate the necessity of employing civilian craftsmen. Placed under the command of a Captain of the Royal Engineers, the detachment of Royal Military Artificers was employed at various tasks, its principal work being the construction of a light house in Halifax harbor.

In July 1807 eighteen Non-commissioned officers and men arrived in Newfoundland to assist in the works on Signal hill. The following year 48 more men were received.

By mid 1814 there had been four companies of sappers and miners distributed in the Canada's, at Halifax and in Newfoundland. The following year a sizeable detachment of another artificer corps, The Royal Staff Corps; arrived in Halifax, being sent on to the Canada's in 1816.

The second company of the fourth battalion, Royal Sappers and Miners was present at Bladensburg in August 1814 and was subsequently employed at Washington in the destruction of public buildings. Together with the Seventh company, first battalion, it took part in the New Orleans campaign.

While visiting Halifax Nova Scotia in August of 2003, I spent time in the "Citadel" (Fort George) which is a rather large stone Fortress over looking the Halifax Harbor. I found in their large museum a display case covering a period of 1793 - 1815; a color lithograph showing a Black Pioneer Private in the Pioneer Company of the104th New Brunswick Regiment of Fencible Infantry. I have not been able to find a copy of the lithograph outside the museum.

Fencible Regiments(*) Both cavalry and Infantry differed from Militia Units raised in time of War, On a permanent basis like the regular Army, but for Local Defense only, they were not to be moved out of England or Scotland (Canada), according to where they were raised, except in the case of invasion.

(*) from the book: *A History of the Uniforms of the British Army - Vol. III* by Ceil C.P. Lawson

Author's Collection

FOOT GUARDS BATTALION   23rd REGT. Of FOOT
YORKTOWN, OCTOBER 1981

WELLINGTON'S PENINSULAR ARMY[115]

After several disastrous sieges, in which very high casualties had been sustained despite the gallantry of the British Troops, Lord Liverpool stated that unless the Army be provided with a sufficiently trained corps of Sappers and Miners, heavy losses will continue. The Engineers who were present, though well-educated and brave, had never turned their minds to the mode of conducting a regular siege.

The slaughter that occurred at Badajor, in Wellington's estimation, was due in part to the fact that the British Army; unlike all other Armies; totally lacked regular companies of Sappers and Miners; and partly to the inexperience of the Engineer Officers in carrying out the last stages of a Siege.

On April 23, 1812, a Warrant was issued for instructing the corps in military field works and were to be sent to Wellington as soon as their training was complete. By August 4th, the name of the whole corps was changed (5 March 1813) from Royal Military Artificers to the Royal Miners and Sappers. Late that same year, Wellington's Army had the first of these new sapper companies and by late spring of the following year he had 300 trained men with him.

The rank and file of the Royal Military Artificers were wearing in the early years of the century a most extraordinary and ugly head-dress, a tall top-hat with brim, looking more fit for civilians wear, and having nothing military about it. Not unlike the hat of the Marines. They also had a shako and a blue coat down to 1813, but changed later to a red coat. It was braided with yellow across the front instead of white.

For further information can be found in Connolly's *History of the Royal Sappers and Miners, Vol. 1 - 1854*

Wikimedia Commons - public Domain
Soldier of the 6th Battalion of Cacadores in 1811, They were referred by Lord Wellington, as the "fighting Cocks" of his Anglo- Portuguese Army during the Peninsular War. Cacadores (Portuguese for Huntsmen).

PIONEERS IN REGIMENTS

General Order, Horse Guards, 18 November 1856 states

"The number of Pioneers in each Regiment is increased to 13, that is 1 Pioneer Corporal and 1 Pioneer per Comapny.

They are no longer to carry a muskey, instead a saw-backed sword, also a shovel, pickaxe and a bill hook.

Gaunlet gloves and aprons cease to form part of the Pioneer's equipment.

Pioneers are to wear their Beards and moustachios unshaven

Journal of Army Historical Research
Volume Four 1925 page 223

Pioneers of 1856.

THE FORT HENRY GUARD c1867

In August 1989 I had a chance to revisit Fort Henry located in Kingston, Ontario, Canada. I brought with me a letter from Mr. Stephen D. Mecredy, Military Interpretation Supervisor. See page 245 for copy of that letter.

I met with several staff members including Mr. Mike Grambe who was kind enough to take me back stage to show me some of the Pioneer gear.

This is what I learned; the Uniforms of the Fort Henry Guard are exact copies of those worn by the British Infantry and Artillery at the time of Canada's Confederation in 1867.

The material used is Serge and Melton cloth brought in bulk in England and shipped here where each uniform is tailored to fit. They last on average about 4 years before perspiration and powder burns take their toll on the fabric.

The Shakos, which is of the 1861 pattern, are made in England from original pattern blocks. All Badges, buckles, etc., are made in Montreal and the leather work, belts, slings and packs are made here at the Fort by the Assistant Quarter-Master and leather Master, Mr. Rick Compeau. He is also a member of the permanent Fort's Staff.

If you have ever seen the Fort Henry Guard go through their Infantry Drill, it is something to watch. The Drill is based on the 1867 Drill manual. What is interesting to see is that the arms remain straight down to the sides as they march to the steady 110 paces a minute.

The weapon they carry and fire are all original Snider-Enfield rifles with a triangular bayonet. All weapons are kept in good working order by the Fort's Armory. The Sergeants carry the shorter two-banded version but with a much longer sword bayonet.

The Infantry, all part of the Fort's Summer Staff, are issued two sets of uniforms. The No. 1 Dress or full dress uniform is worn on special ceremonial occasions, is the evening retreat which is done twice weekly. The

No. 2 dress is worn during practice sessions and when guiding tours.

Mike Gramble wasn't aware that there was no set drill for the pioneers who carried the axe when doing their infantry drill. He showed me the basic moves while I took several photo's as he went through his paces.

Mr. Mecredy provided me with a copy of the manual titled: "Equipment of Infantry" which shows sketches of the Pioneer accoutrements.

I was also able to pick up another set of photo's of another Pioneer, who Mike knew, but I forgot this gentlemen's name. The photo's really give you a good idea just how the Pioneer looked, ready for the march out.

Mike indicated, that like Fort Niagara, the Pioneers when in garrison were returned to their individual companies, but remained as part of the Fort's maintained staff. The normal battalion strength in the British Army of the time required 1 pioneer per company.

Two members of the Drill squad are uniformed as Pioneers, but there was equipment enough to outfit 5 pioneers the equipment includes:

This equipment would be divided up among the five pioneers, as needed;

1 Pickaxe, 3 felling axe, 1 crow bar, 1 shovel with case, 1 spade with case, 1 broad axe and handle with case, 1 saw with case, and smaller tools are hammer, auger, cold chisel, chisel, file saw, and a small tools case. Then you add, 1 billhook with case, 4 swords and scabbard, 5 sword frogs, 5 waist belts, 5 knapsacks, 5 haversacks, 5 water bottles, and 5 aprons with gauntlets.

The above equipment was divided up among the 5 pioneers as this example shows:
Pioneer 1 - Felling axe, broad axe, hand axe, broad and hand axe case, bill hook, and bill hook case. Now on the other hand Pioneer number 5 carries: Crowbar, small tools in case and no bill hook.

Either way, he's carrying quite a load. When I had the felling axe with shovel attached I knew I had a load, as it was rather heavy. That's why on many occasion's I carried the two man cross cut saw since it was much lighter.

The following pages are photo's that I took of Mike and the material of the Pioneer Accoutrements. In a passing thought, Col. John Elting mentions finding two Plates - number 49 and 50 in the back of the book - _British Military Uniforms - 1768 - 1796 -_ by Hew Strachan - Plate 49 - Pioneer - 1791 and Plate 50 - Pioneer 1794

Author's Collection

September 1977 - 200th Anniversary Battle of Brandywine, Pa.

Parks of the St. Lawrence **Les Parcs du Saint-Laurent**

THE ST. LAWRENCE PARKS COMMISSION
LA COMMISSION DES PARCS DU SAINT-LAURENT
FORT HENRY, BOX/C.P.213, KINGSTON, ONTARIO K7L 4V8
TEL 613 542 7388, FAX 613 542 3054, TDD 613 542 2956

January 8, 1993

Mr. William Eisenhauer
107 E Market Street
Apt. 10M
Hyde Parks, New York
112538
USA

Dear Mr. Eisenhauer;

I am in receipt of your letter of 14 November 1992 regarding pioneers in the British Army.

In 1867, Pioneers were the skilled artisans of the battalion and were to be recruited from such trades as carpenters, masons, bricklayers and engine fitters.

I have included copies of the patterns of their leather accoutrements from the 1865 <u>Equipment of Infantry</u>. We do not make them for anyone else.

There is no drill in the manuals for pioneers and their equipment per se. We have developed ours based on what we think is compatible and acceptable.

Sincerely,

Stephen D. Mecredy
Supervisor, Military Interpretation
Fort Henry

SDM:rn

FORT HENRY GUARD c1867

Manual of Arms with pick axe

MANUAL OF ARMS WITH AXE

PIONEER - FORT HENRY GUARD - 1867

AT THE POISE

PRESENT ARMS - WITH AXE

Author's Photo's

PIONEER - FORT HENRY GUARD - 1867

Mr. Mike Grambe - Pioneer - at Order Arms
Author's Collection
Refer back to page 73, Pioneer Austrian Army 1749 - doing nearly the same drill.

EQUIPMENT
OF
INFANTRY.

COMPILED BY

CAPTAIN MARTIN PETRIE, TOPOGRAPHICAL STAFF.

FORMING PART V. OF THE SERIES OF ARMY EQUIPMENTS

PREPARED AT THE TOPOGRAPHICAL AND STATISTICAL DEPARTMENT, WAR OFFICE.

COLONEL SIR HENRY JAMES, R.E., F.R.S., &c., DIRECTOR.

PRINTED BY ORDER OF THE SECRETARY OF STATE FOR WAR.

c1856 - Pioneer equipment for Fort Henry, Kingston, Ontario, Canada

LONDON:
Printed under the Superintendence of Her Majesty's Stationery Office,
AND SOLD BY
W. CLOWES AND SONS, 14, Charing Cross; HARRISON AND SONS, 59, Pall Mall;
W. H. ALLEN & Co., 13, Waterloo Place; W. MITCHELL, 39, Charing Cross;
and LONGMAN & Co., Paternoster Row;
ALSO BY
A. AND C. BLACK, Edinburgh;
ALEX. THOM, Abbey Street, and E. PONSONBY, Grafton Street, Dublin.

Price Five Shillings, with Plates.

ACCOUTREMENTS.

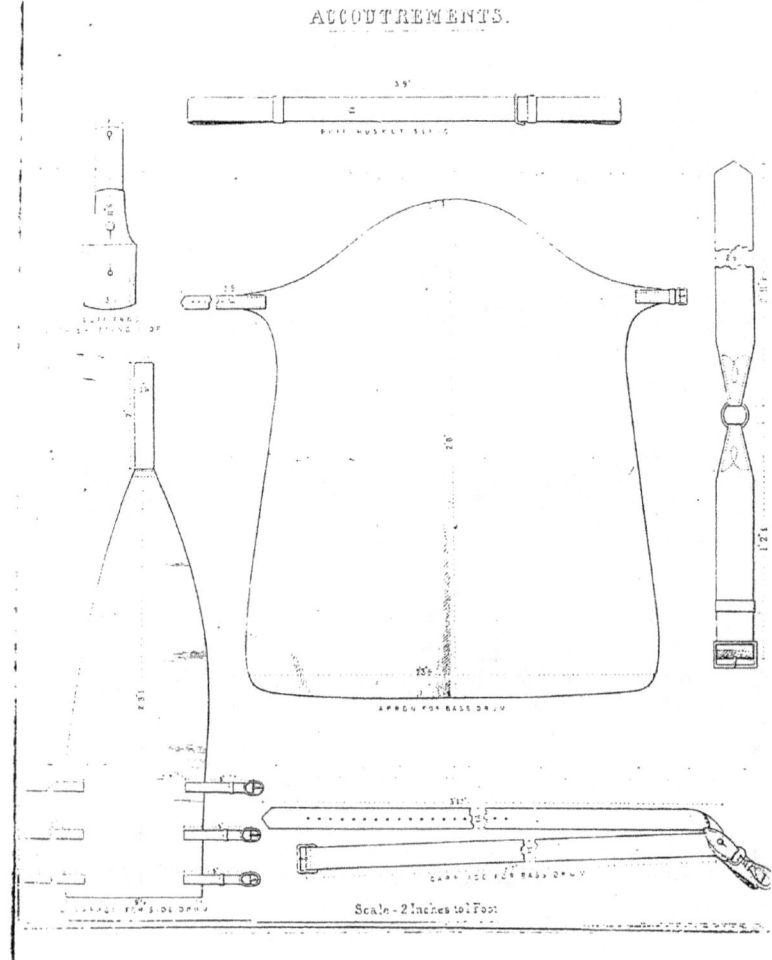

Scale - 2 Inches to 1 Foot

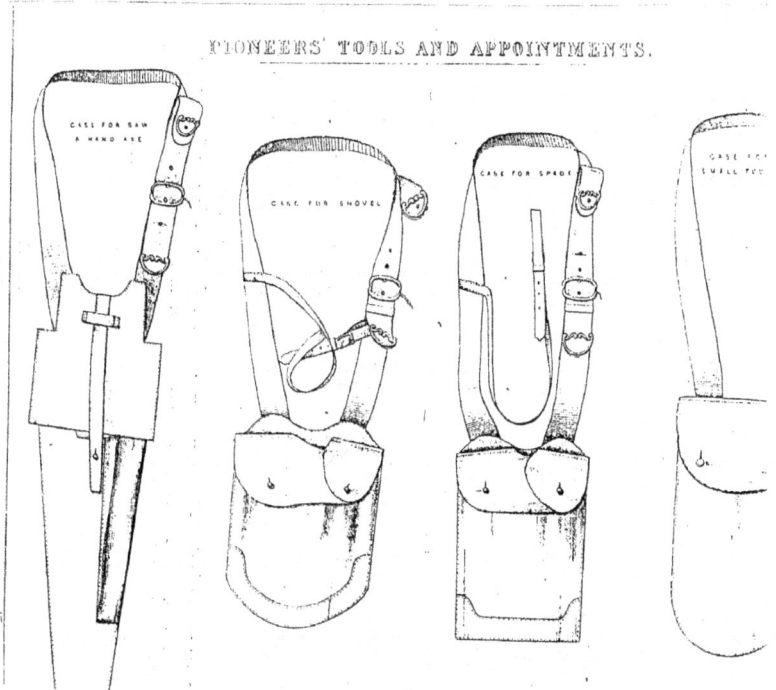

PIONEERS' TOOLS AND APPOINTMENTS.

Scale - 2 Inch to 1 Foot

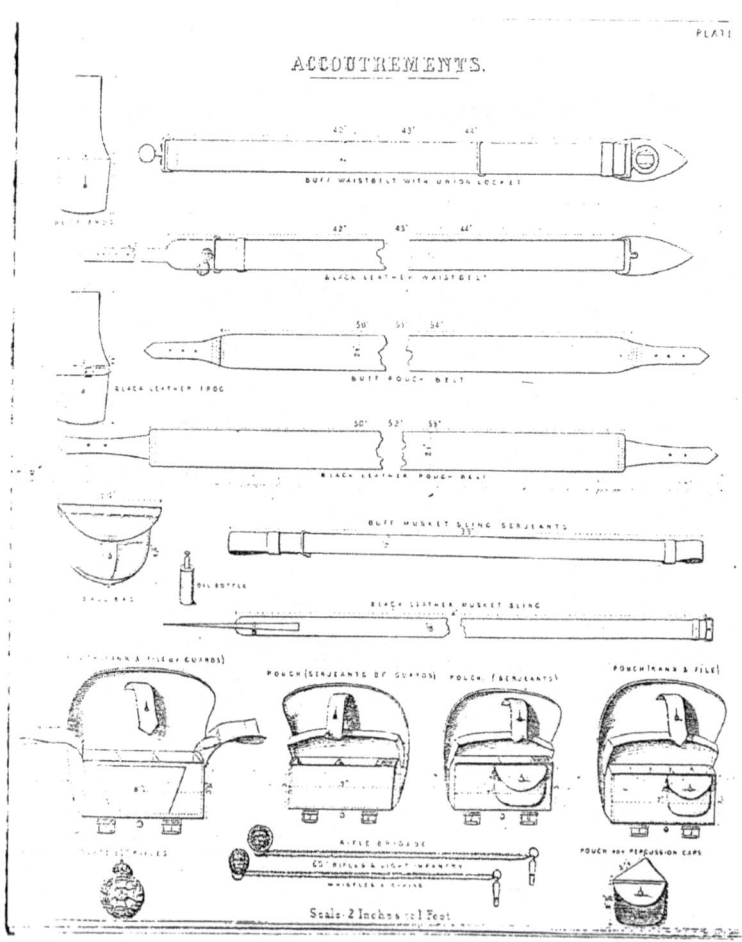

257

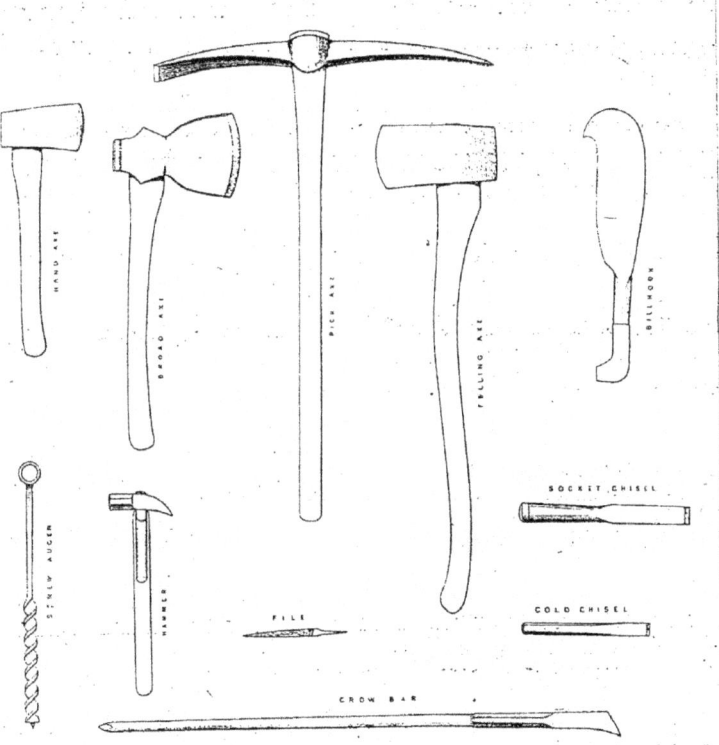

PIONEERS' TOOLS AND APPOINTMENTS.

Scale - 2 inches to 1 Foot

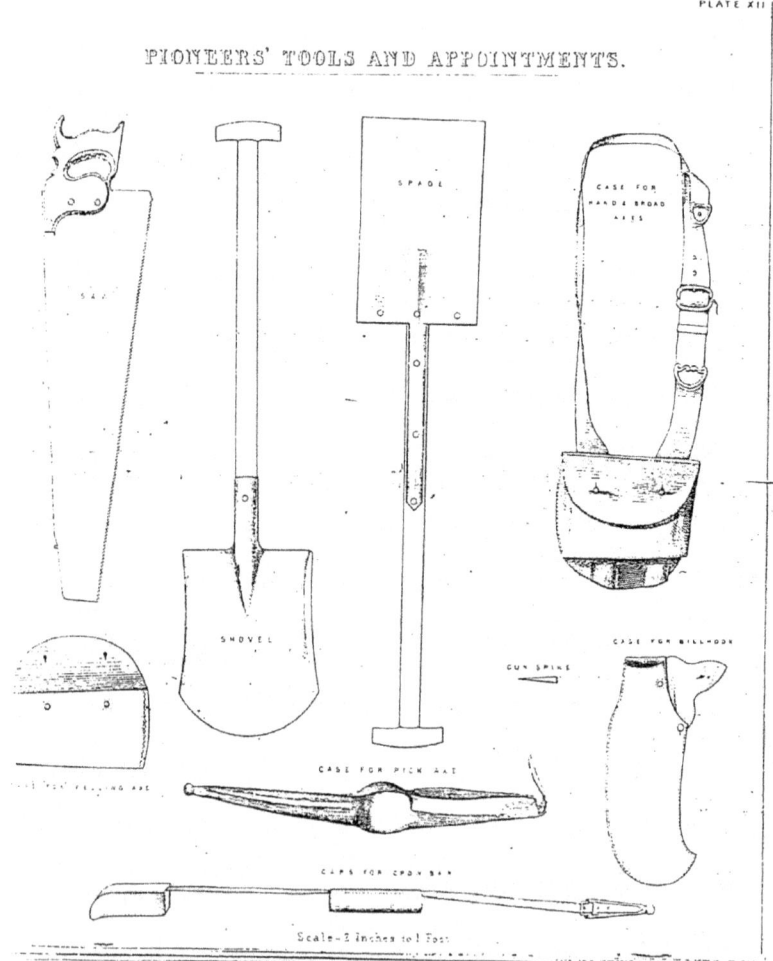

FRENCH ARMY SAPEURS 1766 - 1875

The Infantry sapeurs officially held the title "Soldats - Carpentiers" and were occasionally referred to as "Ouvriers", but this later usage only occurs in the "Controles des Troupes" for the Swiss Guards. Carpenter/ Soldiers were first added to regiments during the Seven Years War by various Colonels on their own initiative, as such they were never formally accepted by the Minister of War and shortly after the war they disappeared.

The Ordinance of 17 April 1766 began the official practice of having 2 Carpenter/Soldiers in each battalion who were to be recruited from the ranks of the 8 Fusilier companies, they were to remain assigned to those companies and could not draw higher pay as a result of their additional duties.

Fig. 59 - Their uniform therefore was the same as the Fusilier and used the same distinctions with the addition of crossed axes in White Cloth - **Fig. 28** - There is some question as to the color The entire uniform was already White thus the crossed axes would not show. The Crossed axe badge was worn on the sleeve of the coat and very possibly a bearskin hat **Fig 58**, which was accorded the sapeurs in an Ordinance of 25 April 1767.

The helmet was made of bearskin (ourson) and shaped like the Grenadier's bonnet but was 3 inches shorter, with a fleur-de-lys on the (calotte), cloth [117] top to the fur grenadier bonnet, normally visible from the rear. It was generally without a plaque except for the Swiss Guards.

The other distinction which seems to have been tolerated for sapeurs was the presence of a beard. It would appear this was against regulations but which is consistently seen on pictures of sapeurs from this period through the Napoleonic era. (Cottreau: passim)

RAGANGE: This was a Chevron, 23 mm wide, set high on the left sleeve in white ribbon (Blue on White Coats). These distinctions otherwise known as "Chevrons d' anciennte", were introduced by edict of 4 march 1771 to distinguish the experienced soldiers. (Nussbau: 1934:30).

These were used to designate veteran troops and a Chevron was added for every 8 years of service. After 24 years of service, the Chevrons were replaced by the veterans Medal - **Fig. 29**. (at bottom)

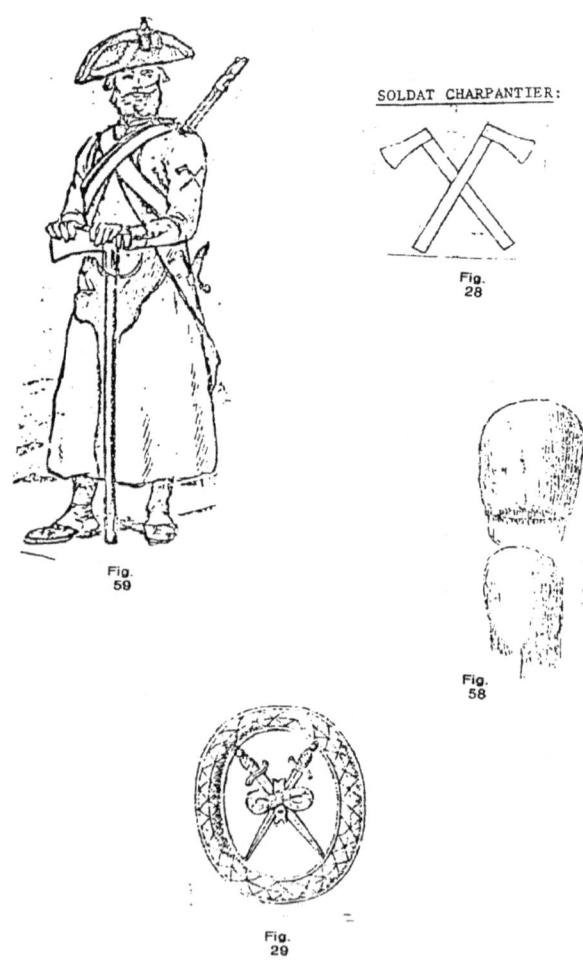

Fig. 59

SOLDAT CHARPANTIER:

Fig. 28

Fig. 58

Fig. 29

VEST - (Veste) - The sleeved vest was worn under the coat was of White cloth and lined with cadis. Vests for foreign infantry in tricot or white estamet (serge), with toile (linen or canvas) (Malibran: 177). The Ordinance of 1786 regulated the color of the cuffs and collar on the veste. For the French line regiments, the cuffs were to be in the color of the coat and collar in the color of the lapel. the collars for all the vests piping in white. For foreign line regiments, the cuffs and collars were to be in the distinguishing color with the collar piping white. (Malibran: 192)

The "Siege" painting shows clearly that the Deuxponts in 1781 differed from this later description having both cuffs and collar in deep sky blue.

The insignia of service and rank were worn on the sleeve of the vest as on the regimental coat. Those of Corporals, appointes and regages were the same; probably blue on the white vest; and were 11 mm wide.

Fig. 32 shows the basic sleeved waist coat. The vest was worn under the coat, until 1821, when it was carried as a separate item of clothing and only worn for drill or stable assignments.

EQUIPMENT: The sappeurs were armed with a Fusil and carried a sword which tended to be non-standard issue, and carried on a shoulder strap which was fitted with a brass plate.

Fig. 57 shows the axe (1786), had a head 298 mm from heal to blade, the handle being 198 mm long. The axe fits into a white buff leather case which closes by means of a small belt and buckle, Fig. 60, (pg 261) the belt on which the axe is hung is made of white buff leather and is 624 mm long and 81 mm wide.

THE APRON (tablier), is in bleached sheep skin approximately 975 mm high and 758 mm wide just below the bib. Its 650 mm in the middle and 839 mm at the bottom. **Fig. 61** (pg 261). The waist band is also provided with straps which tie behind the back.

THE GLOVES Fig. 62 (pg 261) are in the period of 1844 and provide a possible design if they were used.

Régiment de Gatinais - 1779
Frater de Chasseurs

Fig. 32

Fig. 33

263

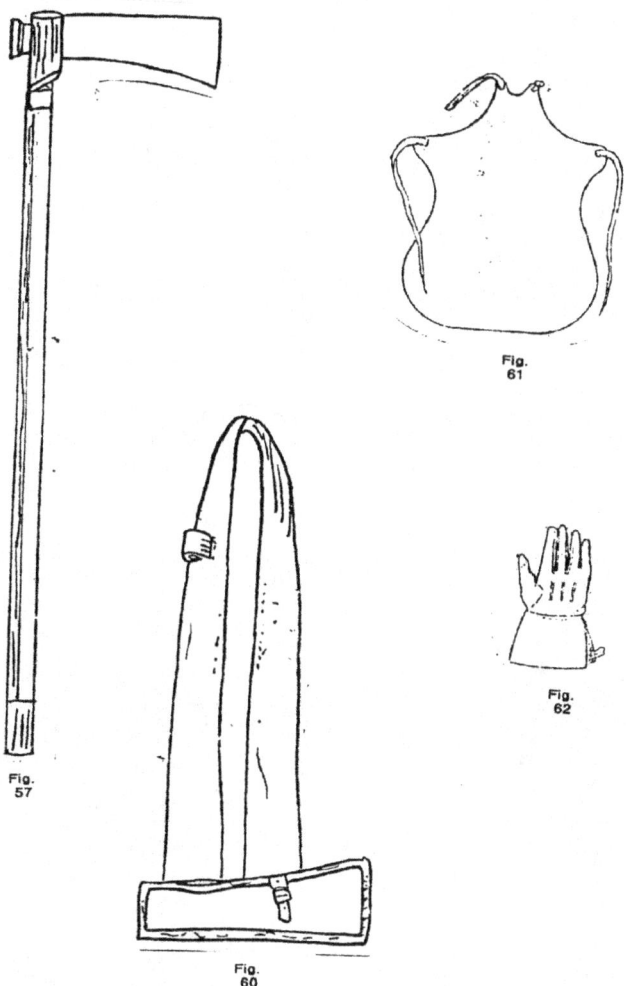

Fig. 61

Fig. 62

Fig. 57

Fig. 60

SOME NOTES [118]

French Sappers are clean shaven during the 1790's or else with mustache only, which goes back to Swiss regiments into the 1780's. The big beards appear c1795.

In France, "Pioneer" means labor unit, often POW's or criminals; these usually are rear-area units, only a few of them served with the Armies.

Sapeur's (English as sappers) are combat units (Sapeurs de Genie') or specially trained and equipped infantrymen or gunners (Sapeur d' infantine/ d' Artillere).

What this book is mostly about are the regular Pioneers of the Infantry Regiments, or Sapeur's d' infanterie.

Just how the French "Soldier-carpenter/ouvner" got translated into "Pioneer" in the Continental Army, Col. Elting doesn't know but the term was present in Steuben's "Blue Book". It disappeared for a time, then General Winfield Scott organizes some in 1814, and this continued through the Mexican War and really reached a high point during the Civil War - Crossed Axe Insignia being a highly prized badge of distinction.

Sapeur en grande tenue de service
Sidi Brahim - 1876

Sapeur de chasseurs à pied
- 1859 -

THE SAPERS AFTER THE IMPERIAL PERIOD

In 1822, the bear skin cap of the sappers had a linen skull cap of a distinctive color, with a lily made of red wool. This Lilly was Royal Blue if the skull cap was crimson, dark pink or the color of dawn. On the left side of the cap a scarlet Grenadier's plume was placed and, in front, a tassel of white thread. This cap stayed without a weighted plate.

A decision of 27 February 1825 said that sappers must be pulled from an equal number of grenadiers and light Infantry companies. Nonetheless, all had the Grenadiers Insignia.

In 1835, the bear fur cap continued to conform with the decisions of 1822, but the background was madder red with a blue "grenade" insignia. There were no more plumes nor tassels. The cockade on the left was surmounted with a flamming pompon made of scarlet wool like those of the Grenadiers. The sappers had, furthermore, a shako with a Grenadier's pompom.

In 1845, one states that the sappers had to wear a beard and moustache (Officialisation of what had existed for a long time). They had the coats and epaulets of the grenadiers. On the sleeves two crossed axes surmounted on a bright linen "grenade" insignia. They always had axes of polished iron, a pectoral plate, and whitened buffalo gloves up to the cuffs. Since 1843 the sapper had no other hairstyle but the police cap and the bear hair cap with designations of only the sappers; such as the shako, which had a leather chin strap.

The axe case was replaced by a knapsack of calf skin covered with black fur, whose body was traversed by a oblique leather girdle at the interior, in which was placed the axe handle. The iron head of the axe was placed across on the top of the knapsack. The description of this knapsack is given in the regulation of March 4, 1845. Refer to sketches on page 270.

In this manner, the marching order of the regiment would have been the following: In front, the corporal-sapper, followed by the Drums and Bugles of the 1st Battalion; behind the drums and music corps composed of 50 musicians. In 1845 also, one speaks of sappers as foot soldiers. They had on the top of each sleeve of the tunic and the jacket; a cut out trophy of linen composed of an axe at the right, a shovel at the left, crossing at a right angle.

From 1845 until 1872 there were no more changes in the uniform. At this period, the definitive bear fur hat and the pictorial plate were taken out. The only distinctions which remained were the axes slung over the shoulder and the "Grenade" on the sleeves.

DISCRIPTION OF THE ENGRAVINGS

Grenadier Sapers of the Imperial Guard - 1857

by J. Hilpert which appeared in "La Gilerne" in 1905.

Hat of Black Fur, which should be without a badge conforming to the regulations and like the one represented by R. Gignoux and L. Rousselot.

(Hilpert shows a brass badge, with an eagle stamped in relief placed on a bomb where the thunderbolt escapes the whole on a background of rays)

Ribbon, white tassels and "rackets", red plume, blue rosette at the center, white and red.

Dark Blue coat with two crossed axes upon a grenade, the whole in a scarlet wool. Epaulets of scarlet wool. On the left sleeve three long silver chevrons in scarlet wool. A white buffalo apron coming from above the coat held by a padded buffalo belt, with a brass grenade badge. Gloves of white leather. Pants of madder linen, white leggings, and black boots. A cartridge pouch and a shoulder belt of white buffalo, each decorated with the head of a lion in copper. Musket sling, knapsack and white straps. The case/cover of the overcoat was blue and white striped material.

Decoration: Silver Military Medal with a center of gold, with a yellow ribbon bordered with green. The carbines of the military police and of the Guard, model 1854, with brass furnishing. Axe of polished iron with a steel edge ending near the handle with a hammer or a pick (6 of each, 13 of a hammer for a Corporal), handle in blackened wood.

INFANTRY SAPER - 1860

According to a photograph, retrospective military exposition, 1889 ~

Bear fur hat, without decorations. Dark Blue coat, yellow collar, yellow buttons, Epaulets of scarlet wool. No axe insignia was visible on the photograph so the curator of The Army Museum placed the axes and yellow "Grenades" on scarlet chevrons at the left. White apron attached around the neck. Gloves and crispins were white, the madder red pants were inserted in the white leggings, black boots. Shoulder straps were of black leather. Over coat rolled up on the dark blue bag.

Decorations: military Medals, Medal of the Italian Campaign (Silver, red ribbon with 5 White vertical rays), British medal for the Crimean Campaign (Silver with a sky blue ribbon bordered by yellow, bar was of white metal.)

Infantrymen's rifle, axe with a black handle, and a copper ferrule

SAPER OF THE FOOT GERDAMERI - (MP) - 1861

According to a photograph, retrospective military exposition, 1889 ~

Black bear fur hat, red cockade from center, red, white, blue plume with red base. Dark Blue coat, on the sleeves, crossed axes upon a grenade, in white thread. Aiquilletts and shoulder knots (cords) of white thread. Yellow buffalo apron, going over the coat, held by a yellow belt with a white border and with a cooper belt stamped with a :Grenade". The cover for the overcoat was light blue, white "Grenade". Musket sling, shoulder strap for the knapsack and white leather "Sword Knot".   Decorations: Military Medal

NOTE: Col. John Elting U.S.A. (Ret) and Alan Aimone provided me with this information on the French Army Sappers

Col. Elting a former Instructor at West Point Military Academy and Mr. Aimone worked in the rare book section at the West Point Military Library.

Author's Collection

French Troops at Yorktown Oct 1981 receiving the blessing before battle

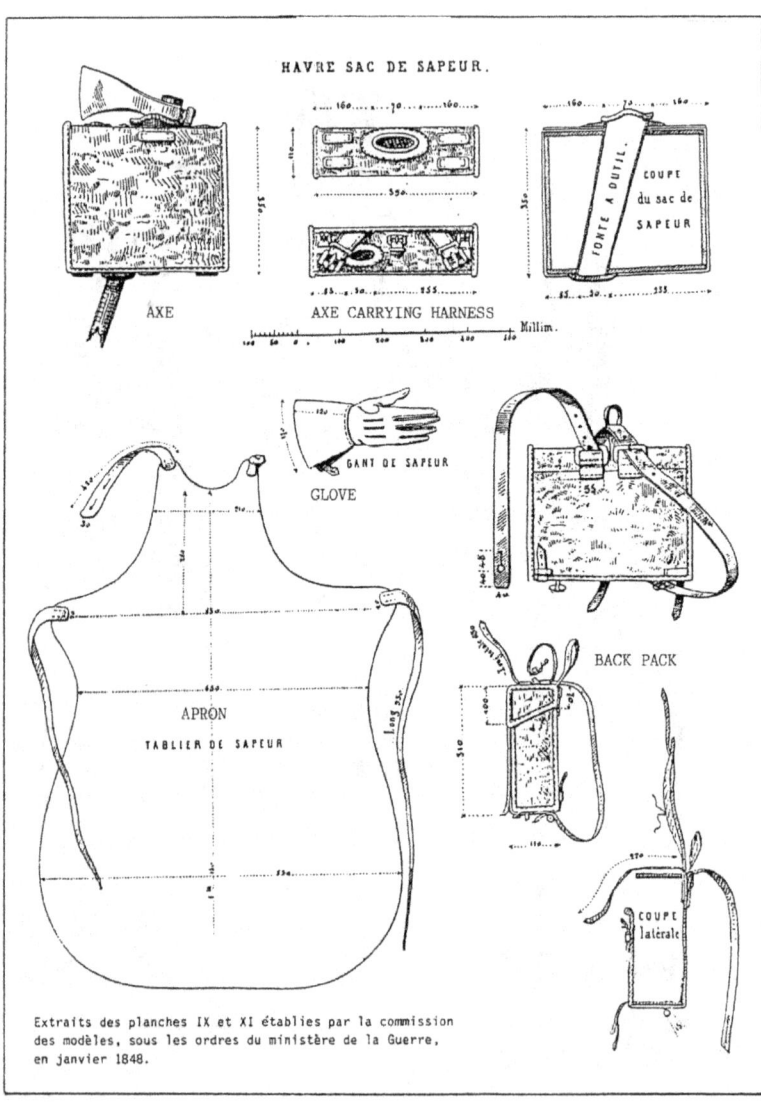

Extraits des planches IX et XI établies par la commission des modèles, sous les ordres du ministère de la Guerre, en janvier 1848.

PIONEERS - CENTER - REPRESENT THE ROYAL WELSH FUSILIERS
YORKTOWN, VIRGINIA - OCTOBER 1981

PIONEERS ON EITHER SIDE - REPRRSENT THE 23rd REGIMENT OF FOOT
c 1775 (ROYAL WELSH FUSILIERS)

BRITISH FORCES IN THE 1st GULF WAR

Several paintings done by Mr. Robin Watt had been done during the 1st Gulf War which are now on display at the National Army Museum in London.

The above painting is of a Pvt. Graham, Royal Pioneer Corps, H.Q., 7th Armored Brigade, 3 December 1990.

The 7th Armoured Brigade; was comprised of the following units:

207th (7th Armd. Bde.) Signals
The Queens Royal Irish Hussars
1st Bn. The Staffordshire Regt.
(The Prince of Wale's)

The Royal Scots Dragoon Grds
(Carabiniers & Grays) 4 Sqns.
40th Field Regt. RA

"A" Sqn. 1st The Queens Dragoon Grds
1st Armoured Field Ambulance RAMC

Senior Pioneer - Staffordshire Regiment - Full Parade Kit

The Staffordshire Regt. on Parade

The Staffordshire Regt. with Pioneers
(The Prince of Wale's)

On Parade at Whittington Barracks
Litchfield, Staffordshire, England

Photo's provided by a Mr. Jeff Elson
Historical Researcher at the Staffordshire
Regimental Museum.

SEPTEMBER 2005 - MEMBERS OF THE 64th REGIMENT OF FOOT IN AMERICA - PARTICIPATE IN THE STAFFORDSHIRE REGIMENTS 300th ANNIVERSARY

SEPTEMBER 10th, 2005 - THE STAFFORDSHIRE REGIMENTAL PARADE GROUNDS - WHITTINGTON BARRACKS, LITCHFIELD, STAFFORDSHIRE, ENGLAND - "THE DRUM HEAD CERMONIES"

The 64th Regiment; since its formation in 1756, has an impressive history. It fought in many well known and lesser known battles during its history. It began with the invasion of Guadeloupe in 1759. Then with the American War; Boston; New York City, Philadelphia, and the SOUTHERN CAMPAIGN. The dawn of the 19th century saw the 64th taking part in the capture of Fort Bourbon and the occupation of Martinique. As the 19th century unfolded the 64th saw extensive action in India. The regiment saw action in the bloody trenches of the First World War. And then again during the Second. Sadly our ancient regiment is a memory, amalgamated to make part of the Mercian Regiment.

The Mercian Regiment (*MER-CIAN*) was formed by the algamation of four existing regiments; *Cheshire, Derbyshire, Nottinghamshire, Staffordshire and the Worcestershire*. The regiment was formed on September 1, 2007 at Tamworth Castle, England. It is called the Mercian Regiment as it is generally located within the ancient English kingdom of Mercia. The regiments cap badge is a double headed Mercian Eagle with Saxon crown. This has been chosen because it forms a link to the regiment's recruiting area, which encompass a number of counties that do not have traditional links, except under the Kingdom of Mercia.

*The above article came from **THE CROWN NEWS LETTER** of Capt. Stannus's Company - 64th Regt. Of Foot (Sept. Oct. 2008)   Author's photo collection*

Note the **STAFFORD KNOT** in center of flag; this flag was flown on the troop ship taking British Troops out of Hong Kong when Britain turned it over to the Chinese government. Mike Grenier on left, Jackie Bradbury on right. On the right is the current **MERCIAN REGIMENTAL CAP BADGE.**

The photo's and article about the Battle of Eutaw Springs, South Carolina were provided by Mr. Roger Chapmen, former Editor of the Regimental magazine called the "GREEN HOWARDS" as this is the current Regimental designation. The 19th Regiment of Foot; Originally raised in 1688, they served under various titles until they were amalgamated with *The Prince of Wales's Own Regiment of Yorkshire and The Duke of Wellington's Regiment, all form The Yorkshire Regiment* on 6 June 2006.

24 Members of the Regimental Pioneers of the 1st Battalion The Green Howard's in Alma Barracks in Minden, West Germany in 1955 under the command of Second Lieutenant R.M. Weare. The Pioneer Sergeant is holding the two ceremonial Pioneer Axes carried on Parade.

Pioneer Sergeant - the only man in the Battalion allowed to wear a beard - Len Gee is talking to the Brigade Commander during an inspection in Minden, West Germany in 1972. Regimental Sergeant Terry Latham MBE is in the background.

~ The 19th Regiment of Foot ~
From Ireland to the West Indies, via
The American War of Independence

In March 1781, the 19th Regiment of Foot (The Green Howards) embarked at Cork, in Ireland, for South Carolina. Twelve weeks later, on 3rd June 1781, the Regiment landed at Charleston to play its part in the American War of Independence. The 30 officers, 30 sergeants and 672 men, under the command of Lieutenant-Colonel James Coates, formed 10 Companies - 8 Battalion and 2 Flank Companies. In the twelve months they were there, the Regiment lost its baggage train, took part in skirmishes, turned the tide at Eutaw Springs and left America decimated in number, but with a new designation.

Corporal - Battalion Company - 19th Foot - 1781

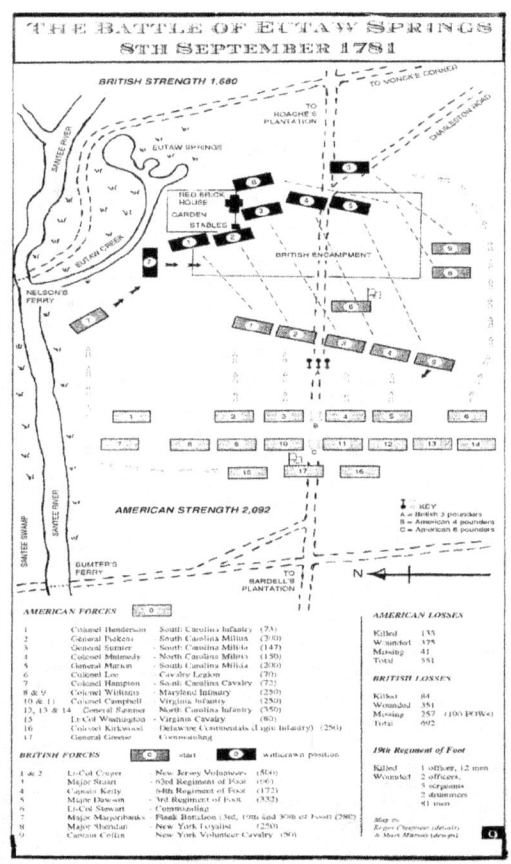

#3 - indicates the location of the 63rd Regt. Commanded by a Maj. Stuart (96)
#4 - indicates the location of the 64th Regt. Commanded by a Capt. Kelly (172)
#7 - indicates the location of the Flank Battalion (3rd, 19th and 30th of Foot) (280)
Under the Command of Major Majoribanks

YORKTOWN - OCT 1981 - LOYALIST REGIMENTS RETURNING TO CAMP FROM REVIEW BY PRESIDENT RONALD REAGAN

BRITISH REGULARS ALREADY HAVE RETURNED TO CAMP - PAY PROPER RESPECTS TO THEIR LOYALIST COUNTERPARTS

Generally, 18th Century events involve the enter family. The family takes part in setting up the camp, and bringing in the firewood for the cooking fire. You must be 16 or older to handle a musket, thus the young men can either be a runner for the officers or take up the fife or drum; both are difficult, and knowledge of music helps.

I took this photo at the Saratoga Battlefield Park in Saratoga, New York
September 17 & 18, 1983

SO THEY LIKE MUSIC

18th CENTURY MILITARY MUSIC

One of my quests is to determine what music or drum beat may have been used to assembly the pioneers prior to the regiments marching out of camp. One of the tunes I found is called "PIONEERS MARCH", in this section. Although this tune comes from a book published in 1785, I must wonder if it dates earlier then that.

Also found in this section you'll find the regimental march of the Royal Engineers, from the book by Derek Boyd, also found here is the regimental march of the Staffordshire Regiment or known to us here in the states as the 64th Regt. of Foot.

Additional materials were provided by Mary Thomas (Stone), Now married to Winston Stone, Commander of the 1st foot Guards (Reenactment unit). Mary is a fifer, so her input was very helpful.

There are comments in regards to the duties of the regimental fifer and drummer, as well as some of the required tunes they had to know. This information was taken from a book by Steven Baule, titled

THE RECONSTRUCTED SONGBOOK FOR HIS MAJESTY'S 55th REGIMENT OF FOOT;
Which served in North America from 1775 to 1778.

Another book provided some additional tunes, and used for reference, was put out by the Corps of Drums Society titled:

A BIBLIOGRAPHY OF DRUM AND FIFE MUSIC, Volume 1 - 1717 - 1815 by D.J. Rowland's B.A. The Honorary Secretary for the Corps of Drums Society is a Mr. Roger Davenport, 50 Station Road, Halstead, Sevenoaks, Kent, England, TN14 7DJ.

I had mentioned earlier of a tune called "English Pioneers Call" or "Round Heads and Cockolds, Come Dig". By the time I had reached this point in the book, I'm not sure if the use of this tune or its actual existence is fact. In one of Col. John Eltings letters dated September 1993, he thinks Kipling may have caught an echo of it, in his poem about the Royal Engineers.

> "We build them good barracks"
> "They say they are bad"
> "That there colonels are Methodist"
> "Married or mad"

On June 6th, 1995 I had written to Mr. Davenport, of the Corps and Drums Society requesting further information on the tunes mentioned; The Pioneers Call, the English Pioneers Call, and the Pioneers March. I received no answer, thereafter I wrote to Doctor Peter B. Boyden, Honorary Secretary to the Journal for the Society of Army historical research, care of The National Army Museum in London. He wasn't able to reach Mr. Davenport either, but he was able to provide another name, Mr. David Rowland's, who was a Bibliography of the Fife and Drum Music for the Corps of Drums Society some years ago.

Below is Mr. Rowland's reply, part was typed, part hand written and the balance of his reply was on the back of the envelop.

6 Saville Place
Clifton
Bristol, England BS8 4EJ
29 February 1996

Dear Mr. Eisenhauer

Thank you for your letter of 18th February.

I've enclosed a Photostat of the instructions and drum beats for the Pioneer march, taken from "The Young Drummers Assistant", (printed by Longman and Broderip; no date; c1785). This book is very rare; I know of only one in Britain (in the Barber Library, University of Birmingham). It is the earliest extant book containing British Army beats we know of.

There are no melody lines of the tunes in that book. For the tune I have turned to "The complete Tutor for the Fife ..... with ..... Celebrated March's and Airs Performed in the Guards and other Regiments etc." . (Published by C and S Thompson; no date, c1770).

The music of the duty tunes and marches in all the extant 18th Century military books is almost always identical; in the days before copyright; publishers copied from each other repeatedly. It was very important for soldiers to recognize the tunes and drum beats, so these did not change over very many years; in my view it was very likely that the tunes and beats in use in the 1780's were the same as those used earlier in the century.

I have looked at two other sources: William Williams (Correctly Nichols ?) ms book, Pawtucket, Rhode Island, 1775, has 45 military fife tunes; Pioneers march is there, in identical notation (even to the placing of the trills), and probably copied from a printed book. (Harris Collection, Brown University's John Hay Library, Providence, R.I.) Winstock (Songs and Music of the Redcoats) queried whether Pioneers March and Rogues March were identical; but Skillern has the well-known Rogues March on pg. 14 under its own title.

I hope the enclosed tunes are of interest, and I wish you well with your re-enactments, and hope these tunes will be heard again.

Sincerely,
David Rowland's
Corps of Drums Society

P.S. - It is believed that fifes were re-introduced into the British Army in certain regiments from 1745 onwards, amongst those regiments serving in Flanders (where they probably copied their use from the German Regiments).The historian, Grose, said his old regiment, the 19th, was the first. In this context I note that you quote a Captain Philip Browne, 1745, referring to the drum beats (i.e. not fife tunes). I am confident that the drum beats of the Pioneers march are almost certainly the ones he heard.

P.P.S. - David Ruthford: "The Complete Tutor for the Fife" (c1776); I've just checked this: it has Pioneers March (tune) identical to C.S. Thompson.

Since I already have a considerable number of tunes which I added herein, I added a few items that Mr. Rowland had sent., especially the one from C.S. Thompson.

Pioneers March. [118]

First Division twice over — Second Division once over —

Rogues March.

The Drum that Rolls, begin at the first Flam, and end at the last.

Adjutants Call.

Serjeants Call.
Long Roll. Long Roll.

Last 5 strokes for the Corporals

The firſt Part of this, twice over, the ſecond Part once.

NB. Each Reveily to be Beat twice over.

General.

The firſt and ſecond Diviſions of the General, to be Beat twice over.

THE CORPS MARCH [119]

In 1856 on the amalgamation of the Royal Engineers officers and Sappers and Miners, to become the Royal Engineers as we know them today, a properly constituted Military Band was decided upon to replace the unofficial Brass Band which had existed at the sappers and miners HQ at Woolwich under Bugle Major David Youle since 1835. The first Band master of the official RE Band was Mr. W.G. Collins - formerly a Band master of the Royal Artillery. The RE Band and string Orchestra quickly took a leading role in the world of military music. In 1950 a minor Staff Band was formed at Aldershot, to assist the band at Chatham in carrying out the many musical duties of the Corps.

The Corps March as we know it today really consists of two tunes in the following order:

Claribel - Old German Tune - composer unknown
Wings - A song, with appropriate words, composed
by a women, Dolores Barnard (there is some
doubt about the accurarcy of the full name)

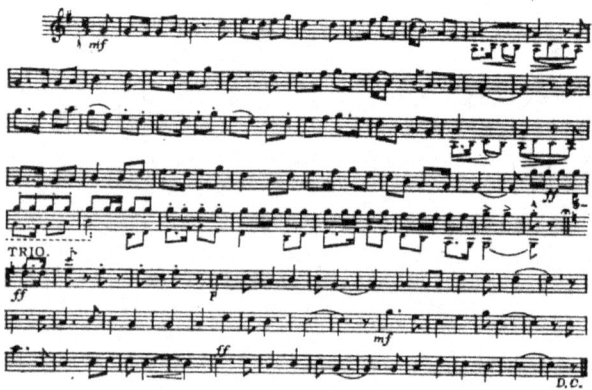

Reproduced by permission of
Captain R. A. Hunt LRAM, ARCM A(Mus), TCL, RE
Director of Music
The Band of the Corps of Royal Engineers

REGIMENTAL MARCH - 64th Foot [120]

"The days we went a 'Gypsyn' was adopted by the Regiment shortly after the 1881 amalgamations. The previous Regimental March of the 64th was "Romaika", while from 1876, the 98th had used "God Bless The Prince of Wales", which continued in use as an Approach march.

64th REGIMENTAL-MARCH
continued

DAILY CAMP DUTIES [121]

Each day, the drummers and fifers of a regiment controlled the activities of the soldier through a variety of calls and beats. These were normally referred to as the "Camp Duty". It was vital that the drummers and fifers knew these calls. It was the responsibility of the Drum Major and fife Major to train them.

In order to avoid confusion, drummers were not allowed to practice around their companies. The drum Major normally took them off to a secluded location. An 1783 manuscript, "Advice to Officers in the British Army" .... that satirized poor practices in the army, mentions that one place where drummers were fond of practicing was near church services. This seems to have caused many a preacher more than a small disruption in his services.

In the British Army, the English regiments played the "English Duty". The Scottish regiments played the "Scots Duty". The Continental army therefore had a chance to hear two different sets of calls from the British. In 1816, the practice of separate calls was abolished in the British Army.

From: Camus, st al.

Drummers and Fifers on the British Establishment

Each Grenadier Company - 2 Drummers and 2 Fifers
Each Light Company - 2 Drummers
Each Battalion and Field Officers (8) company - 2 Drummers
Each replacement (2) company - 2 Drummers

Total per battalion - 24 drummers and 2 fifers

Additional fifers were sometimes attached to the battalion. These were unofficial and normally paid for by the officers. Highland regiments were allowed two pipers instead of the two official fifers.

From: Rules and Regulations for Formation, Field Exercise, and Movements of His Majesty's Forces.

Qualifications and Duties of the Field Musicians

Ralph Smith noted that the following should be taken into account in appointing drummers and fifers:

> "All captains must have drummers and fifers and men to use the same, who should be faithful, secrete, and ingenious, of able personage to use their instruments and office, of sundries languages; for oftentimes they be sent to parley with the enemies .. to redeem and conduct prisoners and diverse other messages."

Additional duties field musicians performed included: carrying out court-martial sentences for the guard room when orderly drummer, and following the battle assisting the wounded. Drum Majors were also responsible for teaching musicians, serving as regimental postmaster, and supervised the execution of court martial sentence. When not supervising the massed drummers of the regiment, the drum and fife majors of the period reverted to performing drummers and fifers for their companies.

Expectations of a Company Drummer

In the 1670's, Sir James Turner commented as to what he expected of a drummer:

"The Drummer ought to be skillful to beat a Gathering, a March, an Alarm, a Charge, Retreat, Travaille or Dian, and the tattoo. If they can do that, well, and carry a message wittily to an enemy, they may be permitted to be droll".
From: Haythornwaite

Expectations for a Drum Major

"The Drum Major is entrusted with carrying officers letters, handling money, and with confidential maters; and who being expected to 'strut' at the head

of the drummers, could not be too great a coxcomb, provided his appearance was not so grand as to be regarded as showing disrespect for his officers"
From: Haythornwaite

Cadences in the 18th Century

Battalion troops in the British Army generally marched at slow or Prussian time. Elite British units, such as grenadiers and light troops, normally marched at Quick Time. Hessian troops serving in North America were required to march at the quick step also. Washington was known to order all his troops to march at quick time on occasion. This was to give the general impression that his forces were made up of elite troops.

British Cadences:
Slow or Common time: 1759: 60/minute   1786 - 70/minute
Quick time: 108/minute   (120/minute *)

Prussian Cadences:
Langsamer March: 60 - 72/minute

French Cadences:
Pas ordinaire: 70/minute
Pas redouble: 120/minute

Continental Cadences
Slow time: 60 - 70/minute
Grand Time: 70 - 80/minute
Common Time: 80 - 96/minute   (75/minute *)
Quick Time: 120/minute

From: Camus, Moon and Steuben
* Sources differ, Steuben recommended 75/minute

Beats and Calls for the Drum and Fife

The following list has been developed from several period and early 19th Century fife and drum manuals and infantry tactics manuals.

The Duty Day

The Reveille or Points of War: The signal to begin the duty day. It was the "Signal for soldiers to rise and for sentries to leave off challenging", Originally one song; this became an extended mix of several tunes by the mid-18th century.

The General - The signal for tents to be struck and preparations made to march.

The Assembly - Is the signal to repair to the color line or colors.

The Troop - The signal for the men to assemble for roll calls, inspections, etc. The first part of The Troop was used as the Adjutant's Call.

The March - The signal for the whole army to move. Each nation seemed to have their own tune before the Revolutation. The Scottish March and The English March were both used by the British Regiments.

To Arms - The signal of alarm. Soldiers were to assemble under arms.

The Retreat - This call was the beat at sun-set. The orders of the day were read and the next day's details assigned.

The Tattoo - Soldiers were to repair to their tents after this call.

The Parley - to signal for a conference with the enemy. It was also used as a signal for church parade.

Other Calls - Though these calls may have less military significance, they were very important to the soldier. These calls varied from regiment to regiment more than the former tunes. As the drum major taught incoming drummers each tune, there was no need to write them down. They start to appear in manuals around the turn of the century.

Roast Beef - To signal the evening meal or to go for provisions. Molly Put the Kettle On, was also used for this purpose by some units.

Peas upon a Trencher - The Traditional tune used for the breakfast meal. A number of variations exist.

Pioneers Call - This call was used for three things, to assemble the pioneers as a fatigue call, and to drum disorderly women out of camp. At least one source notes that the fifes were only to play in the latter case. This could signify that the orderly drummer alone beat this call on other occasions. Note page 215 of this writing.

Rogues March - This call was used to drum the unworthy and condemned from camp.

Drummers Call - This call was normally beat five to ten minutes before other scheduled calls to assemble the field music.

The Doublings - This call exists in several period manuals. It may have been used to signal forming by battalion. Several other uses have been suggested.

The Singlings - This call may have been a version of the troop. It appears to have been used to signal forming by company. Other uses have also been suggested.

The Dead March - Several tunes have been suggested as period funeral tunes "Roslin Castle" was apparently the most common. A quick step was used to return from the burial site. "Merry Men Home from the Grave" was commonly used in this role.

The following quotation is reprinted here, comes from the "EASTERN CAMPAIGN", published by the Colonel's Company, 23rd Royal Welch Fusiliers, (in America). The quotation speaks for itself:

ON MILITARY BEARING

One of those tangible" qualities which distinguish a professional recreated regiment from a half-assed one is "Military Bearing". It is one of those fine details which, when properly done, makes a unit impressive, and when not, or poorly done, makes a unit appear to be "playing at soldier"

Too often, when someone thinks of Military Bearing (or "playing the role"), they think of ego trips, arrogant Officers, and salutes. This isn't proper military bearing. Proper bearing is putting yourself in the role of the soldier whose part you are playing, be he Officer, NCO or enlisted man. Proper military courtesies are a part of playing that role, so also are a good knowledge of history; and an idea of what a soldier of the RWF might have felt just before a battle. Military bearing makes us a real Regiment, instead of a bunch of guys who spend their weekends fighting battles, just for kicks. It is one of those traits which makes amateurs into professionals.

We insist on it.

I believe that I can safely say, that the above quotation fits into
the motto of all British reenactment units.

GOD SAVE THE KING

GOD BLESS ENGLAND

LONG LIVE THE REGIMENT

THE AUTHOR
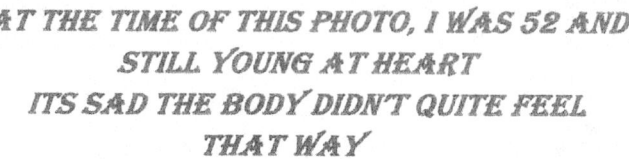

AT THE TIME OF THIS PHOTO, I WAS 52 AND
STILL YOUNG AT HEART
ITS SAD THE BODY DIDN'T QUITE FEEL
THAT WAY
AUGUST 24TH & 25TH, 1996 - NEWTOWN
BATTLEFIELD PARK NEAR ELMERA, NEW
YORK. I HAD JUST COMPLETTED AN EARLY
MORNING SKIRMISH, DOWN, AN OLD
COUNTRY ROAD TO THE BOTTOM OF A LONG
HILL, AND THEN BACK TO THE TOP. I WAS
AMOUNG THE OLDER TROOPS WHO WERE
VERY THANKFULL FOR THOSE WHO
PLANTED THE TREES ON THE ROAD BACK
TO THE TOP., AS THE SPACING WAS JUST
RIGHT FOR BRIEF REST PERIODS.
I DON'T KNOW WHO TOOK THIS PICTURE, BUT
I HAD JUST FINISHED LUNCH AND DEEP IN
THOUGHT ABOUT THE SKIRMISH -
WHAT THE HELL WAS I THINKING

THE 64th REGIMENTAL AND KINGS COLORS

THE STAFFORDSHIRE REGIMENTAL OFFICERS MESS

These two gentlemen with their families I had flow over to England out of Boston's Logan Airport.

SOURCE LIST

1. The Grand Strategy of the Roman Empire - from the First to Third Century A.D. By Edward N. Luttwak - page 14 - The John Hopkins University Press
2. The Roman War Machine - by John Peddie - page 50 - Alan Sutton Publishing Ltd.
3. The Roman War Machine - by John Peddie - page 65
4. Josephus - complete works - Translated by William Whiston, A.M. and the Forward by William Stanford LaSor, Ph.D; Th.D - pages 506 and 507 - Kregel Publications
5. The Roman War Machine - page 135
6. The Roman War Machine - page 45
7. The New College Latin and English Dictionary - by John C. Traupman, Ph.D - Bantam Books

1066 to 1346

8. Correspondence with Col. John Elting - U.S. Army (Ret.)
9. Article "Nothing Barred" - by Major Reginald Hargreaves, M.C. The Article printed in 1944 and provide To me by a Major E.R. Elliott (Ret). Royal Pioneer Corps. Simpson Barracks, Northampton, England. Site of Barracks now a large parking lot.

1400 to 1700

10. War in the Middle Ages - by Philleppe Contamine - pages 200 and 201 - Blackwell Publications
11. The Article "Nothing Barred" by Major Reginald Hargreaves
12. Elizabeth's Army - page 164
13. The Article "Nothing Barred"
14. Elizabeth's Army - pages 25 and 49
15. Elizabeth's Army - Pages 25 and 49
16. Cromwell's Army - by C.H. Firth - page 223 - Methuen - London
17. Art of Warfare in the Age of Marlborough - by David Chandler - page 223 - Hippocrene Books, Inc
18. Notes from Col. John Elting - U.S. Army (Ret.)
19. From Cromwell's Army - by C.H. Firth - page 173
20. From Cromwell's Army
21. Article "Nothing Barred"

1703 to 1747

22. Article "Nothing Barred"
23. A History of the British Army - Vol. II - by Ceil C.P. Lawson - pages 192 and 193 - Kay and Ward Ltd. Current publisher and owner of copyright is currently unknown
24. History of the British Uniform - Vol. II - by Ceil C.P. Lawson
25. The Armies of Queen Anne - by Major R.E. Scouller - Royal Signals - pages 174, 175, 183, 185 Oxford Press - 1966
26. Armies of Queen Anne - by Major R.E. Scouller - page 186 - Oxford Press - 1966
27. A History of the Regiment and Uniforms of the British Army - by Major Robert Money Barnes 2nd Edition 1951 - page 31 - Seeley Services - Current publisher and owner of copyright is unknown
28. The Royal Engineers - by Derek Boyd - page 8 - Pen and Swords Books Ltd. Current publisher And owner of copyright is unknown.
29. Article "Nothing Barred"
30. Treatise of Military Discipline - 4th Edition - 1720 - Chapter 17 - page 248 Original works at the rare book section - West Point Military Library
31. British Army of the 18th Century - by Col. H.C.B. Rogers - pages 84, 85, 89 - Allen and Unwin Publishers. Current publisher and owner of copyright is unknown

1703 to 1747 continued

[32] These Branches are : Engineers and Artillery - Signals were added much later (1920)
[33] The Royal Engineers - by Derek Boyd - page 9
[34] Journal of the Society for Army Historical Research (J.S.A.H.R.) Vol. 5 - Oct/Dec. 1926 - page 97
[35] The British Army of the 18th Century - by Col. H.C.B. Rogers O.B.E. pages 86 and 88

1748 to 1765

[36] Diaries of Lt. Col. The Honorable Charles Colville - May/June 1747 - J.S.A.H.R. Vol. 27 - pg. 53 Edited by J.O. Robson - 1949
[37] The British Army of the 18th Century - by Col. H.C.B. Rogers - OBE - pages 86 and 88
[38] The Royal Engineers - by Derek Boyd - page 10
[39] British Army of the 18th Century
[40] The Royal Engineers - by Derek Boyd
[41] J.S.A.H.R. - Vol. 61 - West Point Military Library
[42] Treatise of Military Discipline - 4th Edition c1720 and the 5th Edition of March 1759 - Both Original works are in the rare book section - West Point Military Library
[43] The Manual of Exercise - Kings Regulations of 1764 - Original Copy at the rare Book Section - West Point Military Library
[44] The Royal Engineers - by Derek Boyd - page 11
[45] Enlisted from the Royal Navy into Webb's Regt. Which served under Marlborough in 1708. British Army of the 18th Century - by H.C.B. Rogers O.B.E. - page 63
[46] British Army of the 18th Century - page 63 - Allen and Unwin Publishing - current publisher And owner of copyright is unknown.
[47] J.S.A.H.R. Vol. 12 and 29 - West Point Military Library
[48] An 18th Century tern used to identify local farmers.
[49] Piquet - a detachment of either Grenadiers or Battalion soldiers to act as additional support Should they run into a larger enemy force
[50] Lord Brome was the future Lord Cornwallis of America and India
[51] The Diary did not identify who Sanford was, possibly a Brigade Commander
[52] The Army of Frederick the Great - by Christopher Duffy - pages 123 and 125 - Hippocrene Books
[53] Instrument of War - Vol. I - The Austrian Army in the Seven Years War - by Christopher Duffy Pages 232 and 299 - The Emperor's Press - Current publisher and owner of copyright is unknown.
   (*) **Jean-Baptiste de Gribeauval** - highly accomplished French artilleryman, then serving with the Austrian Army as a General c 1760
   (*) **Field-Marshal (Count) Leopold Daun** - prime mover of military reforms and directed the main Austrian Army from the spring of 1758 until the end of the war.
   (*) **Franz Moritz Lacy (1725 0 1801)** - was Austria's first Chief of the General Staff (1758)
   (*) **Count Wenzel Anton Kaunitz** - Foreign Minister to Queen Maria Theresa - Empress of Austria.
[54] Inspection returns of July 1767, Regimental review while in Limerick, Ireland, by a Major General Lord Blayney.

1765 to 1770

[55] Public Record Office - KEW, Richmond, Surry, England - March 1984
   A Mr. Loren Daniel Lillis of Dimondale, MI was of great assistance in providing me with The "War Office Numbers and the mailing address as to where to write.
[56] British Military Uniforms - 1768 - 1796 - by Hew Strachan - Pages 159, 169, 170, 171, 202 - Arms and Armour Press - Current Publishers and owner of Copyright is unknown

1765 to 1770 period continued

[57] British Military Uniforms 1768 - 1796 - by Hew Strachan - Appendix 4 - Page 175 under "Pioneers" - Pages 175, 186, 216, 221, 222, 237, 271

1770 to 1785

[58] This return was provided by a Mr. Rene' Chartrand - Parks Canada - (Ret.)
[59] Notes of the Dress of the Royal Highland Emigrants - 1775 - 1778 - by Mr. Rene' Chartrand
[60] An extract from "With the British Army in Philadelphia, 1777 - 78 - by a Mr. John Johnson Attempts to locate Mr. Johnson have not been successful.
[61] At the time of this writing, Mr. Farmer was the Curator of the Fort Niagara Museum
[62] From J.S.A.H.R. - Vol. 7 - July 1928 - Diary of Lt. John Baker - pg. 86 1928
[63] History of the Sapers and Miners - by T.W.J. Connolly - Vol. 1 - London 1857 - from assorted notes Book currently out of publication and the Copyright is "Public Domain".
[64] Royal Engineers - by Derek Boyd - page 11
[65] The Continental Army - by Robert K. Wright, Jr. - U.S. Army Center of Military History - Fort McNair, D.C. At the time of this writing, attempts to local Mr. Wright were unsuccessful.
[66] The Organization of the British Army in the American Revolution - by Edward E. Curtis - page 8 North American Book Dist. - Hamburg, MI - Current Publishers and owners of the Copyright is Unknown
[67] The Organization of the British Army - Pages 109 and 110
[68] British Forces in North America - 1774 - 1781 - J.S.A.H.R. - Vol. 16 - by C.T. Atkinson Page 237 - 1936
[69] Guides were considered knowledgeable for the area they lived and worked in.
[70] The British Army of the 18th Century - by Col. H.C.B. Rogers, O.B.E. - page 208
[71] The Provincial Corps of the British Army - 1775 - 1783 - J.S.A.H.R. - Vol. 54 - 1976 - pg. 91
[72] Public Archives of Nova Scotia - 6016 University Ave. - Halifax, N.S. - B3H 1W4
[73] The Negro in the American Revolution - by Benjamin Quarles - Pages 106, 113, 115, 122, 135 University of North Carolina Press - Chapel Hill, N.C.
[74] The American Provincial Corps - 1775 - 1784 - by Philip R.N. Katchner - Attempts to contact Mr. Katchner have been unsuccessful. Pg. 91,92
[75] Some notes on the American Provincial Uniforms - 1776 - 1783 - by Albert W. Harman - J.S.A.H.R. Vol. 49 - 1971 pg. 91, 92
[76] William L. Clements Library in Ann Arbor, Michigan - The Clinton and Wray Papers
[77] The Provincial Corps of the British Army - 1775 - 1783 - Volume 54 - 1976 by Philip R.N. Katchner Page. 91 Color plates from the book of the same title - Publisher motor books International Pubs. And Wholesalers, Inc. - Osceola, WI.
[78] The Negro in the American Revolution - by Benjamin Quarles - page 140
[79] The Negro in the American Revolution - Pages 171 and 172
[80] Carleton Photostats and the Negro in the American Revolution - Bottom of Page 178
[81] The Negro in the American Revolution - Page 178
[82] The National Geographic Society Magazine - April 1975 - "The Loyalists" by Kent and Ted Spiegel
[83] History of the Royal Sapers and Miner - by T.W.J. Connolly - London 1857
[84] History of the Royal Sapers and Miners - from assorted notes.
[85] Infantry Clothing Regulations of 1802 - Vol. 19 - J.S.A.H.R. - page 103
[86] Infantry Clothing Regulations of 1802 0 Vol. 19 -1940 - J.S.A.H.R. page 103 - W.Y Carman
[87] The Royal Engineers - by Derek Boyd - page 30
[88] History of the Royal Sapers and Miners - by T.W.J. Connolly - London 1857
[89] The Royal Engineers - by Derek Boyd - page 44

[90] History of the Royal Saper and Miners - Vol. 1 - London 1857
[91] The Royal Engineers - by Derek Boyd - page 18

1770 to 1785 period continued

[92] From War Office Records - Public Record Office - Richmond Surry, London, England
[93] From the War Office Records - Public Record Office - London - England
[94] From the Osprey Series #267 - The British Army - 1660 - 1704 - Text by John Tincey the Color Plate by Gerry Embleton - Osprey Publishing - Elms Court, Chapel Way, Oxford, England
[95] Col. John Elting U.S. Army (Ret) - mentions the Pioneer - Foot Guards, 1745, in Vol. II of "History Of the Uniforms of the British Army" - by C.P. Lawson - page 18 - Kaye and Ward Publishing London, England - Current publisher and owner of copyright unknown.
[96] British Infantry Uniforms from Marlborough to Wellington - by Liliane and Fred Funcken Current publishing Company and owner of copyrights is unknown
[97] From the Book "Uniforms of the Seven Years War" - 1756 - 1763 - by John Mollo and Malcolm Mc Gregor - drawing number 135 - Hippocrene Books, Inc. N.Y., N.Y.
[98] The Osprey series - Kings Georges Army - 1740 - 1793 Infantry - by Stuart Reid and Paul Chappell Pages "C" and "E"
[99] Color enlargement taken from a color plate of the British troops in Boston c1775. Company of Military Historians Journal - artist is Peter F. Copeland..
[100] The Gentlemen in the photo's of this article, provided me the article and help make my apron pattern. We worked together at the 200th Anniversary of the Battle of Monmouth.
[104] Article found in "The New York Historical Society Quarterly" - Volume 64 - January 1960 - Page 53 By Richard J. Kike, Curator of the Museum, part of a larger article on "The Briton's Who Fought At Stoney Point", Uniform descriptions of "the Corps of Royal Engineers"
[105] British Military Uniforms - 1768 - 96 - by Hew Strachen - Page 299 - White Hats in 1772 with Hair Cockades, did not change in 1778 for Engineer Officers. The dress for 1786 as a plain double breasted Red Coat with orange-yello collar and cuffs, white breeches, waistcoat and skirts. Working dress, plain Long red coat almost a tunic, was replaced by linnen in summer.
[106] From the Book "Thin Red Line" - by DSV and BK Fosten - Windrow and Greene
[107] Refer to "British Military Uniforms" - by Hew Strachen - page 189
[108] Brigade of the American Revolutation, currently Headquartered at the New Windsor Cantonment, Washington's Last encampment, New Windsor, New York
[109] British Military Uniforms - 1768 - 96 - by Hew Strachen - Pages 181 and 185, plates 39. Uniforms of German, American, British and French Armies of the War of the American Revolution - 1775 - 1783 By Lt. Charles M. Lefferts - page 192
[110] From the Reference materials - "European Weapons and Warfare - 1618 - 1648
[111] European Weapons and Warfare
[112] European Weapons and Warfare
[113] Drawings of Vauban's "Les Saps" from the West Point Military Library - Rare Book Section Military Dictionary Comprising Technical Definitions - by Col. H.L. Scott - 1861
Other sources are Mr. Brian L. Dunnigan's Book "Siege 1759 - The Campaign against Niagara" And a - Le Blond "The Military Engineer", London, 1759

PIONEERS - BRITISH - 1856 / ARTICIFERS - CANADIAN - 1792 - 1867
SAPEURS - FRENCH - 1866 - 1875 / AND A FEW MODERN COMTEMPORIES

[114] British Military Artificers in Canada - 1760 - 1815 - by Glenn A. Steppler
J.S.A.H.R. Volume 60 - 1982 - Page 239
[115] From the Book Wellington's Army - 1809 - 1814 - by Sir Charles Oman -
Green Hill Books - 1913 - Pages 284, 285, 286, 299.
116 was eliminated
[117] Interpretations of French terms done by Col. John Elting, (US Army Ret.) - (**) indicated
Col. Eltings interpretations. Also reference materials provided by Col. John Elting; from his
Book "French Army Sapeurs - 1766 - 1875"

SO THEY LIKE MUSIC

[118] Traditional Military Music - taken from the book "The Reconstructed Songbook for His Majesty's 55th Regiment of Foot" - by Steven Bauled and provided to me by Mrs. Mary Thomas Stone, Fifer for the recreated 1st Foot Guards, U.S.A. and wife of its commander, Mr. Winston Stone.
[119] "The Corps March" - from the Book "Royal Engineers" - by Derek Boyd - Leo Cooper Ltd. London - Publishers
[120] "The Staffordshire Regimental March" - From the Book "The North Staffordshire Regiment" (Prince of Wales) by Hugh Cook - Leo Cooper Publishers
[121] Notes taken from "A Bibliography of Drum and Fife Music - Volume 1 - 1717 - 1815" By a D.J. Rowland's B.A. and provided to me by a Mr. Roger Davenport, "Honorary Secretary for The Corps of Drums Society", Seven oaks, Kent England

INDEX

A

Appointments – (1702) – page 50
Artillery, Infantry and Pioneers – (1685 – 1693) – page 37,38
Artillery, Pioneers, Trench Master, Engineer and Master of Ordnance - (1415 - 1560) pages 37,38,39
Army of Rome - 3rd Century B.C. pg. 18
Austrian Army – (1757 – 1761) – pages 72,73,74
A Museum of Early American Tools - by Eric Sloane
American Country Furniture by David T. Smith
Nick Engler and Mary J. Favorite
Avalon Forge - 409 Gun Road - Baltimore, MD. 21227 - Cat. Available 301-242-8431
Arrowhead Forge - Rt. 1 Box 26 - Wilmot, S.D. 57279 - Cat. Available 605-938-4814
American Machine and Tool Co. - 4th Ave. and Spring Street - Royersford, Pa. 19468-2519
Catalog Available 215-948-0400

B

Battle Road, Arlington, Mass. April 1981 – Page 198
British Army - Miners - (1727) – page 50
British Army's Field Forge's – Page 50
British in North America – pages 239
Bench Tools - The Best of Fine Wood - by Taunton Press

C

Calis - British Garrison - (1346) page 36
Charles the II - (1660) - page 43
Commissary Generals Office in New York City – (1782) page 87
Company of Black Pioneers – Page 91
Continental Army under Washington – (1775) – page 86
Chapmen, Roger - former Editor of the Regimental Magazine "THE GREEN HOWARDS" (19th Regt. of Foot.) provided Photo's of Regimental Pioneers and an article on the Battle of Eutaw Springs, N.C. pages 276 & 279

D

Daily Camp Duties – page 291
Diary of a Lt. John Baker in Boston – (1774 – 1776) – 4th Regiment of Foot – Page 86
Diary of Captain Philip Browne – (1737 – 1746) pages 52,53
Diary of Sgt. William Todd – Pioneer – 12th Foot (1760) – pages 69, 70

E Evolution of the Pioneer Cap/Helmet – page 136

F
Formation of Royal Company of Articifer @ Gibraltar 1772 – page 86
Fort Niagara – 8th Regiment of Foot in Garrison – page 85
Forth Henry Guard – (1867) – page 248
French Sapeurs (1766 – 1875) – page 259
Fortifications - pg. 222

G
Glossary of Artisan Titles and Terms – page 220
Guards Regiment – (1716) – page 117
George Metz - Roman Army 1st Century - pages 23, 24, 25, 33 & 33

H
Humphrey de Lilleul - King Edward the 1st - (1066) First recorded Engineer - page 35

I
Infantry Clothing Regulations – relative to Pioneers – (1802) – Pages 103

J
Josephus -War of the Jews – page 21
Jeffery Elson - Staffordshire Regimental Researcher, pages 273 to 275
James Mathews - pages 26, 27, 28,29,30,31,32
Journal for the Society of Army Historical Research - Field Forges of The British Army- Vol. 61 1983 - Pages 54, 55, 56, 57 & 58 by W.G. Child

L
Letter – The British Museum – 28 March 1984 – page 146
Letter – To The Staffordshire Regimental Headquarters – April 1999 – pages 155, 156 & 157
Letter from Park of St. Lawrence – January 1993 – page 246

M
Market Days in Williamsburg, Virginia – pages 165 & 166
Master of Ordnance, New Model Army- (1559) – page 39
Military Bearing – page 292
Military Discipline – 1720 and 1759 - Position of Pioneers in the Ranks, Order of March for Pass in Review, Battle Formation and Line of March – Pages 58, 62, 63, 64, 65 & 66
Mr. Eric Manders – The Kimble Papers – Orderly Books of Generals Howe, Clinton and Jones – (1775 - 1778) pages 88 & 89

INDEX

A

Appointments – (1702) – page 50
Artillery, Infantry and Pioneers – (1685 – 1693) – page 37,38
Artillery, Pioneers, Trench Master, Engineer and Master of Ordnance - (1415 - 1560) pages 37,38,39
Army of Rome - 3rd Century B.C. pg. 18
Austrian Army – (1757 – 1761) – pages 72,73,74
A Museum of Early American Tools - by Eric Sloane
American Country Furniture by David T. Smith
Nick Engler and Mary J. Favorite
Avalon Forge - 409 Gun Road - Baltimore, MD. 21227 - Cat. Available 301-242-8431
Arrowhead Forge - Rt. 1 Box 26 - Wilmot, S.D. 57279 - Cat. Available 605-938-4814
American Machine and Tool Co. - 4th Ave. and Spring Street - Royersford, Pa. 19468-2519
Catalog Available 215-948-0400

B

Battle Road, Arlington, Mass. April 1981 – Page 198
British Army - Miners - (1727) – page 50
British Army's Field Forge's – Page 50
British in North America – pages 239
Bench Tools - The Best of Fine Wood - by Taunton Press

C

Calis - British Garrison - (1346) page 36
Charles the II - (1660) - page 43
Commissary Generals Office in New York City – (1782) page 87
Company of Black Pioneers – Page 91
Continental Army under Washington – (1775) – page 86
Chapmen, Roger - former Editor of the Regimental Magazine "THE GREEN HOWARDS" (19th Regt. of Foot.) provided Photo's of Regimental Pioneers and an article on the Battle of Eutaw Springs, N.C. pages 276 & 279

D

Daily Camp Duties – page 291
Diary of a Lt. John Baker in Boston – (1774 – 1776) – 4th Regiment of Foot – Page 86
Diary of Captain Philip Browne – (1737 – 1746) pages 52,53
Diary of Sgt. William Todd – Pioneer – 12th Foot (1760) – pages 69, 70

E Evolution of the Pioneer Cap/Helmet – page 136

F
Formation of Royal Company of Articifer @ Gibraltar 1772 – page 86
Fort Niagara – 8th Regiment of Foot in Garrison – page 85
Forth Henry Guard – (1867) – page 248
French Sapeurs (1766 – 1875) – page 259
Fortifications - pg. 222

G
Glossary of Artisan Titles and Terms – page 220
Guards Regiment – (1716) – page 117
George Metz - Roman Army 1st Century - pages 23, 24, 25, 33 & 33

H
Humphrey de Lilleul - King Edward the 1st - (1066) First recorded Engineer - page 35

I
Infantry Clothing Regulations – relative to Pioneers – (1802) – Pages 103

J
Josephus -War of the Jews – page 21
Jeffery Elson - Staffordshire Regimental Researcher, pages 273 to 275
James Mathews - pages 26, 27, 28,29,30,31,32
Journal for the Society of Army Historical Research - Field Forges of The British Army- Vol. 61 1983 - Pages 54, 55, 56, 57 & 58 by W.G. Child

L
Letter – The British Museum – 28 March 1984 – page 146
Letter – To The Staffordshire Regimental Headquarters – April 1999 – pages 155, 156 & 157
Letter from Park of St. Lawrence – January 1993 – page 246

M
Market Days in Williamsburg, Virginia – pages 165 & 166
Master of Ordnance, New Model Army- (1559) – page 39
Military Bearing – page 292
Military Discipline – 1720 and 1759 – Position of Pioneers in the Ranks, Order of March for Pass in Review, Battle Formation and Line of March – Pages 58, 62, 63, 64, 65 & 66
Mr. Eric Manders – The Kimble Papers – Orderly Books of Generals Howe, Clinton and Jones – (1775 - 1778) pages 88 & 89

N

Negro Soldiers in the British Army's Service – Pages 91, 92, 93, 94 & 96
New Royal Warrant - (1669) - page 43
  New Uniform and Corps Colors – (1700) – Pages 46, 47

O

Organization of Artillery Trains – (1669) – page 43

P

Pioneer – 12th Regt. of Foot – (1761) – page 120
Pioneer – 23rd Regt. of Foot – (1775) – page 123, 124
Pioneer – 27th Regt. of Foot – (1785) – page 127, 128
Pioneer - 28th Regt. of Foot – (1759) – page 119
Pioneer – 29th Regt. of Foot – (1768) – page 121
Pioneer – 42nd Regt. of Foot - (1771) – page 125
Pioneer - 60th Regt. of Foot - (1755) - page 131 & 172
Pioneer – 66th Regt. of Foot – (1815) – page 132
Pioneer – 7th Regt. of Foot – (1789) – page 129 & 130
Pioneer – Battalion Company – 64th Regiment of Foot (1775) – pages 161 to 165
Pioneer – Battalion Company – Guards – (1772 – 1750) – page 117; 118
Pioneer – King James Army – (1688) – page 116
Pioneer Helmet – 59th and 64th Regiment of Foot – page 158, 159, 164
Pioneer Organization – page 62
Pioneer/Articifer Camp – pages 187 to 195
Pioneers of Yorktown, Virginia – October 1981 – pages 133 & 167
Prussian Army – (1754 – 1761) – pages 71 to 74
Public Record Office – Company of Pioneers for Service in Portugal – (1762) – pages 77 to 82

Q

Queen Elizabeth I and Pioneers - (1400) page 37 & 38
Queen Mary I – New Pioneer Uniform (1559) – page 37 & 38
Queen Mary II, Corps of Articifers – (1700) – page 44 to 47

S

Salaries of Queen Anna's Army – (1701 - 1714) page 48
Sapeurs after the Imperial Period – (1822) – page 265
Second Series of War Office Records – French Corps of Pioneers –
  April 1795 to December 1799 and the organization of the Corps – pages 104 to 112
Siege of Leith, Scotland - (1560) - page 38
Siege of Somersetshire - (1650) - page 42
Siege Work - (1346) page 36
Sieges of Lisle (Lille) and Tournai – (1709) – page 50, 51
So They Like Music – pages 261 to 282
Strategy and the Roman War Machine - page 19
Soldier - Articifer Company (1783) page 102, 103

T
Target Practice – (1756) – page 54
The Author – pages 300, 301
The Soldier – Articifer Company – (1772 - 1789) page 125, 126
Today's British Army's Pioneers/Sapeurs – Page 273 to 275 & 278, 279
Tumbrels, Field forges, forge carriages, Furrier wagons, bread & ammunition wagons - pg 54 to 58
The Work Bench - by Scott Landis
The Woodwrights Shop - by Roy Underhill
The Weekend Woodworker Annual by Rodal Press
Book Readers Service - 33 East Minor St. Emmaus, Pa, 18098

U
Uniforms and Accrutrements of the Battalion Soldier and Pioneer c1775 – pages 169 174 to 179
Unit Returns – January 1774 to September 1781 – Provincials, Guides and Pioneers – pages 94 to 98

V
Victoria and Albert Museum - September 1981 – Color of Regimental Coats – page 180

W
Warrants and Returns of 1768 – pages 83, 84
Wellington's Army – Page 242
William III & New Uniform - (1689) page 44
Wood Craft Books: Country Woodcraft by - Drew Langsner
  Home building & Woodworking in Colonial America - by C. Keith Wilbur
Woolwich, Warren, England – Royal Military Academy for Engineers – (1741) – page 39
Woodcraft - 210 Wood County Industrial Park - P.O. Box 1686 - Parkersburg, WV. 26102-1686
Catalog Available 800-225-1153
Woodworkers Supply - 1108 North Glen Road - Casper, Wyoming 82601
Catalog Available 800-645-9292

THE AUTHOR

By the time I finally reached Texas for the winter months of 01; at 56, the one thing I had to do was ride a horse.

Now folks, I'm far from a John Wayne, I'm sure he was watching me get on and painfully getting off. But a ride along the beach area was nice indeed.

During the winter months I continued to work on my manuscript.

You are now looking at the finished work; god only knows how many times I had to do a rewrite as the publisher wasn't happy. Making this chore more difficult was the simple fact that I'm not a writer by any stretch of the imagination.

I sincerely hope that each rein-actor gets something out of this work and even takes up the call to be a "Pioneer". I can proudly admit; that from 1978 until my retirement I was the only pioneer constantly on the field. I saw many oh so briefly come and go. The proudest moment, was at Yorktown in 1981, when there were 22 of us leading the Regiments onto the field. Without my documentation and Major Larry Bradbury's help, the powers that be would not have allowed that to happen. Yorktown was our shining moment for sure. Those of you who were with me on that day; I bet when you think about that moment you have goose bumps.

I'd like to hear from you folks, if I've gotten something wrong or misquoted something please feel free to contact me. Good or bad, your thoughts are more important to me then you can imagine. I do miss those weekends in the field, smoky camp fires; the friendship of sharing hot days or soggy campsites. God bless you all.

thepioneer.articifer@yahoo.com

www.ingramcontent.com/pod-product-compliance
Lightning Source LLC
Chambersburg PA
CBHW060554230426
43670CB00011B/1821